# SMALL SHOES, Impossible to Fill

## *Maureen Howley*

Maureen Howley's *Small Shoes, Impossible to Fill* shines for its heartfelt honesty, vivid imagery, and authentic voice, capturing not only personal struggles and family history but also the resilience, wit, and warmth of her mother's life in a way that feels both intimate and universally moving.
*Nicola Kearns, Author*

A fascinating, beautifully and sensitively written story of one small Scottish woman's life that resonates in our own memories and emotions.
*Pauline Minnis, Teacher of Communications and English*

…written with intimacy and authenticity. The dialogue is lively and balances well with the descriptive and historical narratives, and internal musings.
*Mary Manandar, retired Technical Officer, WHO*

# Copyright

This paperback edition by Maureen Howley

Imprint of Jasami Publishing & Productions CIC
Glasgow, Scotland

ISBN 978-1-913798-74-1

Copyright © Maureen Howley 2025
Cover Design Joy Dakers Copyright © 2025

All rights reserved. No part of this publication may be reproduced, stored in a retrieval system, or transmitted, in any form, or by any means (electronic, mechanical, photocopying, recording or otherwise) without the prior written permission of the publisher except for brief quotations used for promotion or in reviews.

The story is original, and all details are proprietary. All rights reserved.

*Dedication*

For Mum,

With me every page of the way.

…She faces life head-on, says here I come.

She never walks when she can run,

Won't sit it out if she can dance,

Lives every day as if it's her last chance…

                              My song for Mother's Day, 1994

# Family Tree: Alec Coulter and Teresa Gardner
## Grandparents of Terri Reilly (Teresa Coulter)

**Alec Coulter**=Annie Brown (m 18/7/1903)     Robert Wilson=**Teresa Gardner** (m 5/9/1900. Div.1937)
b1879 d1925  b1883 d1965                        b1878 d1953   b1877 d1959

Children of Alec Coulter and Annie Brown:
**Alec**  Isabella  John  Nan  Emma  Cathy  George  Bill  Jenny

Children of Robert Wilson and Teresa Gardner:
Isabella  Rose  **Martina**

Alec Coulter=Martina Wilson (m 13/7/1928)
1904-1952          1905-1989

Children: **Teresa**  Alec  Robert

Joseph Reilly = Teresa Coulter (2/9/1952)
1928-1997         1929-2021

Children: **Maureen**  Paul  Colette  Bernard  Joseph

Martin Howley=Maureen Reilly (m 27/9/1980)
1951-              1956-

Children: Mark  Paul  Sarah

*Table of Contents*

Part 1 Growing Up                           6

Part 2 Growing Stronger                   118

Part 3 Growing Wiser                      244

Epilogue                                  366

Author's Note                             367

Acknowledgements                          368

The Rubáiyát of Omar Khayyám              371

About the Author                          372

# PART 1
## *GROWING UP*

## 1. Maureen. Sligo, Ireland. 12th June 2020
### *Ending and Beginning*

I walk away from the building carrying a plant under one arm and a boxed cake under the other. My husband follows behind, laden with an assortment of gift bags and a plastic box brimming with office paraphernalia. My face mask is soggy with tears and slowly disintegrating. I do not look back.

I planned my retirement, wrote the letter and filled in the forms. I am ready to leave the role of Assistant Director of Public Health Nursing. The stress has ceased to be compensated by job satisfaction or my wonderful colleagues. Too few solutions for too many problems, too many complex issues for too few staff on the ground. I love my job, but it is time to move on.

Markievicz House in the heart of Sligo is named after Countess Constance Markievicz (née Gore-Booth), a revolutionary, social reformer and the first female to be elected to Westminster. It is home to Sligo/Leitrim/West Cavan Community Services and has been my base as a public health nurse (PHN) for the past twenty years. As the resident choir director for the last seven of those years, I have presided over the musical entertainment at several retirement parties and written lyrics for humorous ditties to celebrate the day. It never fails—everyone becomes the perfect employee on the day they retire. Today, it is my turn! And a virus named Covid-19 has arrived in time to make the final day of my working life even more challenging.

Covid made its presence felt at the beginning of 2020. It started with rumours from China, then rumours became reality. The World Health Organisation (WHO) designated the virus as a Public Health Emergency on 30th January and Italy was in full lockdown by 9th March. We watched the horror unfold in their hospitals during graphic news reports, as corridors overflowed with patients on makeshift trolleys. Some flayed their arms and gasped for every painful breath, others just lay with staring eyes, resigned to their fate. Doctors wept on camera, overwhelmed by the number and severity of Covid-19 admissions. Relatives wailed in despair on hospital steps, while cities and towns across Italy became ghostly, deserted places. On 11th March, Covid was declared a pandemic, with the global death toll surpassing 4,000. Ireland imposed a total lockdown on 17th March, St. Patrick's Day. The UK delayed another crucial week before responding.

Markievicz House is normally a hub of activity, with a variety of clinics operating downstairs and a range of health care professionals based in upstairs offices. The building was deserted as employees worked from home where possible and access for the public was suspended. Corridors echoed and cafe areas, normally buzzing with chatter and laughter, became sombre, silent spaces. We stood in awkward queues, 2 metres apart, waiting to boil the kettle or use the toaster. At spread-out tables, we pontificated about where all this might lead and how long it would last. We whispered comments about the news of daily deaths and devastation in hospitals. Doctors and nurses now resembled astronauts from a distant planet in their Personal Protective Equipment (PPE). It felt as if we were living in a parallel universe where aliens might appear at any moment.

After a few weeks, I began working from home myself. Having been hospitalised the previous year with asthma-related respiratory issues, my son Mark was concerned and suggested a simple, practical arrangement. He would collect my post daily from Markievicz House, leave it in a folder for me to deal with and return it the following day. The rest of my work could be done by phone. With the approval of my lovely boss, Maire, the system worked well for almost three months.

April and May were bright and warm. On my early morning 2-kilometre walk—the distance permitted from home—I often felt in awe of nature. Glencar Lake sparkled as though thousands of diamonds had landed on its surface, the surrounding mountains mirrored in its shimmering stillness.

Our daughter, Sarah, living in Dubai, had planned to get married on 18th April in Ireland, but like so many other weddings and gatherings, it was cancelled. The cherry blossom trees on my daily walk became a bittersweet reminder of her chosen theme. Every morning, I stared up at the soft pink clusters on their burgeoning branches and told myself:

*She's fine. She's safe. We're all healthy. That's all that matters. We're the lucky ones.*

And it was true. The weather might have been beautiful, but not everyone was fortunate enough to have a scenic walk within two kilometres of home. Families confined in overcrowded high-rise flats, with no access to a garden or park, struggled to cope. Struggled to survive. Parents working from home tried to manage children with no school, no routine, no space and no way to let off steam.

\* \* \*

I returned to work the week before my last day to empty my desk and organise the files for my successor. After three months without meeting anyone, I was anxious, disoriented and somehow out of sync with myself. So many of the Markievicz House stalwarts were missing. People in face masks busied themselves quickly and quietly. Covid had sucked the lifeblood from the building. A heavy sadness sat like a stone on my chest. I felt like a stranger instead of a long-standing member of staff.

\* \* \*

The beautiful spring weather has transitioned into a bitterly cold summer. Indoor parties have been banned and only a designated number of individuals are granted permission to attend my retirement. They gather in the grounds at the back entrance to Markievicz House in Spartan groups, arms folded against unpredictable, easterly gusts. My legs tremble under a ridiculously flimsy dress as I stand alone at the door, like an actor waiting backstage for my cue, the signal to join an outdoor party. It does not feel right to be at a party, especially one for me. I walk out, smiling, the muscles in my face twitching with nerves and cold. Flattering speeches and undeserved compliments follow. Oh God, I am that perfect employee!

   I'm stunned and delighted when my choir appears, dressed in 1960s costumes, their huge smiles flying in the face of the arctic conditions. They sing a personal song written for me, with the gusto and warmth I have come to love. I adore every one of them and feel overwhelmed with gratitude and a strange sense of grief. A microphone is thrust into my hands, now trembling in tandem with my legs. Smiling eyes are fixed on me, their expectations like emotional bullets. I want to run. I don't. What I want is to reverse the clock, to return to life before Covid, before retirement. Instead, I mutter words I cannot recall, failing to express how much I have valued two decades of fulfilling work and the friendships formed along the way. This is not how I imagined my last day. This is not how I imagined my *Retirement Do*.

As the group disperses in search of heat, I slip into the bathroom, close the toilet door and sit in a cubicle, dabbing my eyes with a square of toilet paper. I need a few moments alone. I compose myself, exit the cubicle and wash my hands, staring at my masked reflection as I follow the five-step guideline taped to the wall. By the time I leave the bathroom, I am ready to face the future. My next step has already been mapped out. I am heading to Scotland to look after my terminally ill mum. I want her to die with dignity, surrounded by love. I cannot, and will not, allow her to be admitted to hospital and have her final moments witnessed via iPad held by a healthcare professional in PPE.

My resolve is disintegrating in sympathy with my paper face mask as I walk away from my working life. No physical contact. No farewell hugs. I will never forget the loneliness of that walk.

Covid has taken over the world. I am a retiree. My mum is dying. And, oh yes, my husband has prostate cancer.

*  *  *

## Maureen. Dublin. 11th June 2020

The day before I retire, my husband, Martin, and I are in Dublin. We sit in the private consulting rooms of a urologist who has an American twang and a matter-of-fact delivery. The Perspex screen between us and his mask makes it difficult to discern facial expressions or even a reassuring smile.

'It's most likely cancer, Mr Howley. We'll know more after the biopsy, but the MRI pretty much confirms it.'

He turns his laptop towards us so that Martin can see the offending black area on the scan. If he thought the picture would reassure us, the consultant was mistaken. He pushed some information leaflets under the screen.

'Take these home and think about how you want to proceed, Mr Howley.'

He wants to dismiss us, move on to the man waiting outside.

Martin looks at me then says, 'We don't need time. We've decided to go the robotic surgery route. When can you do it?'

And indeed, we have spent many hours discussing options. I have reviewed studies and familiarised myself with prostate-specific antigen (PSA), the Gleason Score (a method of assessing the severity of prostate cancer), treatment options, survival rates and side effects of both surgery and radiotherapy. We are ready for this conversation, but it is still a shock to hear the word 'cancer.' We are in the throes of a pandemic and are lucky to be offered treatment at all. By the time we leave the building, Martin is pencilled in for surgery on the 25th August 2020.

'We can't even go for a cup of tea to process all this,' Martin says.

I squeeze his hand. 'Bloody Covid,' I say.

* * *

## Maureen. Aboard the ferry to Scotland. 16th June 2020

Five days after the trip to the urologist and four days after retiring, we are aboard the Stena Line ferry from Belfast to Cairnryan. It will probably be the last time Martin and our sons, Mark and Paul, will see their grandmother, known as Mama. Covid travel restrictions mean weekend trips will be impossible. The sea is calm and the ship quiet, with passengers and crew Covid-aware and fearful of human contact. It feels very different from our many previous sailings across the Irish Sea: no children laughing, no noisy feet thumping across the deck, no gregarious passengers enjoying a tipple in the bar or a coffee in the cafeteria. We head for a semi-circle of armchairs.

'God, it's great to sit down and take off this mask,' Martin says, throwing down the bag of provisions and peeling off the mandatory blue face covering.

We all follow suit.

'Jesus, I thought I'd never make it from the car park to the deck,' I say and plonk myself down beside him. 'The stairs don't usually bother me, but the mask makes it hard to breathe. And my glasses steam up. I couldn't see my hand in front of me.'

Martin laughs and reaches for my hand. 'We've made it this far. Relax.'

The lads are unfazed by masks, stairs or glasses. They head off to explore the food options, despite our plentiful supply. It reminds me of when they were boys, travelling back and forth to Ireland to visit

Martin's family. As soon as we boarded, they'd be off exploring the ship. I smile at the memory, grateful for a flash of normality.

Martin goes in search of the loo and I sit back and take stock. I stare through a dirty window at the grey sea, vaguely aware of a safety announcement as the boat lurches away from the dock. My emotions are muddled and erratic, refusing to settle, like bubbles blown into the air but never caught. As the ferry picks up speed and the familiar outline of Ailsa Craig appears on the horizon, my overriding emotion is fear. Am I ready for this responsibility? Despite all my years of nursing, will I have the competence and confidence to look after my own mother until the end? I worry about Martin. Am I letting him down by leaving so soon after his cancer diagnosis? What if something happens to him when I am away? He returns and settles beside me, retrieving the flask and paper cups from the bag. He pours two coffees and hands me one.

'Penny for your thoughts.' He smiles and adds, 'Good coffee!'

We have become the kind of coffee snobs we used to mock. Since Paul's first trip home from Guatemala with bags of coffee beans and Mark's investment in a grinder and fancy machine, we now turn up our noses at *instant,* preferring to carry a flask of our own brew.

I pause and take a sip, grateful for its warm, aromatic comfort.

As if reading my mind, Martin says, 'Take it a day at a time, love. You'll know exactly what to do for your mum when the time comes. Just be there for her. That's enough. Isn't that what you've always done when she's sick or needs you? And there's nothing you can do for me. I just have to wait for the surgery. And you'll be back for that. So stop worrying and hand me a tea biscuit.'

The lads rejoin us, having found tea and sandwiches—both available in our packed provisions—and are soon scrolling on their phones. Martin also has his head down, despite claiming he *never uses the thing.*

I reach into my handbag for a notebook and pen. Writing has always helped me make sense of life, of the world. And God knows, it's hard to make sense of anything, large or small, in June 2020. I start with a list of plans for Scotland. I like lists.

\* \* \*

My fear of finding Mum sickly, feeble, dying could not have been further from reality. On our arrival, she is standing in the doorway, hair styled, full makeup applied and a welcoming smile that shows no sign of dimming. She is wearing her floor-length, furry, sleeveless waistcoat over brown trousers and a bright orange blouse, coordinated with ankle boots and matching accessories.

Terri Reilly is not going anywhere anytime soon.

## 2. Terri. Perth, Scotland. 16*th* June 2020
### *Reflection: Hello, I'm Terri (with an i)*

I'm finding it more and more difficult these days to do the things I've always done. It takes longer to get washed and dressed, put on my makeup and curl my hair. Sometimes, I can't even be bothered cooking. I'm ninety-one, but it has nothing to do with my age. I had radiotherapy for bladder cancer a few weeks ago and it has floored me.

My eldest daughter, Maureen, is coming later today and then I'll be able to relax. I can manage on my own, but it will be good to allow myself to be looked after for a while. Maureen's good at that. It's been hard work to keep going recently. Yesterday, I had to lift the basin of clean washing upstairs to the airing cupboard by resting it on every third stair. I just didn't have the energy to carry it all the way up. My daughter-in-law, Lorna, is very good to me. Since the radiotherapy, she brings me soup to heat in the microwave and a Costa coffee to cheer me up. She also offers to do the washing in her house, but I'm very fussy about sorting colours and textures into separate loads. She tends to mix them. I don't want to take any chances!

My husband, Joe, used to say, 'Growing old isn't much fun, but the alternative's worse.'

He was right. Joe's *alternative* came twenty-three years ago and I've lived on my own since then. It's been a good life and I think I've made the most of it. I survived bowel cancer thirteen years ago, as did my two youngest sons, Barney and Joe. We discovered a family gene. It's the same one that killed my father, several of his siblings and some of my cousins. They were all in their forties. Of course, we didn't know about the gene when they died. Barney was diagnosed with bowel cancer in 2007 and we were all tested. Joe, the youngest in the family and me, the oldest, had the gene and also active bowel cancer. All three of us had surgery in 2008. Thankfully, my eldest son, Paul and my daughters, Maureen and Colette, didn't have the gene, which was a relief.

2008 was also the year Colette's husband walked away from their marriage without so much as a by-your-leave. Yes, it was a tough year for the whole family. But we got through it. I have a bag on my tummy now, instead of going to the toilet the normal way. It behaves most of the time and I simply get on with it. Maureen's a nurse and the only one who has anything to do with my ileostomy. She was a great help to me in those early months. It took me a long time to accept it. I asked the poor young doctor to let me die, but I'm delighted to say he ignored me. I have a system now. It isn't always the same as the colorectal nurse's system, if you know what I mean, but the bag's on my tummy, not hers. I've also had skin cancer on my face, head and legs. I had an excellent plastic surgeon for more than twenty years. He's retired now, so I hope I don't need any more bits taken off.

I think this new bladder cancer means my *alternative* isn't a million miles away, but I try not to dwell on it. One consultant told my son Joe there was nothing else they could do for me. Then another doctor suggested a session of radiotherapy. I said *yes* because doing something was better than doing nothing. No wonder they say, *Doctors differ and patients die*. When you get to a certain age, some doctors don't think you're worth the effort.

At least I have my marbles—or most of them. For instance, I know I'm never going to vote for the Scottish National Party (SNP), even if my son Barney and his family pray for my conversion. I still cook the best mince in Scotland. Maybe even the world, according to my grandchildren. I believe in mind over matter. Always have. I don't believe in devolution. I loved being in business and hated having to retire at seventy-eight. I can still dance, albeit for short periods, and before this clampdown stopped me going out, I knew the price of pink grapefruit in every supermarket in Perth.

*\*\*\**

I stopped driving a few years ago because of my failing eyesight. That was very hard. I was a good driver. When I first moved here, I drove from Perth to the flower shop in Kilmarnock most days. Over 80 miles each way, but I didn't mind. I loved working. To my horror, I discovered one of the staff members was stealing. It had been going on for quite a while by the time I found out. There I was, trying to keep the business afloat by paying wages from my personal credit card. All the while, she was robbing me blind. I lost heart after that. I stopped fighting the inevitable bankruptcy.

I hated letting people down. Staff. Creditors. It's easy to say 'staff' and 'creditors', but not so easy when you know their names and you've worked beside them or done business with them for years. I was humiliated. I felt stupid. Mortified. I paid back every possible penny after the shop closed. I worked hard all my life and would have liked to retire with some dignity. Not give up the business because it failed. But hey-ho, that's life. It's all in a day's march.

I retired in 2007. And the following year, I had other fish to fry, what with the cancer and the surgeries. God works in mysterious ways. I've always had a Guardian Angel looking out for me. He was kept very busy during those years. I had to recover from the trauma of losing the shop and my bowel! It wasn't easy to let go of either. But I got on with it. And I'm still here to tell the tale.

* * *

I enjoy taking the bus into town. Sometimes even to Glasgow. People are very good and always help me. I shop in Primark. Since my surgery, I can wear a size 8. I go in and do a bit of reconnaissance, then wait for the prices to drop before I buy. I used to tell the family, *time spent in reconnaissance is never wasted*. It's still true. I keep an eye on the stock. The very large and very small sizes are the last to sell, so I nearly always pick up a bargain. Sometimes, I go to the charity shops on the High Street. My daughter Colette loves them too and we always have a good root for a bargain when she's here. I ask for help with labels and sell-by dates in the supermarket because I can't read them now. I'm told everyone wears a mask in shops these days. You can use a paper one or make your own from a bit of material and ear loops. I can't hear very well either, so even if I *were* allowed to get close enough to ask a question, I couldn't hear the answer.

Mind you, my son-in-law Martin says, 'Terri, you don't see well, and you don't hear well, but you miss nothing!' And of course, he's right.

This Meltdown, or Clampdown, or whatever they call it, means people my age are confined to barracks. It's called shielding, or sheltering, or something. I heard someone on the news say it's just a way of keeping old people out of the way. But my son Barney, who is a GP, says it's to protect the National Health Service. I don't mind. I'm old enough to remember life before the NHS. When we were sick, my father used to treat us with remedies from his big book. I often wonder what happened to that book. He had a wonderful cure for a cough: a thimble of whiskey, sugar, liquorice and a few other ingredients I can't remember. But it worked. If we had a sore throat, he would fill a big sock with salt and say, 'Wrap that around your neck. It'll draw the infection.' We couldn't afford to run to the doctor for silly things the way they do now.

I miss my Soroptimist friends and my pals in the Keep Fit class. I also had a wee job on Mondays in the hospital canteen in Perth. After a lifetime in business, it was great to be involved again. I used to advise Alma, the boss, about staffing issues or organising the café during busy spells. And I never allowed anyone to close the shutters before half past four. Some of the others tried to stop serving early so they could clean up, but I always said, 'If we're open until 4:30, we serve until 4:30. That's business!'

'You're our Coffee Queen, Terri,' Alma announced one morning during my shift. 'Did you hear that gentleman? Best latte his wife ever had, including Costa's. Made her day when he brought it to the ward, he said.'

And I have to admit, I was tickled pink. It's good to know you're still useful. Not just useful, but doing a good job. That's very important. Even when you're old. *Especially* when you're old. From then on, I was known as the Coffee Queen. I took the responsibility seriously. That's how responsibilities should be taken. Always. But if I'm honest, it was better that the Clampdown closed the café than me having to hang up my overalls. The café was busy and my eyesight just wasn't up to it anymore. Imagine if the Coffee Queen had lost her crown by spilling coffee on a visitor or worse, a member of staff.

I was a volunteer with the Perth Street Pastors until last year. We went into town once a month in groups of three, from ten o'clock until three in the morning. We wore special hats and jackets so people could recognise us. And we carried bags with lollipops and flip-flops for sore feet or sore heads. I met so many lovely people. Some were sad. Some just wanted to talk. I also got lots of hugs. Now and again, I might have made a small difference in someone's life. It felt good. I loved it. The Street Pastors operate in lots of countries, and I was the oldest volunteer in the world. I even made it into the *Perth Gazette*. Something to be proud of.

Now the clock is ticking and Maureen, Martin and my grandsons will be here soon. I want to look my best. It's time to get going.

\* \* \*

### Terri. 17th June 2020

Maureen arrived in the car with Martin, Mark and Paul last night. It did my heart good to see them all coming through the door. In the blink of an eye, my wee house was full to the brim. Mark and Paul are big men now and take up a lot of space.

I didn't think they'd all be allowed to visit me with this Clampdown and all the restrictions that go with it. But apparently, it is one of the perks of having cancer!

Mark and Paul have brought laughter and happy chaos into the house. Mark is my first grandson and it's been a long time since we ran together in the park with Heidi, my German Shepherd dog. I taught Mark about the power of raw energy and he couldn't eat enough cucumber and raw carrots when he was a wee boy.

'Look, Mama. Raw energy!' he used to shout, running ahead of me with Heidi at his side.

When we lived in Skelmorlie, Mark couldn't wait to jump into bed in the mornings with Joe and me. He used to call it *the football pitch* because it was such a big bed. He's so tall now, he probably needs a football pitch to himself!

The boys have great appetites. I remember one time they were staying here with me and I made my special mince for them. I thought there would be enough left for dinner the next night, but they got up early the next morning and ate it cold for breakfast. My friends in the Keep Fit class had a good laugh when I told them.

\* \* \*

### Terri. 19th June 2020

As suddenly as they arrived, Martin and the boys disappeared. Like snow off a dyke, as we used to say. It was lovely to see Martin. He has cancer too, but says he's 'grand.' That's the Irish word for fine. We had a good talk while Maureen and the boys went for a walk, comparing notes on our cancer.

'Sure, you look as good as ever, Terri,' he said. 'And still as tough as old boots!'

I think that's what they call a backhanded compliment, but the two of us have always enjoyed a bit of banter. He looks after me when I stay with them in Ireland.

'You'll be tickety-boo after the surgery,' I told him. 'After all, you're still a young thing. Even if you're not as tough as me.'

He laughed at that. Martin's nearly seventy and doesn't think he's young. But I'd love to be seventy again.

\* \* \*

Maureen has made coffee and we're sitting in the living room, relaxing.

Out of the blue, Maureen says, 'Mum, I want to write a book about you. About your early life growing up in the Gorbals. I never met Alec, your dad, my grandfather. You could tell me about him. And I want to know more about your army days. You've always said you lived a lifetime during those years, but I don't know much about them. What do you think?'

To be honest, I'm taken aback. Of course, we've discussed bits and pieces over the years, but the idea of a book is a bit different. It's daunting. My mind's in a whirl. Maybe my life wasn't that interesting. Maybe I won't want to talk about the messy bits. Maybe she'll give up after the first chapter. God, that's a lot of ifs, buts and maybes! I realise Maureen's waiting for an answer. Yes, it's scary, but since when have I been scared to tackle something new? I spoon the last of the latte froth into my mouth.

'You know, Maureen, that's a good idea. It'll give us something to talk about. Apart from this virus and my cancer. Do you know what I mean by that?'

'I think I do, Mum,' she says.

I wonder why she's smirking. 'Let's play it by ear,' I say. Anyway, my Keep Fit pals will be very impressed by the idea of me being in a book.

\* \* \*

## Terri. 22nd June 2020

Maureen has been here for almost a week. Every morning, she asks what I want to wear and heats my clothes on the radiator. That's my little luxury. She gives me breakfast in bed, another real treat. Then she brings her tea in and sits next to the bed while we plan the day. There's not much to plan, but it's the best treat of all. Sometimes we chat for ages. Then she does the washing and I help with the bundles because, as I've said, I'm very particular about my washing.

Maureen is wonderful, but I miss having the run of my own house. I'm fussy about how I do things. It's not just down to my army training. I was always keen on order, unlike my mother. Her life was chaotic. When my brother Alec and I came home from school for lunch, she'd sweep the breakfast dishes from one end of the kitchen table to the other to make space for food. Usually, mashed potatoes and milk. I'd happily have cleaned the table, but I got a swift slap for my efforts once. After that, I ignored the mayhem, even though I hated it. Funnily enough, I don't remember being angry when it happened. Just shocked.

My mother worked the afternoon shift on the trams at that time. Alec and I would let ourselves in after school, pour a cup of milk and sit at the kitchen table with our homework. When I'd finished and Alec had given up trying, I decided to tidy the cupboards in the scullery. They were grubby and disorganised, full of the same bits and pieces. I laid everything out on the table and wiped down the shelves. I was thinking about the ideal way to replace them when the door crashed open. The storm that was my mother arrived in the scullery. To say she wasn't happy is an understatement.

'Mum, I was just trying to help… I'll put them all back… It'll just take…'

But she was too furious to listen. And of course, Alec sat with his head down and his mouth shut.

I was startled when the slap stung my cheek. I had no time to recover before Mum grabbed my hair and dragged me across the kitchen floor into the scullery. She was shouting, but I had no idea what she was saying. Then it was over. She let go of my hair as if her hands were on fire. I must have picked the wrong day. She wasn't one for hitting us. My father would never have allowed it. And anyway, she was usually all noise and bluster. That's the only time I remember her lifting her hand.

When my father came home, it was as if nothing had happened.

'Fritters and eggs for tea!' Mum announced with a smile.

We all loved her fritters: sliced potatoes dipped in flour and water batter. She always dried the slices in a dish towel before dipping and they were delicious. My father was delighted when he came home to a happy household.

'How about a double portion for a working man?' he asked and we all laughed.

Mum put everything back into the cupboard, thrown in with no order at all. There was never any mention of the incident again.

That was Tina Coulter. Once she got whatever was bugging her out of her system, she was fine. Sometimes it took the rest of us longer to recover. But her outbursts never lasted long. She could go from a summer breeze to a gale-force wind before you had time to register a change in the weather.

I would love a portion of her fritters now, but I couldn't eat them. Since the bowel surgery, I've lost weight and my false teeth are too big. I can't chew properly. The best set of false teeth I ever had was made for me in the army. In those days, people thought false teeth were great. They gave you a lovely, white smile. My husband Joe got his as a 21st birthday present. Can you imagine that happening now?

### 3. Maureen. Perth. 23rd June 2020
*The Real Journey Begins*

Martin, Mark and Paul return to Ireland, and Mum and I settle into our routine together. Eleven o'clock is coffee time and as I sit back on the sofa, I feel more at ease than in a long time. I top up our lattes with hot water from the flask, a habit acquired from Mum.

Having coffee together has always been one of our favourite shared pastimes. When we are out and about, Mum likes frothy cappuccinos with plenty of cocoa powder, and I prefer a latte extra hot. But whether we have our coffee in cafés or at home, in Scotland, Ireland, or elsewhere in the world, it remains our special time. As Mum tucks into a custard tart, I set my phone on the table beside her, ready to record our conversation of the day. I have wanted to document her stories for a long time, but it never felt right to interrupt our coffee and cake with a notebook and pen, as if I were a reporter.

'You don't have to write a book about me just because I've reached the ripe old age of ninety-one,' was her initial response.

But after some thought, Mum agreed there were a few stories worth sharing.

'I suppose life was different back then. The Great Depression and the Second World War were tough for everyone. Maybe I should share my thoughts about those times. At least until the shops open up again.'

And that was that. I was writing a book about my mum, or rather, about Teresa Coulter. That was the name she was given when she entered the world on 2nd May 1929, the eldest of three children and the only daughter of Alec and Martina Coulter. Documenting Mum's story is not only about legacy and historical context, though they are important. I want to protect our relationship as mother and daughter, not allow it to be reduced to patient and carer as her health deteriorates. We are both excited about our shared journey into the past.

\* \* \*

## Maureen. 24th June 2020

In our first chat about childhood yesterday, Mum told me her mother, Martina Coulter, always known as Tina, was useless. Not as a person, but as a mother. She used that very word: *useless*. It was a huge statement and I have thought about it overnight.

This morning, as we enjoy our coffee, I ask, 'Can you remember when you first realised your mother was useless?'

On reflection, it is a very direct question. No gentle lead-in. I had spent the night ruminating, but Mum wisely spent it sleeping. She looks a little surprised.

Just as I am about to change the subject, she says, 'I suppose I always knew. But it wasn't her fault.'

Intrigued and a little embarrassed at my insensitivity, I try to ask a more open-ended question, the kind therapists use. We sit with our morning lattes and two strawberry tarts in front of us as I start the recording.

'Why don't you tell me about Tina when she was young?'

Without hesitation, Mum launches into a monologue about her mother, taking me back to 1924, when Tina was nineteen. Her tone is more formal than usual. I think she is keen to explain why Tina's parenting fell short at times. I am reluctant to break the spell by probing. Her expression is unusually intense. I let the moment unfold.

'My mother, Tina Wilson, was born in Oatlands in the Gorbals, the youngest of three sisters. Isa, the eldest, died in her late twenties, but I don't know why. Maybe she had a heart condition. It was never discussed. Unlike Tina or Rose, the middle sister, Isa, was quiet and reserved. She had a good job in McVitie's, the biscuit factory, as secretary to the boss. He must have thought highly of her, because she got both sisters' jobs as packers there.'

As Mum continues the story about the day Tina interviewed for the job at the biscuit factory, I have a picture of what Tina looked like and how she behaved. I can see her clearly with her petite frame and blond curls, the belligerent edge to her voice, the way she holds her head high and walks with a swagger. The germ of an idea begins to form.

*What if I write Mum's stories as if I am part of them, like an actor in the film rather than a member of the audience?*

The idea energises me and I must have a silly grin on my face, because Mum stops and asks, 'Maureen, are you alright? Did I say something daft or funny?'

'No! God, no, Mum. I'm sorry. I was just thinking about Tina getting ready for her interview and trying to look the part. Please go on. I'm engrossed.'

## 4. Tina. 27 Wolseley St., Gorbals, Glasgow. 1924
## The Lodger

Tina Wilson had known for years that George Lynch, the lodger, wasn't paying rent to her mother in the usual way. Bastard! He and her mother deserved each other.

When her father came home after working as a commercial traveller, Tina hated watching him try to please her mother. He brought presents from his travels and wanted to take her dancing or out to the pub to make up for being away. It was sickening. It wasn't his fault that the job meant travelling for a couple of weeks at a time. They would all sit at the dinner table and George Lynch would talk about his work in the psychiatric hospital. Her stupid mother would fawn over them both. Tina couldn't wait to get away from the whole sordid situation.

Her father, Robert, was working again, so *he* was back in their bed. Half the day was gone and they were still in there. Her mother, Teresa, didn't even try to hide it anymore. She was probably sleeping off the effects of last night's booze. Tina supposed she should be grateful George Lynch wasn't a drunk like her mother. Her sister, Isa, was too innocent to notice what was happening under her nose and Rose was too consumed with herself to care.

Tina put the finishing touches to her makeup, double-checking her appearance in the hall mirror. Finger waves in her hair, pinned back off her face, skirt not too tight, blouse not too low, heels not too high. Her interview at the McVitie & Price biscuit factory was at two o'clock and she wanted to look her best for Isa's sake. Isa was a good girl, gentle and caring. Tina didn't want to work in the packing room of a factory, especially since her sister, Rose, was already on the line. But she couldn't find anything else and Isa had organised the interview. It would have to do for now. She pulled her new cloche hat carefully over her curls.

'That's me off then,' she shouted through the closed bedroom door.

She didn't wait for an answer because she expected none. There would be no 'Good luck, Tina. Hope it goes well, Tina,' from her mother. She threw on her good brown coat, slammed the front door and headed down the three flights of stairs out onto Wolseley Street in the heart of Glasgow's East End. Bridie Doogan from the landing below was scrubbing the middle stairs. Tina nearly fell over her bent figure and narrowly missed kicking over the bucket of soapy water.

'Watch where yer going, Tina Wilson. Yer not too old for a slap, ya know.'

Bridie had five children in the *room and kitchen* below them and was well used to swiping at kids, whether they or not they deserved it and whether or not they belonged to her. Greasy hair straggled from under the headscarf tied around her head and she had no top teeth. Bridie was no advertisement for motherhood.

'Late for an interview, Mrs D.'

'Oooh! lah de dah… Interview, is it? You'd do better to do yer mammy's turn at the stairs. She hasn't done them for months!'

'I'll mention it to her when I get back, Mrs D,' Tina shouted as she ran out of the tenement Close.

*Yeh right. That'll make a big difference!*

'Bloody rain,' Tina said to the empty street. 'Typical. And me with no umbrella, of course.'

Lifting her handbag over her head, she ran to the tram stop. The factory was at St. Andrew's Cross. At least she wouldn't have to change trams. Her hair was strawberry blond this time. Well, that's what it said on the bottle. And now she would look like a drowned strawberry rat by the time she arrived at the factory. Tina noticed the crowd at the tram stop. A good sign. She genuinely didn't want to disappoint Isa by being late. The number 3 to University via Charing Cross arrived within minutes. Tina elbowed her way onto the footboard and squeezed into the seat closest to the door. She wiped her damp handbag with her coat sleeve, thinking about the imminent interview. She couldn't help smirking at the idea of all three sisters working in the same factory. Mind you, Isa was the boss's secretary, not a biscuit packer. She wasn't like Tina. Isa kept her head down, worked hard and hated any kind of confrontation. Definitely not like Tina.

*  *  *

Mr Graham's office was located at the top of a flight of open stairs just inside the front entrance to the factory. The sign on the frosted glass door said *Manager*. The smell of cigarette smoke and old newspapers hit

Tina as soon as she stepped inside. The boss drew deeply on a Player's non-tipped cigarette and stubbed it out in an already overflowing ashtray. She stood in front of his cluttered desk as he scanned her with his small, grey eyes. Tina instantly disliked the man.

*I'm not one of the biscuits on your conveyor belt, you stupid git,* she thought, but said nothing. Instead, she pulled herself up to her full five feet two, clutched her handbag and waited for him to speak.

'Take a seat, Miss Wilson. So, you're Isa's sister.'

She sat on the edge of the uncomfortable wooden chair and was about to retort, 'And who the hell else might I be since I'm the one with the appointment?'

'Yes. Tina, short for Martina. Her youngest sister,' she said instead.

'And you want a job here?' he continued, as if she hadn't spoken.

Again, the temptation to tell him it was obvious she wasn't here for a cup of tea or to listen to his bullshit. She decided not to sound desperate.

'Yes,' she said with what she hoped was a demure smile. Then Tina sat up straight and stuck out her chin. 'I do...' then added, '...Mr Graham.' It nearly choked her.

He gave her the biscuit inspection again. She kept her head high, meeting his slimy gaze.

'You'll be packing boxes. Start on Monday.'

With that, he lit up another cigarette and went back to his paperwork. Not much of an interview. But then, Tina knew she would get the job. Isa was a great worker as well as beautiful and gentle. The boss had no choice if he didn't want to upset her.

'Thank you,' Tina said with her back to Mr Graham and her hand on the doorknob, trying to summon her most polite voice.

'Arsehole!' was what she wanted to say.

It was a shit job, but it would give her enough money to go dancing and pay for her hair to stay strawberry blond. As she walked away from the factory, she couldn't help wondering if Mr Graham looked Isa up and down like he did with her. He was a real slime ball.

It was still raining, but Tina didn't care. She lifted her chin towards the sky, closed her eyes, and shouted, 'Do your worst,' as the rain pummelled her face.

\* \* \*

Tina tackled the stairs of 27 Wolseley Street with less energy than earlier that day. She was on the middle landing, pondering what she would buy with her first pay, when she heard the shouting. It was coming from upstairs. Her father's voice. Something wasn't right. She gripped the banister and took the remaining steps two at a time. Even before she reached the door, Tina knew. Maybe she should have turned and run back down the stairs and out into the wet street. But curiosity got the better of her and she secretly hoped her father was laying into George Lynch with his fists. By the time she threw open the door, the drama seemed to have fizzled out. Her mother was sitting on the kitchen chair, crying noisy crocodile tears and the lodger was standing beside her like a big drink of water with nothing to say for himself.

'What's going on here?'

It was a stupid question, but Tina could think of nothing better to say. Her father wasn't in the room and neither of the other two idiots said anything.

Robert Wilson was in the bedroom. He had pulled the big brown suitcase from the top of the wardrobe onto the bed and was wiping thick dust from its surface. Tina had never seen the case used. Her father always took the small one on his travels. She knew he was upset because his cheeks were wet and smudged from where his dusty hand had wiped his face. She instinctively ran towards him.

'Oh, Da, don't go. Can't you stay and get rid of *him*?'

She flung her outstretched arm in the direction of the kitchen without turning her head. As soon as the words left her mouth, she wanted to grab them back. Too quick to speak, as always. The only thing she was good at was saying the wrong thing. Or opening her mouth at the wrong time. Or both, like now. Her father lifted his head slowly from the suitcase. He looked so hurt. When he spoke, his voice was barely a whisper.

'You knew.'

'I'm sorry, Da. I didn't tell you because I didn't know what to say. What to do. I'm so sorry. He's a bastard. Please, don't go.'

Her father began throwing his clothes into the open suitcase, grabbing them from the drawer and the wardrobe. Hangers clattering onto the floor was the only sound, apart from her mother's snivelling. Finally, he closed the suitcase, clicked the lock into place and put it on the floor. Then he came to Tina and put his arms around her.

When her father finally let go, he just said, 'Don't swear, Tina. It's not ladylike.' As he was about to leave the room, he turned and added, 'You don't want to turn into your mother, do you?'

Then her father, Robert Wilson, put on his cap, lifted the two suitcases and walked out of 27 Mosley Street, and out of their lives. Tina stood, rooted to the spot, desperate to run after him, but unable to move. She thought about Isa and Rose, still at work. What would they say? The job didn't seem important anymore. All Tina wanted to do was get out of this place. She kicked the bedroom door closed, threw herself onto the bed and bawled into the pillow.

## 5. Terri. Perth. 24th June 2020
### *Reflection: My Mother Tina's Story*

I close my eyes and try to let the past wash over me. That's the thing about the past—you can't change any of it, no matter how hard you try. It's yours and that's that. And sometimes talking out loud is harder than thinking about it.

As a child, I remember believing I didn't belong in my own life. I was desperate to escape, like Tina. I had no intention of staying and being part of the future laid out for me. But this story has also stirred up more recent, unhappy memories. Memories that involve hurting Maureen.

Tina wasn't always a great mum to me, but let's face it, her mother hadn't set much of an example. After Robert Wilson walked out that day, Tina didn't see her father again until she was in her thirties. He wanted to divorce Teresa Wilson and remarry, but she refused. When he asked his two remaining daughters for help, Tina agreed. She went to court and testified that her mother had been living with George Lynch for years. Tina's mother and sister never forgave her. But I always thought it was a brave thing to do.

Robert Wilson remarried and had another family. He and Tina met now and again and my brother, Robert, is named after him. I suppose nowadays they'd all be friends, but the world was a different place then. I'm glad Tina's lingering memory of her father wasn't of him walking out the door.

I adored my own father, Alec Coulter. He died on 15th September 1952, during my honeymoon. My mother didn't cope well and spent a lot of time in our house, crying and smoking. When she was in her early fifties, she answered an advert in the newspaper and got a job in New York. She was happy there, coming home for holidays to stay with us, which was fine. I could cope with her for short periods. Then, twelve years later, Tina had a row with her male friend and quit New York. After some persuasion, she eventually returned to the States to sort things out. Joe and I didn't have much money, but we scraped enough together to pay her fare. It was worth it to get her out of the house.

Colette was nine at the time and when she tried to run away from home because of my mother's behaviour, it was the final straw for Joe. She had to go!

Maureen has come back into the room. It must be lunchtime because she is carrying a tray. I sit up and gather myself together.

'Have I been asleep?'

'Just a snooze,' she says and smiles.

She lays the tray down on the coffee table. Her smile fades and she has that worried look on her face.

'I hope I didn't upset you or tire you out this morning.'

I take a moment. Sometimes I can say the wrong thing. Maybe I'm a bit like my mother that way. I struggle to find the right words. I don't want to get this wrong.

'I was thinking about George Lynch,' I say. 'I was thinking about all the trouble he caused. Not just in Tina's life but in yours.'

I feel awkward and don't trust myself to say any more. Maureen comes over and clasps my hand between hers again. Her face is bright and her eyes are shining with love.

'It's alright, Mum. I'm glad you told me the story. It was an important part of your mother's life. And Tina's past affected yours, too. George Lynch definitely affected my life. But it was a long time ago. Let's not waste our time or breathe on him. You and I are here today, enjoying each other's company. We are writing a book together. That's exciting. That's here and now. To hell with him!'

Maureen distributes the goodies on her tray. The subject is closed. I am grateful and very relieved. My grandmother, Teresa Wilson, wasn't a nice woman. And she drank too much. After she died, I kept in touch with George Lynch because I felt sorry for him. When he was in his eighties, the tenements around the Gorbals were pulled down. I brought him to live with us. Joe had just opened the flower shop in Shawlands. Staff were expensive and I had to work a lot. George was there, which meant I didn't have to pay a babysitter. I thought the children were safe. I was wrong.

The day Maureen told me was one of the worst in my life. We were sitting in the conservatory of her house in Edinburgh and she just blurted it out. She was married, Mark was seven and she was pregnant with Paul. She had already told Martin, but even he didn't know for a long time after they were married. It can't have been easy for him to hear. But I've never discussed it with him. Maureen has told me I made hurtful and inappropriate comments at the time. I honestly didn't know what to say. It was such a shock. I couldn't take it all in. Eventually, I said something like, 'Oh, Maureen.' And then, because I couldn't think straight, I said, 'How could it happen when the other children were in the house? I trusted him. I thought there was safety in numbers.' Not finding the right words. Saying the wrong thing. And then the worst bit. 'Why didn't you tell me?'

I remember Maureen visibly bristling. Her eyes changed from sad and upset to cold and angry.

'I couldn't tell you or anyone else. Don't you get it, Mum? I felt guilty. I was ashamed. And now you're making me feel guilt and shame all over again.'

That hit me hard. I think I cried. It was me who felt guilty. My own daughter couldn't talk to me. Why couldn't she talk to me? Why did she not tell me? But when would it have been the right time? I was working six days a week and had four children younger than Maureen. She was sensible and responsible. When I think about it now, there was no right time for her. There were signs. I should have noticed them. Should have known. But I was too busy. I had no idea. Things weren't the same as nowadays, when sexual abuse is on the news and people talk about it. Even priests are going to jail for the crimes they committed years ago. Joe's heart would have been broken if he'd been alive. He would never have recovered.

I understand it all better now. I wish I could go back and do it all differently: Pay more attention. Spend more time listening. Not let it happen. Ask the right questions. Say the right thing. But, as I've said, you can't change the past. Any of it. It's yours and that's that. I can only live with it and let it wash over me when I close my eyes.

'Mum. Are you alright?'

Maureen's worried look is back. I drag my thoughts into the present.

'You're right,' I say. 'No more wasted time discussing that man. When can we talk about the army?'

We both laugh.

'I love you, Mum,' she says.

A rush of love takes my breath away, then gives it back, strong and calm.

'And I love you, my darling girl.'

## 6. Maureen. Perth. 24th June 2020
*Between the lines*

Mum is snoozing after lunch. I am in the 'wee' room upstairs, where I have engineered a writing area. Perhaps *engineered* is an over-the-top description for an Ercol sofa, a suitcase and a tray. There is no space for a desk with the assortment of furniture in this tiny room. I remind myself that good writers don't need a fancy environment.

I close the laptop without re-reading the first fictionalised account of one of Mum's stories. Tina's job interview was also the day her father left home. Mum wanted me to understand why Tina's mothering skills left something to be desired. That was the real story. But it had an impact on me. An unexpected repercussion. There was no way Mum could talk about the day Tina's father walked out without mentioning George Lynch. His name must have been difficult for her to say. It was certainly hard for me to hear. I thought I would struggle to write the story, but being inside Tina's head provided perspective and distance.

I was sexually abused more than fifty-five years ago and have lived with the consequences ever since. I have accepted its ramifications and worked hard not to let it ruin or define my life. However, it would be foolish to deny or diminish the devastating fallout. Sexual abuse is like an octopus whose tentacles reach far beyond the abuse itself, ambushing your life when least expected.

From the vantage point of hindsight, education, life experience and time, I understand it was not my fault. I am also aware that some decisions in my life were tainted by this early experience. Initially, I trusted too easily and then found it hard to trust at all. My intellectual and emotional responses have often been at odds with each other. The insidious guilt is hard to slough: I allowed it to happen. Did not refuse. Did not shout. Did not stop it. For a long time, I also lived with the guilt of not telling anyone.

After bottling it up until I was in my thirties, I talked to my sister, my husband and my mum. In that order. Another ten years later, I told my two closest friends from school. It was a shock to discover they were already aware of my secret. I had confided in them individually when we were at school. When it was happening. We were all eleven years old and my friends had no idea what to do with the information, or even what it meant. How could I have forgotten? I felt hugely relieved, knowing I had reached out to them, even if it changed nothing. The knowledge was therapeutic. I think it helped me forgive myself.

I understood why Mum was angry at the man she had invited into her home. I understood why she was hurt that her eldest daughter had not opened up to her. I understood she did not blame me. Of course, my rational brain understood everything. But my emotional brain was in tatters. Never, not even in the far corners of my mind, did I ever blame my parents. It was not my fault, but it was not theirs either. We were living in different, less enlightened times. Mum and Dad were busy in their flower shop, working to provide five children with the education and opportunities they had been denied.

It may have been happening to other girls in my school. or on my street, or in my city. But I thought I was the only one. Now that historical sexual abuse is openly discussed, I know that I was certainly not alone. Mum and I moved on after that day and had never discussed the subject of George Lynch since then. Until yesterday.

Yes, trauma is complex and victims are diverse. Mum and I were both victims of George Lynch. My body was abused. Her trust was abused. When I first told Mum, we were both hurting, but unable to find a mutual path to cope. The story of Tina in 1924 triggered a different discussion, still painful, but shared in a new way. I wanted Mum to know that I loved her for all the times in my life she has been by my side. Supporting me in so many ways, too many to count or recall. She did her best. Always. And that's all any of us can do.

* * *

I let go of the past and return to the present, daydreaming. Wouldn't it be amazing to finish this book before Mum dies? I imagine her holding it, surrounded by family and friends. Of course, there's no Covid in my daydream. How thrilled she would be, knowing her stories are captured on its pages. But the daydream balloon bursts. Who am I kidding? I have journals filled with impending writing projects, deadlines never met and goals not achieved. I have read books about how to write a novel, how *not* to write a novel and everything in between. Spoiler: none of them came with a magic formula! I have attended workshops, both in person and online, and watched countless YouTube videos. I have dabbled for years writing poems, essays, songs and ditties. I have a half-written play, known as a WIP (work in progress), although in my case, progress has ground to a halt. In 2012, I helped to compile an anthology by Sligo women in mid-life, aptly titled *Mid Life Slices*. I was very proud of that book. But it was published eight years ago.

I place the tray and laptop on the sofa and wrestle my legs from either side of the suitcase. Stretching my aching limbs as I stand at the window, I find myself talking to the garden.

'I'm a dabbler. A dabbler! What makes me think I can write a whole book? By myself?'

Unsurprisingly, the garden has no answer. But I hear my own voice.

'So what if you're a dabbler? You have a laptop, a notebook and a pen. And, most importantly, you have your mum. So dabble. Get on with it. One story at a time.'

I sit down again, leaning back against the bulky cushions on this uncomfortable couch and close my eyes.

I think of Tina, not as a nineteen-year-old girl, but as a mother and grandmother. I never knew my grandfather, Alec Coulter, but my gran lived until she was eighty-five. The story I have just written reminds me of something Gran told me: she had no memory of sitting on her mother's knee. No memory of ever hearing Teresa Wilson say, 'I love you.' Gran Coulter was not afraid to speak her mind, but I felt overwhelmed with sadness for her that day. She never alluded to it again. I don't think Tina knew how to handle vulnerability, especially her own. She was a complex character: fierce and funny, yet also fragile and defensive.

I am struck by how closely the past and present are linked and by the way one generation quietly shapes the next. I want to know more about Tina and Alec Coulter during Mum's formative years. I am also keen to learn more about Mum's other grandmother, Annie Coulter.

My goal is to understand more about the people and events that shaped my mother's life, including the influences before she was even born.

## 7. Terri. Perth. 25<sup>th</sup> June 2020
*Reflection: Annie Coulter, My Grandmother and Inspiration*

It feels strange talking to Maureen about my grandparents when I am ninety-one, grandmother to fifteen and great-grandmother to three.

I may have been named after Teresa Wilson, but she wasn't much of a mother to Tina or a grandmother to me. Annie Coulter, my father's mother, was a different kettle of fish. She was my role model growing up, as well as my beloved grandmother. The Coulters lived in the top flat of 209 Thistle Street on the corner with Hospital Street, a tenement building in one of the better areas of the Gorbals. It was much bigger than any of the places we stayed. Nowadays, it would be referred to as a penthouse. It had an inside toilet in the hall known as the water-closet. That was a huge luxury and was one of the many reasons I loved staying there as a girl. Thistle Street was my safe place, my haven.

\* \* \*

**Annie Coulter. Thistle Street, Gorbals. March 1925-Life Goes On**

It was six o'clock on a cold and foggy March morning. The corner tenement at 209 Thistle Street in the heart of the Glasgow Gorbals was already wide awake.

Not for the first time, Annie Coulter on the top floor thanked God that her husband, Alec, had never been a drinker. She could hear the Ryan children on the floor below howling their objections to being pulled from their bed to make way for their father after his overnight shift at the Singers factory. A few early morning pints in The Seaforth Bar hadn't helped his mood and he roared to be heard above his three screaming children.

It had been an eventful week. A terrible week. The worst week. But it was Monday and Annie always did the washing on a Monday, so that's exactly what she was going to do today. She bent down and dragged the large tin bath from under the bed recess in the kitchen. The older boys and girls had left for work and the others were still asleep. She unfolded the wooden chair from beside the cooker at the scullery door and lifted the old bath onto the seat. The mangle was next. Sliding it across the scullery floor from its home beside the sink, Annie placed it carefully behind the chair. A cast iron pot on the cooker was already full of boiling towels and the brass kettle was heating on the kitchen fire. This was a routine Annie had followed for twenty-two years, since the day she married Alec Coulter, the love of her life. And now he was gone. She needed routine. It would keep her sane. It would stop her from screaming out loud like the Ryan children downstairs.

Annie sat at the kitchen table and began sorting the clothes in front of her. Condensation dribbled down the big bay window. She closed her eyes and let the comforting smell of steam envelop her. On the street below, she could hear the clip-clopping of the coal man's horse and cart on the cobblestones, his distinctive cry of 'Coal up. Coal up.'

But Annie would not be lowering her bucket for filling this morning. She listened to the Gorbals coming to life: the rumbling and grinding of the tram, the squeaking of shutters being lifted, Mr and Mrs Fogell enticing early morning customers with chat and the smell of freshly baked black bread.

By now, the pavements would be pulsing with men and women heading to factories and shops. Annie pictured Alec talking to Max and Yetta Foggell, lunch tin under his oxter, tea mug swinging from two fingers in that familiar way of his. Pain pierced her heart with raw grief. Renegade tears slithered from her closed eyes. She straightened her back and dabbed them with the corner of her apron, reprimanding herself. There was twice as much washing to be done this morning because she hadn't done any last Monday. The past week had all been a blur.

\* \* \*

That Friday, during her afternoon visit to Alec in the Royal Infirmary, the professor had come to the bedside and announced that the bowel surgery had been 'a huge success'. Alec's gaunt face, as white as the starched pillow behind his head, stretched into a beaming smile when he heard the news. It made her heart flutter. Annie wanted to hug Sister Baker, who stood like a sentry beside the professor in his stiff white coat. But she resisted the urge, lifting Alec's hand and kissing it gently instead. Even that small gesture elicited a disapproving glare from Sister Baker.

*If only I'd known it was going to be our last kiss and our last moment together, Alec. I would have thrown my arms around you, kissed you properly and whispered something meaningful,* she thought now, her hands mechanically organising her family's clothes into bundles for washing.

She had said, 'I think I'll treat the children to a bag of Soor Plooms on the way home to celebrate!'

Alec's smile got even bigger. 'And don't forget to buy a quarter of treacle toffees for their mother.'

*Our last conversation was about sweeties, Alec.* And the tears stung again.

The day after that final visit was Saturday, and Annie had busied herself with the shopping and cleaning. She wanted to have the place spick and span for when her Alec came home. The house was quiet by evening time. Alec Junior and his brother, John, were at St. Francis Church Hall playing pool. They were close in age and great pals as well as brothers. The older girls were out dancing, the younger ones with friends. George was upstairs reading, while William and Janet were tucked up in bed. Annie was preparing the vegetables for Sunday dinner when she heard hammering on the door. She wiped her hands down the front of her apron, rushing to the door before the noise wakened the children. Grace Devlin from number 203 along the street was standing there in her nursing uniform. Her face was as pale as her uniform, her beautiful features tight and drawn, making her look terrified. Annie was about to ask her what was wrong when she burst into loud sobs. Annie quickly ushered Grace inside before the neighbours had time to come out for a nosy.

'Come away in, lass, and sit yourself down. What about a wee cup of tea? And you can tell me all about it. Things are never as bad as they seem after a cup of sweet tea.'

But Grace could not be soothed, so Annie sat beside the weeping girl, and gently stroked her hand.

'Mrs Coulter, I'm so very sorry. Mr Coulter's... there was... they did... I'm so very sorry. Oh God, I'm so sorry, Mrs Coulter.'

Grace buried her head in her hands and continued to cry as if her heart was breaking. There was no sense to the words coming from her mouth, but Annie knew exactly what she was saying. After more tears and a little coaching, Grace explained there had been 'complications' and Alec had died, despite their efforts to save him. They had planned to send a policeman to tell Annie, but Grace was working on the female surgical ward next door and wanted to break the news herself.

*What a kind thing for you to do,* Annie thought, before her brain froze and shut down. She remembered little else about that night.

* * *

Now, Annie stirred the pot of boiling towels and made a mental note to go to the house and tell Grace's mother what a kind and thoughtful girl she was. Annie wasn't sure if she had even thanked her at the time. Grace must have thought her very cold-hearted. She hadn't screamed or even wept. She just recalled feeling completely numb. Annie wasn't one for wailing tantrums. They were undignified and rarely altered the outcome. She had witnessed too many screeching women in the Gorbals. She was not one of them. Her abiding memory of that night was the image of the gloating professor.

*Not such a great success after all, Professor,* she thought, giving the towels a final poke and turning off the heat.

Annie opened the kitchen window to let out some of the steam. No more time for remembering or feeling sorry for herself. Alec was gone and she had to get on with life.

*You have nine bairns to rear and the rent to find every month, Annie Coulter,* she whispered to herself, gulping in a mouthful of fresh air from the open window. *Today is Monday and on Monday you do the washing.*

She lifted the washtub to the sink and half-filled it with cold water from the brass tap. Back on its wooden chair, Annie added hot water from the kettle until it was warm enough for sluicing, then plunged in the towels. She hand-wrung them, fed them through the mangle's rollers, and cranked hard to squeeze out every drop she could. It didn't look like a good drying day, so she hung the towels on the pulley in the scullery, keeping the clothes horse beside the fire for the other bits and pieces. She enjoyed watching the mangle flatten wrinkles from the wet cloth, sometimes saving her the bother of flat-ironing. Annie's mother had given it to her after she married, and she often shared it with neighbours who couldn't afford one, sparing them the cost of the steamie.

'I don't need it anymore,' her mother had said. 'Anyway, my old hands aren't up to the cranking.'

Annie didn't believe her, but Mrs Brown had looked so pleased that she gratefully accepted the gift as well as the inevitable lecture on cleanliness.

'Don't ever let your family wear dirty clothes, Annie,' she'd said in that stern yet gentle way of hers. 'It's a sign of ignorance 'round these parts. Get yourself a routine for the washing and stick to it. It doesn't matter if the clothes are old. As long as they're clean, they can be worn with pride.'

Her mother was a wise woman and Annie had followed her advice from that day on.

Even when the babies were barely out of the womb, Annie insisted one of her sisters come over to do the heavy lifting of the basin and mangle. Monday washday went ahead as normal, with laughter and chatter as they worked. Luckily, she had never delivered a baby on a Monday.

*I wish you were here to give me one of your wise lectures today,* Annie thought, topping up the water in the tub and lifting the Janet's vest from the pile. She immersed it in the warm water, dabbed it with Sunlight soap, and rubbed it gently on the rippled glass surface of the board. It wasn't soiled, but the steady motion comforted her as she moved the little white garment up and down.

Poor wee Janet was only four and would have no memory of her father. Alec had always made time to play with her on the kitchen floor after work. It wasn't fair. But life wasn't fair for many people nowadays. It was just how the cookie crumbled. You had to keep going or fall apart, and there was no point in that.

*So, no tears today, Annie. No tears!*

She had not been allowed to see Alec at the hospital on the Sunday morning when she gathered herself together and made the journey across town. She knocked on the swing doors of the ward, the same doors she had breezed through just two days earlier. A nurse eventually poked her head out.

'I'm Mrs Coulter. I've come to see my husband, Alec. He passed away last night.' Annie swallowed hard, but she could hear her voice quivering. 'I couldn't come before now.'

The nurse whispered as if it were the middle of the night and the patients were all asleep.

'Oh. Yes. Mrs Coulter.'

Her head disappeared back inside. Annie had taken the two older boys with her for support. They stood facing the closed doors, holding hands, a lost-looking trio. Annie was about to turn away when Sister Baker barged through like a drill sergeant on parade.

'Mrs Coulter, did Nurse Devlin not inform you that Mr Coulter was no longer a patient here? I am sorry for your loss, but Mr Coulter died peacefully and has been removed to the morgue. You should not have bothered coming all this way. I am sure you have enough to do with a funeral to organise. These are Mr Coulter's belongings.'

Sister Baker took a brown paper parcel from under her arm and thrust it at Annie. Without another word, she disappeared back through the ominous grey doors, which swung back and forth in her wake. The three of them stood in silence until the doors to the ward where Alec Coulter had spent his final hours also stilled.

The rest of the Coulter household was coming to life on this brisk March morning. Annie heard the girls upstairs getting ready and the younger ones stirring in the bedroom down the hall. It was time to clear the table for the breakfast rush. She could finish later when the house was calm again. Life went on, though it would never be the same. But it was Monday, and Annie always did the washing on a Monday. So that was what she was going to do.

## 8. Terri. Perth. 25th June 2020
### *Postscript for Annie Coulter, a Remarkable Woman*

Maureen is sitting beside my bed with her cup of tea on the window ledge. She has been looking into the historical context of when Annie Coulter was widowed. She reads from her notebook, then stops abruptly for a mouthful of tea, looking pensive.

'Annie Coulter was widowed at the age of forty-one with nine children,' she announces as if it's something I don't know. 'That was before the Welfare State. Before the NHS. Before Children's Allowance. Even before Means Testing, which didn't come into effect until the beginning of 1931. The widows of insured men got 10 shillings after 1926.'

I put in my tuppence worth. 'Well, that would have been no use anyway, because Alec Coulter wasn't insured. He was a journeyman.'

She puts down her notebook.

'It's outrageous when you think about it. Annie would have been left to go cap in hand to the State or charitable institutions looking for help. There was nothing else. No wonder women and children ended up in the Poor House. Thank God that didn't happen to Annie.'

I agree with Maureen. 'My grandmother was a proud and dignified woman. I can't imagine her going to the authorities to be scrutinised for a pittance.

'And very little pity,' Maureen adds.

\* \* \*

We're downstairs now and have finished our morning latte. Maureen is still trying to work out how Annie managed her finances after her husband, my grandfather Alec, died.

'The thing about history, Maureen,' I say, 'is that it's just life when you're living through it. The Depression started in 1929, the year I was born. My grandfather had been dead for four years by then. I don't remember any discussions about money when I stayed in Thistle Street. Annie never looked worried or stressed to me. 'I know that when she was first widowed, my grandmother visited the local priest to ask for help. He examined her neat appearance: smart coat and hat, shiny shoes, gloved hands. Then sent her on her way. He didn't notice her darned clothes, the shoes held together with nails and filled with paper, or the hat and gloves that were old and frayed. All he saw was a woman who stood straight and looked him in the eye. Annie's maiden name was Brown and the family was Protestant. She had converted to Catholicism to marry Alec Coulter. That same week, the Minister from her old church visited the house, bringing a financial donation, cakes from the ladies of the parish, and coal for the fire. Who could blame Annie for going back to the Church of Scotland? No one… apart from my mother, who used to say, *she sold her soul for a bag of coal*.'

Maureen laughs and abandons her notebook.

'It seems to me, Annie Coulter was a strong, resourceful woman. Turns out you didn't get it from the breeze!'

I smile at the compliment, happy to go on talking about Annie.

'My grandmother was what you'd call *perjink*. Do you know what I mean by that? It's an old-fashioned word. A combination of neat and precise. And that's exactly how I remember her. She always drank her tea from a china cup and had a little bowl with nutmeg and a tiny grater. I was fascinated. We were lucky to find a clean cup without a chip in our house. And my mother wasn't a woman anyone would have called perjink!'

As I talk, I can see myself sitting with Grandma Coulter. I feel the love, the sense of awe. I grab a tissue to dab my eyes. I'm not talking about history anymore. I'm not even wondering how Annie Coulter managed to provide for her family. I'm back in my childhood. And it feels good. Like last week. Not more than eighty years ago. I don't want to stop. I think Maureen is enjoying my story too.

'When I stayed with my grandmother, I slept beside her in the big double bed. She always brought me breakfast in bed in the morning, the way you do. When you put the tray on my lap and open the curtains, it reminds me of those happy days in Thistle Street. Grandma Coulter would pull open the long, heavy curtains. I think they were brocade. She probably made them herself. Then she would come over to the bed, punch the pillows behind my head and lay the tray gently on my lap. An orange cut into neat segments, a soft roll my grandmother would spread with real butter, not margarine. She flattened it with the palm of her hand and cut it into quarters. There was always a white linen napkin folded neatly at the left side of the plate and a tall glass half-filled with milk in the right-hand corner of the tray.

She'd say, "Now then, lass. Breakfast is the most important meal of the day." Then she'd leave me to enjoy every morsel.

'I look out over swaying bushes and a tree in the garden these days. But when I sat up in the big bed in Thistle Street, I could see the chimneys on the rooftops of the tenements across the road. Their smoke curled into the sky. I was mesmerised by the patterns and shapes it made. Nothing on the ground mattered. Years later, I visited the National Museum in London. I saw a copy of a painting by Vincent Van Gogh. It was called something like *Stars at Night* or *Starry Night*. It reminded me of those trails of chimney smoke. I don't think I've ever told anyone that before.'

Maureen smiles as she clears the coffee cups.

'Thank you for sharing your lovely story, Mum,' she says, and goes off to do her own bits and pieces. I'm ready for a snooze.

*Oh, Grandma Coulter, I wish I'd told you what an amazing woman you were. And that you played an important part in my life, long after those days in Thistle Street. I like to think I got my 'mind over matter' attitude from you.*

I feel my wet eyes closing. I'm very tired. I hope I dream about Thistle Street.

## 9. Terri. Perth. 25<sup>th</sup> June 2020
### *Reflection: Moving House. My First Memory*

I'm back in bed after a lovely day remembering and chatting about my special grandmother. I haven't thought about those happy times for so long. Annie lived in Thistle Street until well after I was married. But we moved a lot when I was growing up.

My earliest memory is sitting on the edge of a wheelbarrow during a moonlight flit. We called it moonlighting because people went from one tenement to another during the night under the light of the moon. Nowadays, they want you to pay your bills online and send lots of letters when you don't!

The Factors worked for the landlords. They were supposed to be responsible for maintenance in the tenements, but no one dared ask about repairs. It was grounds for eviction. In some parts of the Gorbals, the houses were very bad. Toilets on the landing overflowed and poured down the stairs. Rats often ran amok. But they still came to collect the rent, bringing a couple of heavies to protect them from angry tenants. They didn't bother to come after people who flitted during the night because there was always someone ready to move in. No matter what state the place was in.

I remember the cold metal rim of the wheelbarrow on the back of my legs that night. But it's the sadness in my father's eyes I'll never forget.

### 10. Alec Coulter. The Gorbals. July 1932
### The Moonlight Flit

Alec Coulter finished putting the last of their belongings into the wheelbarrow.

*Belongings,* he thought. It was a rather grand word to describe the collection of bits and pieces at the bottom of the rusty barrow.

'Be careful with those cups,' his wife Tina snapped. 'They'd better arrive at the new place the same way they left the old one!'

He looked at Tina, standing in the mouth of the tenement close, their home for the past nine months. They had both liked the place and it was near his mother, Annie, and his family in Thistle Street. But he couldn't keep paying the rent and the Factor was due the following day. This was their only option, but Alec hated it. He didn't answer Tina. He knew she didn't mean to sound sharp. None of this was her fault. She was angry at the world, not just him.

They had been married for four years. He lost his job in the docks two months later and hadn't found one since then. He felt so useless. It had been hard for everyone since the Crash in '29, but that didn't make him feel any better. Their beautiful daughter, Teresa, had been born that year, so there had been a silver lining. But silver linings did not pay the rent. And now they also had baby Alec. Three generations of Alec Coulter. His father would have been proud. He died of bowel cancer seven years ago and Alec still missed him every day. His mother, Annie, had always referred to them as Alec Senior and Alec Junior. The name had stuck, even though, technically, he was Alec Senior now that he had no father and an Alec of his own.

"We should have christened the baby Bert. Or Davey. Or Jim,' Tina had shouted at him one morning out of the blue. 'Anything but Alec. Your mother won't let go of your father's memory, so you have to be Alec Junior and he has to be wee Alec. Otherwise, no one will have a clue who we're talking about'!

He had let it go. The way he let most things go. It was the only way to keep the peace. His mother had suggested they all move to 209 Thistle Street until his finances improved, but Alec knew it would have been a

Impossible to Fill

disaster. Annie and Tina were poles apart, his mother, quiet and dignified, his wife, an opinionated firecracker. She was a live wire, alright. Maybe that's what had attracted him to her in the first place. She was different and unpredictable. But Tina and his mother were oil and water, and it was better to keep them separate because they were never going to mix. Alec looked up at the expanse of ink blue sky and smiled to himself. *No guiding star to show them to the new stable.*

'I'm glad you think this is funny,' Tina said.

He shone his torch in his wife's direction. Wee Alec was wrapped in a shawl in one hand and a large bag of clothes hung from the other. Her petite frame was drowning in layers of clothing to make them easier to carry. She wore two hats, her face nearly lost under the brim of one of them. Her heavy winter coat wouldn't close over multiple layers and she had a pair of huge goloshes on her small feet. Even Tina would have to admit she looked comical, dressed for a snowstorm on this warm July evening. But, as she had just reminded him, tonight was not the night to be funny.

'Stop dreaming and start walking,' she barked, as if reading his thoughts.

Alec looked down at little Teresa, pressed close to his leg as if afraid to let go. Her coat was buttoned over her pyjamas, the hem bunched under mismatched wool socks in her little slippers. Her favourite red hat was pulled down to her eyebrows, a woolly scarf tied tight under her chin. She looked lost and disoriented.

*The poor wee thing is probably terrified*, he thought and his stomach knotted with guilt again. *What kind of man am I, dragging my family from one dismal tenement flat to another in the middle of the night?*

Alec knelt beside his daughter and tried to smile. He could feel his lips quivering and concentrated hard to steady his voice. 'Now, my little Treasure, we are going on an adventure. We are like the wise men who walked beneath the stars. We are going to our new Kingdom, where all will be well.'

Teresa loved stories and he shone the torch and saw her little face light up with anticipation. He half expected her to announce that there were no stars that night, but all she said was, 'Go Daddy.'

Abbotsford Place, their destination, was certainly not a Kingdom. It was overcrowded and they did not even have their own kitchen. But it was in a safe area of the Gorbals and that was important these days.

Small Shoes

There was so much unemployment and desperation that gangs of men were taking the law into their own hands. Alec ignored Tina's derisive tutting at his story and swallowed hard, pushing the rising bile back down his throat. He was grateful for the darkness that prevented his little girl from seeing his shimmering tears. Alec lifted her into his arms, cuddled her and set her on the edge of the wheelbarrow. He knew she would be looking at him with her trusting blue eyes. He should have said more to reassure her, but he couldn't speak. And he had no words of reassurance to offer.

Tina was a practical woman, not a dreamer like him. They had sat at the kitchen table the previous night, looked at their meagre funds and made the decision to do a Moonlight Flit.

'Stop feeling sorry for yourself, Alec Coulter,' she had said, pausing to add, '...Junior. Aren't most of the men out of work 'round here? Just get on with it.'

How many times over the past four years had she told him to 'get on with it'? The 'it' changed depending on the situation and tonight it meant leaving their tenement in the dead of night without paying the rent. A new low point. The Gorbals used to be a nice area, built to house all the men and their families who came to Glasgow to work on the railway and the docks. They flooded in from Ireland and the Highlands in the hope of a better life. There had been plenty of employment then. But the war, the Wall Street Crash and the Depression had taken their toll all over the world. Now, they all hung about on street corners smoking cigarettes and trying to keep from under their wives' feet. Sometimes, one of the lads got excited about a possible job at the docks or in one of the local factories, but the next day he would turn up on the corner with a face as long as his arm. No one asked any questions.

Alec bent his knees and lifted the back of the wheelbarrow off the ground. He concentrated hard to steady himself and smiled into the darkness. 'Right then, off we go into the night, Princess.'

Tina came up beside him. 'Just get on with it, Alec!' she hissed into his ear.

Alec's grey overcoat and cap were soon damp with salty sweat that dripped into his mouth. They hadn't far to travel. Along Eglinton Street into Bedford Street, then round the corner into Abbotsford Place. His friend, Jimmy Rafferty, had vouched for him and there was only a week's rent needed to secure the place. Alec lowered the wheelbarrow to rest his arms for a moment, checking that the key was in his pocket.

'Daddy, can I walk now?' Teresa asked quietly. 'My legs are hurting.'

He was about to say 'Of course,' when Tina piped up. 'It's too dark to walk. We'll be there soon.'

He lifted Teresa down, took a blanket from inside the barrow and draped it over its edge. Then Alec carefully placed his daughter on the blanket. 'Now, isn't that nice and soft?' he said, with as much enthusiasm as he could muster. He could hear Tina tutting again behind him.

'Yes, Daddy,' Teresa said.

He didn't need to look to know his precious daughter was smiling up at him. Alec Coulter Junior lifted the wheelbarrow full of their worldly goods and trudged along Eglinton Street. His arms and back ached, but not as much as his heart.

## 11. Terri. Perth. 26*th* June 2020
### *Reflection: From the Gorbals to a Tent*

I'm sitting with the dregs of my morning latte. The sun is shining through the living room window and making me feel delightfully sleepy. Some days I feel tired, other days I feel *very* tired. Anyway, I'm happy to be left in peace to snooze.

Maureen and I have been discussing the time when my father took us to live in a tent on a campsite in Skelmorlie. I was about four or five at the time, but it's hard to pinpoint my exact age in these stories. I think Maureen gets frustrated at times.

'You can't have been four, Mum,' she said this morning. 'You told me you were four in the story about moonlighting.'

And, of course, she was right. But as I pointed out, 'When you're ninety-one, all those early memories merge or get mixed up. I was a wee girl. That's all I know.'

Maybe I was just three when we moonlighted, but I'll keep the thought to myself. Anyway, it makes no difference to the story. It's just the idea of the thing!

After the moonlight flit, we stayed for two years in one large room in Abbotsford Place. We lived and slept in that room, with a communal kitchen which even my mother described as a disgrace. But the shared toilet on our floor of the house was clean and that was important to me. I think the Irish woman next door took it upon herself to make sure it stayed that way. My father told me the buildings on our road were home to the wealthy Tobacco Lords at one time.

Dad took me to the big library on Rosamund Street when I was seven or eight. He wanted to prove the Gorbals was not a slum, even if that's what the newspapers called it. We flicked through photographs of the way it used to look before neglected tenements became overcrowded and greedy landlords took advantage of the need for cheap housing.

We read about how the Potato Famine in Ireland and the forced eviction of crofters in the Highlands caused a huge influx of people into the city in search of work. We looked at photographs of men in the shipbuilding yards, proud to be part of the industry. The same with the railway and the Singer factory. The Gorbals itself wasn't known for its industry. The area was mostly shops and pubs, but it was near the city centre and within easy reach of industrial work. There was also a thriving Jewish community, with wonderful tailors and shops that sold all sorts. My parents weren't great Mass goers and I often went alone. But if I had no clean white socks, I could ask for a few pence and run round the corner for a pair on Sunday morning.

When things became too much for Mum in Abbotsford Place, Dad decided it would be a good idea to move out of the city for a while. He bought a tent and practiced putting it up in our one room, much to my mother's annoyance. It was made of thick, dark green canvas and was big enough to stand up in the centre. My father had never set up a tent before and it took a lot of effort. I remember him trying to fit lots of poles together, especially the big one holding up the roof. It was called a *ridge pole*. I never forgot the word because he said it so often.

'The ridge pole must be secure. The ridge pole is the most important one. As long as the ridge pole is secure.'

He showed us the guy ropes but couldn't try them out on a hard floor. We buttoned and unbuttoned the flaps on either side of the entrance to the tent until we got it right. My brother Alec and I thought it was great fun, but my mother just tutted a lot and threatened to leave if my father didn't take it down.

'Soon enough I'll have to sleep in that thing,' she said, or something similar with more swearing.

\* \* \*

We lived in a campsite in Dundonald for a few weeks before moving to Skelmorlie on the Firth of Clyde. Funny to think that years later, my husband Joe and I bought a house in the same village. It was a beautiful red sandstone building on the coast road, which had once belonged to Lord Kilmarnock. The house is now divided into three separate homes. Ours was on the first floor with magnificent views of the Clyde. I'm not sure where the campsite was in Skelmorlie, only that it was high on a steep hill with a long walk down to the water. I have no clear picture of Dundonald, but I remember the tent and the field in Skelmorlie as if it were yesterday.

I'll never forget my first gulp of Clyde Coast air: cold and salty, with a faint smell of fish. Not the kind you'd cook, more like a flavour in the breeze that made my eyes and nose stream. It felt as if we'd landed on another planet, not travelled thirty miles from Glasgow.

The tent was always a mess. I hated that, but we only slept there. We had free rein to play in the surrounding fields. My mother didn't ask questions as long as we weren't under her feet. Someone had built three wooden swings at the top of the site and all the children gathered there, waiting for their turn. We also tied ropes to the campsite poles and swung around them. I thought that was more fun. I was a real tomboy.

I suppose that's why I fell on a broken milk bottle outside the caravan beside our tent. I'd been jumping from stone to stone. I remember my mother screaming and my father wrapping a towel around my knee, lifting me into his arms and carrying me to the doctor in the village. It must have been a long way and I still don't know how he didn't drop me.

Some of the details about that day are vague, but others are as clear as a bell. The doctor stitched the wound while my father held me down. One hand pushed on my shoulder and the other on my leg, pinning me to the couch. He was speaking gently into my ear, which seemed at odds with what was happening. The rest is blurry. When I was older, Dad told me the doctor hadn't enough thread in his needle and had to do it all over again. That's why he had to hold me down. My father wasn't an angry man and never swore. But he told me, when that 'eejit doctor' asked him to come back in a week to have the stitches taken out, he shouted, 'Not bloody likely,' and walked out without paying.

He carried me back to the campsite, and we stopped off at Mrs Farrell's shop on the hill. I think she must have been shocked by the blood on my father's shirt because she fussed over us both. Tea for him, a lollipop for me, and a pot of her homemade jam to take away. I'm laughing to myself now because I had no idea I still remembered Mrs Farrell or her shop. Her Scottish accent was so strong I had trouble understanding her. Funny the things that pop into your head once you start digging. I didn't feel a thing when my father took the stitches out. I still have the scar on my knee.

I used to love it when my father took me fishing at the pier in Wemyss Bay. I rode on the front of his bicycle as we whizzed down the hill into the village with the wind blowing my hair and stinging my cheeks. The faster he went, the better I liked it. He would park the bike and sit on the stony shore with his rod dipped into the Firth of Clyde. I would balance along the thick wooden rafters underneath the pier, arms outstretched. I felt safe and happy, listening to the waves slapping against the pillars and watching the screeching seagulls.

I close my eyes and let the warm summer sunshine work its magic.

## 12. Tina Coulter. Skelmorlie. August 1934
### Living in a Campsite

Tina stood at the mouth of the tent, hands on her hips and apron fluttering in the wind. At 29 and a neat 5 feet 2, she was petite, but far from fragile. No one messed with Tina Coulter.

'Teresa, come away from that caravan. How many times do I have to tell you? That sour-faced old trollop'll use any excuse to come over and moan into my face.'

Tina wiped her wet hands down the sides of her apron. It was a hell of a way to live. A tent in a muddy field, they had the cheek to call a campsite. They were stuck at the top of a bloody big hill in the middle of nowhere. Oh, and then there were the trollops like her next door, who thought they were high and mighty because they had a caravan with a solid roof over their heads. Without waiting for a response from her daughter, Tina turned and marched back into the large green canvas tent, their home for the past eight weeks. It was cold, wet, and desolate. Like living in a foreign land for Tina, but Alec and the kids loved it. She had never heard of Skelmorlie until Alec's brother John got a job on some big estate. Even then, she hadn't taken much heed, except to note that it was somewhere near Largs, where Glaswegians with money went for holidays or expensive ice creams on a Sunday afternoon. How could you remember a name like Skelmorlie? It sounded like some sort of disease, or maybe a type of fish.

Tina had wanted to move back to the Gorbals after the Dundonald campsite fiasco, but Alec was determined to stay out of the city. It's not as if she'd loved Abbotsford Place. The outside of the building was better than a lot of tenements, but the inside was just as bad as the rest. Some greedy landlord made every room into a separate house for desperate families, like them. They had been in Abbotsford Place for two years since the moonlight flitting all crammed into one room. Every floor of the tenement shared a toilet and a kitchen, and Tina couldn't decide whether the smell from one was worse than the other. God knows what those Irish women cooked, but it stank. So, here they were, in a place with a name like a fish instead of smelling like one. And, of course, Alec had John on his side, both ganging up on her.

'Think of the children running around in the fresh air, Tina. Think of the freedom, Tina. It's just for a few months, Tina. You'll love it, Tina.'

Tina had to admit she had a soft spot for John. He wasn't as serious as his mother, even if he was working for a bloody Earl! He knew how to have a bit of a laugh, especially with the children. She had given in and although she would never admit it to Alec, it wasn't all bad. At least they didn't have to put up with her mother screeching from the street in Abbotsford Place after a few too many drinks. Teresa Wilson wouldn't be caught dead in a tent, so it had its advantages. She'd threatened Alec that if they didn't get out of Dundonald, she would move in with her mother. But there wasn't a snowball's chance of that happening. She was still living with that bastard, George Lynch. Tina couldn't have cared less if she never clapped eyes on either of them again. But this place was still a soggy field in the back arse of nowhere. Half the time, she didn't even think she spoke the same language as the locals, especially that stuck-up biddy in the shop.

Alec was sitting on the fold-up camping chair with a library book in his hand. Without lifting his head, he said, 'I wish you wouldn't talk like that in front of the children, Tina. And anyway, she's not a trollop. She's just trying to get by like the rest of us.'

Alec always saw the best in everyone. It was one of the reasons she fell for him in the first place. He was so different from her. But after seven years of marriage and a husband with no job, she just found his tolerance irritating.

'If she rattles that window one more time, 'trying to get by' will be the least of her worries!'

'Oh, Tina!'

He put down his book and came over to put a hand on her shoulder as if it would somehow, magically, calm her. It had the opposite effect.

She turned on him.

'Tina, don't shout! Tina, don't swear in front of the children! Tina, don't complain! Tina, you're lucky to have a tent to live in!'

She pushed past her husband and stomped out of the tent again. There was nowhere else to go. She couldn't throw on her coat and swan off to meet her pals or go to the bingo. Tina knew Alec would follow and try to make peace. He didn't like conflict. Unfortunately, she thrived on it. She couldn't help herself, the words were out before she could stop them. It had always been her problem and, God knows, it had gotten her into bother more times than she cared to remember. Her mother called her 'gobby', but who was she to talk? Her mother had been involved in more fights in the Close where she lived than the local stray cat!

Alec joined her, and they watched in silence as Teresa jumped from stone to stone across the muddy patches. She was very sure-footed, which was just as well because it was no easy job washing a filthy dress with no sink.

'I'll make a cup of tea,' she said, deciding it was time to stop bickering. Tina saw her husband's face visibly relaxing and broadening into a smile of relief.

'That's a great idea, Tina,' he said, as if she had suggested cooking him a steak dinner.

Having set the kettle on their little camping stove in the awning of the tent, Tina slumped into the one decent chair they had brought with them. It had been a gift from Alec's mother, Annie Coulter, and you couldn't deny it was comfortable. But who gives their son a wedding present of one chair? Alec said it was because his mother wanted to give them good chairs and could only afford one at a time. Mrs Coulter was the next best thing to a saint and it wasn't easy being married to the son of a saint. Annie managed the household budget on very little and always looked well-dressed. She baked and made clothes. And to top it all, she still had time to drink tea from a china cup! Yes, it was nauseating! But how could you not admire a woman who had brought up nine children on her own? The truth was that Tina would have given her eye teeth to be more like her saintly mother-in-law. Sometimes, she felt like a useless wife and mother, but she'd never admit that to Alec.

'I hope you're not looking for a biscuit,' she said to him now, slouching back in Mrs Coulter's chair.

Alec was sitting in the camping chair, his head stuck back in his book. He didn't answer. Probably didn't even hear her.

\* \* \*

Her husband may not have had any qualifications, but Alec Coulter was cleverer than the 'dimwits' who wouldn't give him a job. When they were courting, he'd tried to get Tina to go with him to the Gorbals library, one of his favourite places. But it wasn't her thing.

What she did love was going with him to the billiards hall. He'd been playing a match with his brother, John, in St Francis church hall the night they met. Alec was a champion and always claimed he lost that match because he was distracted by her. There was nothing he didn't know about Pool, from the history of the game to playing the winning shot. He could have gone professional, but he wanted a steady job, not one that meant travelling the country. These days, there was no shortage of billiards teams, not with so many men out of work. But Alec had lost heart. Somewhere along the way, they had both lost hope.

There wasn't much Alec didn't know about being a doctor, either. When Teresa had horrible yellow crusts on her face with impetigo and wee Alec had a bad throat and a nasty rash with scarlet fever, it was their father who had treated them. That Doctor Flanagan was a quack. Tina had heard Mary Fitzgerald talking to Millie Doyle outside the butchers. She hadn't left a tooth on it.

'That bleedin' man nearly killed my Stan. Calls himself a doctor. He went in with his blood pressure and came out with the same blood pressure and a bill for two and six!'

Tina wanted to chime in. *It's a wonder you haven't killed him yourself, Mary. He's a lazy good-for-nothing layabout.* She kept the thought to herself, which wasn't like her at all.

'Maybe we'll have a biscuit after all, Alec Coulter. If you take your nose out of that book and fetch them from the tin.'

## 13. Alec Coulter. Skelmorlie. Summer 1934
### *Stormy Weather*

Alec didn't notice the wind picking up at first. Barrhill Campsite sat at the top of a hill, with stunning views of the Firth of Clyde, but no protection from the elements. Fresh, blustery weather was part and parcel of life here. A healthy, if persistent breeze.

The storm that night took them all by surprise. It was mid-July and there'd been nothing to hint what lay ahead. It struck without warning, before anyone had time to bring in the belongings they'd left outside to make space inside the tents. A summer wind turned into an angry gale within minutes. Thankfully, the Coulters were all indoors when the sharp flapping of tarpaulin became more than background noise. The fibres of their tent stretched and tugged violently with the sound of snaps and cracks all around. It was like being attacked by a massive whip, as the storm's force attempted to pull their home free from its moorings.

'Daddy, I'm scared,' said Teresa in a tiny voice, while wee Alec shrieked in competition with the wind.

Tina stood frozen, unable to move. Alec knew he would have to act, and quickly.

'Tina, wrap all the breakables in clothes and towels. I'll make a secure area in the middle of the floor. The roof'll be okay if the tent holds. It's a good quality canvas and the ridge pole is strong. We'll be fine. But keep the children away from the sides.'

She didn't move. His heart lurched at the fear in her eyes.

He softened his tone. 'Tina, I need you. We can do this. Please. Let's see to the children.'

Outside, pots, pans and pieces of metal clattered and clanged as they hurtled through the air. The rhythmic jangling almost sounded like a percussion band, a strange contrast to the roaring storm. Every sound felt magnified: snapping ropes, shuddering poles, tearing canvas and flying debris merged into a single cacophony of unpredictable terror. Suddenly, something slammed into the side of the tent, denting it briefly before flying off. Tina screamed. Teresa and her wee brother followed suit. He was about to intervene when Tina shot to her feet, galvanised into action. She calmed the children and moved them to the centre of the tent.

When they'd done all they could to protect themselves and their belongings, they lay close together, each holding a child in their arms. Alec was confident the tent would hold, but there was a stone in his stomach that refused to budge. Through the din he could hear the occasional frantic shouts of people trying to secure their tents or banging on neighbouring caravans, seeking shelter. Alec thought briefly of the woman next door and hoped she was safe, then let the thought go. Tonight his only responsibility was here, with his family. Peering through the dark at the shapes of his sleeping wife and children, he couldn't help smiling. Tina was snoring despite everything. Life with Tina was often like living in the middle of a storm, but there was always hope of better weather to come.

He must have dozed off because the tent was brightened when he opened his eyes. Alec gently slipped his arm from under Teresa without waking her, shook it to restore circulation and eased himself out from under the pile of bedding. He wasn't sure when the storm had abated, only that it had gradually quietened, as if nature had run out of energy. He unbuttoned the tent flap and stepped outside. His body was stiff, his mind foggy with exhaustion, but the tent was still standing and his family were safe. Teresa crept up behind him, slipping one small hand into his and rubbing her eyes with the other. He turned to look at their home: bedraggled, torn at the edges, splattered with mud. Their home was a mere tent on a hillside. Hardly worthy of the word. Hardly an ideal shelter in a storm. Hardly the decision of a sane man.

He had struggled to pay the rent, it was true, but Alec had genuinely believed it would be good for Teresa and wee Alec to get away from the Gorbals: the smog, the overcrowded tenements, the sickness, the despair. He'd read about Dundonald one day in the library. Families were moving to a campsite there to escape the slums and noisy neighbours, in search of fresh air and space. All you needed was a decent tent from Black's and the bus fare from Glasgow. It had sounded ideal in the newspaper. Alec wasted no time gathering what they needed. But every other slum dweller had read the same article. It was a disaster. The location might have been right, but the problems of overcrowding, sickness and lack of sanitation were the same.

His brother John worked on the Eglinton Estate in Skelmorlie and knew of a campsite nearby. It ticked all the boxes, but had taken all of John's charm and a bag of toffees to convince Tina to try one more move. She agreed to give it a week. That was two months ago. Barrhill Campsite had space, a sea view, and decent people. Families like them, desperate to escape the tenements and rents they couldn't afford. Alec had made the mistake of comparing it to a holiday.

'This is not my idea of a holiday, Alec Coulter,' Tina snapped. 'Start with four walls and a front door. Oh, and a proper bed would be good.'

She blustered for a while, Tina's usual way of handling situations she didn't like. Then she lifted the kettle with attitude, made a cup of tea and sulked for ten minutes. The second cup of tea was for Alec. The signal he called *white smoke*. A silent truce. Until the next outburst. Yes, Tina was feisty, but also witty, with an opinion about everything and an answer for everyone. He'd loved that about her when they first met. Her fearless, 'say it as it is' attitude. He was her opposite, reading up on a topic before giving an opinion. Alec also knew she sometimes used her sharpness as armour. Life hadn't been kind to her. She wasn't always easy to live with, but Tina had a big heart.

How was he going to put this right? Teresa tugged at his trouser leg.

'Daddy, is the world still here?' she asked.

Alec looked around at the ravaged campsite.

*How on earth am I going to persuade Tina to stay one more night here?*

'The world is most definitely still here, Teresa. It just needs a bit of cleaning up to get it back to normal.'

Wee Alec came out to join them. He clutched both of his daddy's legs. 'I want to help too.'

The campsite resembled a battlefield with craters of muddy water, clothes, shoes and toys scattered and soaked. A piece of a pram, sodden blankets and pages from torn books fluttered in the lingering breeze. These were the possessions of families who hadn't been so lucky. People moved slowly, surveying the damage. No morning greetings, no children laughing, no neighbourly banter. Just low voices and the heavy hush of hopelessness.

Alec lifted his son into his arms. 'Well, of course you can help. It's all hands on deck today. But first, let's give your mother a cup of tea.'

He ushered his children back toward the tent, a hand in each of his. Alec was about to throw open the flap when Tina barrelled through it, almost knocking them over. She stopped, surveying the devastation.

'Just as well there's no trees in this bl…' she paused. '…swamp.' Then she looked up at the sky and shouted. 'Halleflamin'luia!'

It was the last thing Alec expected. His wife, as predictable as the weather. Maybe that's why he loved her. They laughed. So did the neighbours who had heard her.

Maybe he was a coward, a dreamer, a useless provider. But right now, Alec Coulter felt nothing but gratitude for Tina, for their children, for all they still had.

## 14. Terri. Perth. 27ᵗʰ June 2020
### From a Tent to a Cottage

The trees are swaying in a lively breeze today. It reminds me of the campsite, always windy at the top of the hill. That's probably why a summer storm affected us so badly.

I'm taking my time getting dressed. My outfit for the day is laid out. I've decided on a navy and green theme. I'm very slow now, but I like to do as much as I can for myself.

Maureen interrupts my train of thought.

'Ready for coffee, Mum? I'll give you a hand with the trousers and we can go downstairs together.'

As she bends to help me, she adds. 'I think Phoebe is bringing cappuccino and Bakewell tarts soon.'

Phoebe is my lovely granddaughter. That's my cue to get a move on. Maureen helps with my hair and makeup. She's not as professional as Colette, but good enough. I make my way downstairs. They're steep, but I have a rail on one side and make a point of wearing suitable footwear, never slippers. I settle myself on my sofa as Maureen scuttles around preparing for our imminent visitor, then flops down on the big couch.

'Did you go back to the Gorbals after the storm in Skelmorlie?' she asks.

I'm distracted because I know Phoebe will arrive any minute.

'No is the short answer, Maureen. We ended up in a cottage in Symington for a few months afterwards.'

That got her attention. 'What! Do you mean the village on the way to Girvan? We used to pass nearby for years when we travelled between Scotland and Ireland. I've never heard you talk about living in Symington. I'm stunned, Mum. How on earth did...'

She halts mid-sentence as Phoebe comes into the room laden with goodies and brimming with energy. The rest of the story will have to wait till later.

\* \* \*

I can't believe it's now the back of four. I ate very little at lunch time and caught forty winks after Phoebe left. I feel bad about not eating because I know Maureen likes to keep me well fed. I ask her to bring me a cup of hot water and sit while I finish the story about Symington. That will please her and get me off the hook. But where will I start? How much does Maureen want to know? In some ways, the positives and negatives were much the same as Skelmorlie, only we lived in a cottage, not a tent.

My mother got her four walls, a roof and a floor, and we had bedrooms and beds. But she was even more isolated there, with no neighbours for miles. The scenery was beautiful, but that made no impression on Tina.

Maureen is waiting. I'd better start talking.

My father cycled from Skelmorlie to Glasgow the day after the storm to collect his dole money. He left with a very sad look and came back that evening with a big smile on his face. He said a man in the queue told him about cottages in Symington with low rents and possible jobs nearby.

'But how on earth did your father persuade Tina to leave a campsite and go to a cottage in a small Ayrshire village?' Maureen asks.

It's a fair question. I think about the answer.

'The funny thing about my mother was, she shouted her mouth off a lot but never really went against Alec. I think we stayed about a month, maybe six weeks. I've a vague memory of going to the school once or twice, but I don't remember any details. We arrived at the end of summer and the cottage looked lovely from the outside, but even then it was musty and damp inside. The walls were wet in places, and the house got colder and colder. We had a coal fire, but it never seemed to heat the place.'

'God, Mum! That sounds like you went from the frying pan into the fire,' Maureen says, adding, 'if you'll pardon the pun!'

Pun aside, she has a point.

'It wasn't all bad,' I say. 'We had some good times. But my father got very sick in Symington. His bad lungs from the flour mill couldn't cope with the dampness. That's why we left.'

I pause for a moment, allowing the memory to settle.

'One morning, he came to sit on the bed where Alec and I slept. It was very early and still dark outside. He looked so white. I remember wondering why he had sweat running down his face when it was freezing.

"Our adventures are over for now,' he told us. "We're going to stay with Grandma Annie for a few weeks. Won't that be fun?"

'I was delighted. But even as a child, I knew things weren't good if we were all moving into Thistle Street.'

I only realise I'm crying when Maureen says softly, 'I'm so sorry, Mum. I didn't mean to upset you. I had no idea Symington would be such an emotional story.'

'Neither did I, Maureen,' I admit. 'It's just that going back in time stirs up lots of feelings. Some are harder to put into words than others, and sometimes I'm hijacked. But that's okay. Anyway, that story has a happy ending. We stayed in Thistle Street until my father recovered. Then we moved to Coburg Street in the Gorbals, where we lived until after the Blitz in 1941. I was happy there.'

Maureen shakes her head. 'But if you think about it, you had one hell of a year. I've worked it out. It must've been 1934. Two campsites and a mouldy cottage. That's some adventure for a five-year-old.'

And I have to agree.

## 15. Maureen. Perth. 28th June 2020
### A Breath of Fresh Air and Music

My younger sister, Colette, comes charging through the front door, followed by my brother, Barney, who struggles with a huge suitcase.

'My God, Colette! What have you got in here? A crate of champagne?' he groans.

'No. Just the one bottle,' she retorts, throwing down her handbag and wrapping her arms around Mum without stopping to take off her jacket.

Mum is so tiny these days and I worry Colette might suffocate her with affection. But they cling onto each other until Mum realises Barney is standing in the background and breaks free.

'Thank you for picking Colette up from the airport, Barney. Can you stay for coffee?'

Barney kisses Mum gently on the cheek and promises to return later. He disappears and we three ladies sit down together in the living room to catch up. My mother's chair is a two-seater wicker sofa, originally designed for use in a garden or conservatory. It is neither suitable nor comfortable, but she likes it. A few years ago, she compromised and allowed me to fit a pressure-relieving cushion on the seat, but there was no chance of her agreeing to a new chair. The vacant seat next to Mum on the sofa is her 'office'.

'I like to keep things nearby, then I can put my hand on them quickly. Do you know what I mean by that?' Mum asked, using one of her favourite expressions and not expecting an answer. 'I know exactly where everything is in my office.'

She smiled, and I knew the discussion was over and the subject closed. The 'office' is home to out-of-date copies of the Daily Mail, large envelopes with questionable contents, flyers for events long past and brochures full of *great buys*. And that's only the top layer. But there are times when you just have to hold your tongue.

Colette spreads herself generously on the larger sofa under the window and I squeeze into the office beside Mum, careful not to upset her filing system.

'Looking good, Mum,' Colette says as she scrutinises our mother, but can't help adding, 'I still think that hairdresser should be shot.'

She is referring to Mum's most recent hair colouring at the hands of her long-standing hairdresser. It has been at least six months since the last visit pre-Covid, but Colette is not a great one for letting things go. Mum and I grin at each other.

'I mean it. It's way too dark and I told him so at the time.'

'Coffee?' I suggest.

Lattes for Mum and me, and decaf with lactose-free milk for Colette. We talk about her flight, the weather in the South of France and her job as a singing teacher. I watch Mum's face light up as she engages in the chat with Colette. Terri Reilly loves an excuse to dress to the nines and add a bit of bling. She has attended lots of glamorous occasions in Monaco with my sister over the fifteen years Colette has lived there. Mum's trips to Sligo are a little less exciting. Still, whether in Monaco or Sligo, her sense of style is legendary and she leaves her mark wherever she goes.

Mum's friends in the Soroptimists marvel at some of their trips with Terri. I was within earshot when they were swapping stories at Mum's 90th birthday party.

'When we were in India, Terri wore her full regalia of pull-me-up/push-me-in girdles, tights, and a skirt, blouse and jacket. I wouldn't mind, but it was 90 degrees and the rest of us were fainting fast in flimsy dresses,' said one lady, much to the amusement of the others.

'And, have you ever heard of anyone walking the Great Wall of China in heels?' asked another, causing more hilarity in the huddled group.

'Only Terri Reilly could take a two-day train journey through Russia with no proper hygiene facilities. And still emerge with her hair and makeup done, looking fresh and ready for the day's action.'

'I remember that trip…' added another friend. 'Terri had more luggage than anyone. We were staggering along the platform with our small cases, exhausted and dishevelled and there was Terri, as glamorous as ever, waltzing along. Followed by a porter carrying her huge suitcase on his shoulder.'

I walked away from the table but heard the tail end of the next comment.

'…always managed to get someone to help her. Usually a man!'

*Yip, that's my mum*, I thought.

As I sip my coffee, the second of the day and likely cause of insomnia tonight. It hits me again how much Mum and Colette resemble each other. Not just that they're both petite and stylish. They have similar mannerisms and a dynamism that instantly engages people. After Colette's husband unceremoniously left in 2008, my talented sister crawled, then walked, then ran, then flew. And she has been flying ever since, teaching and performing. We are all very proud of her. The other day, Mum asked me to promise I would always look after Colette. It was not said in any profound or maudlin way. It was just on her mind.

'Of course, Mum. Haven't I always?' I said. 'I'm there for her and she's there for me. That's how it works.'

Colette has already brought a breath of fresh air into the house and Mum and I both respond to her energy. The three of us are very different women, yet very close. I think we complement each other, although I doubt we could live in the same house for long. Colette will go through Mum's wardrobe and coordinate her outfits. She will organise Mum's jewellery drawer and select a necklace for the day. She will apply Mum's makeup with dexterity and skill, and style her hair while providing a running commentary about the hairdresser who should be shot!

'Look good to feel good,' she will say.

And Mum will love it. And she will indeed look and feel better.

By six o'clock, the champagne from the suitcase has been opened and we toast to being together for the first time in too long. Let the fun begin!

* * *

## Maureen. 30th June 2020

Music is and always has been an integral part of my life. Dad used to say the most effective way to learn was by *osmosis* and that's how it was with music. My memories are all linked to the melodies accompanying them and the year they affected me.

In our house, music was mainly the domain of my dad, whose family were singers or musicians, or both. Pre-television, they used to congregate on a Sunday afternoon and enjoy making music together. We have old vinyl records of them all singing.

In the month before I retired, when Mum was recovering from radiotherapy, I began asking her about the music from her past. Not only did the question spark memories, but she started singing snippets of songs over the phone. Terri Reilly was usually out and about: at Keep Fit, working in the café, or just perusing the shops in town. Covid stopped all that and she had time to think about the past, including the songs she remembered. I have chatted to Mum on the phone every night for over twenty years and this was a completely new departure for us.

I think it's fair to say our mum is not a singer. But the sound and tone of her telephone songs evoked memories in me, too. She used to sing *Hush-a-by-Baby* to the children and sometimes she would sing *Nellie Gray* if one of us was sick or needed a cuddle. Mum sang that story as if she were invested in every word, feeling each emotion. Listening to her always made me cry. But what I remembered most was the contrast between the sad song and the comfort of my mother's arms. No one was going to take me away.

*Oh my poor Nellie Gray*
*They have taken you away*
*And I'll never see my darlin' any more*
*I am sitting by the river*
*And I'm weepin' all the day*
*For you've gone from the old Kentucky shore.*

During those phone calls, Mum sometimes sang a few lines of a song and other times she just wanted to talk about the memories rekindled by the melody. When I told Colette about this new treasure, she was thrilled. She encouraged Mum to sing a little every day, often joining in to make it easier. And always recording Mum's efforts. We started to prompt her.

'What song do you have for me today, Mum?'

'I haven't thought of one yet,' might come the reply. Then, without warning, she would break into '*Oh, the Grand old Duke of York, he had so many men*' or '*Little Sir Echo, how do you do?*' or '*I'm gonna take you on a slow boat to China*' or even '*The Music Goes Round and Round, oh oh oh oh…*'

Realisation dawned: music had been a big part of my Mum's life too. It just wasn't something she had ever discussed.

During one call, she said, 'My father's family, the Coulters, used to sing when they had a party. They just didn't show off as much as the Reillys.' I laughed and Mum added, 'Well, I suppose they weren't as accomplished as the Reillys either. Everyone sang at parties in those days and they all had their own song.'

'Did you have your own song, Mum?'

'No, I wasn't one for singing in front of relatives. But my father's song was *The Minstrel Boy*.

Without a pause or preamble, she sang the first few lines.

*The Minstrel Boy to the war has gone*
*In the ranks of death, you'll find him*
*His father's sword he has girded on*
*And his wild harp slung behind him.*

I could hear her voice trembling and knew she was crying at the other end of the phone. Time does not alter the memories and emotions stirred by music.

\* \* \*

It has been three days since Colette arrived, bringing with her a CD of every song Mum mentioned or sang during those precious phone calls of musical discovery. We have finished our morning coffee and Colette produces the CD with a mischievous look on her face. She inserts the disc into the player and with outstretched arms, says, 'Come on, Mum. On your feet.'

Colette is great for getting Mum going. She takes her by the hand and helps her out of the chair. The CD player hums to the beat of Kenny Ball and his Jazzmen playing *The Music Goes Round and Round*. It is a song we all know well and a favourite of Mum's. She has always been a terrific dancer and even now, with terminal cancer, she still has an incredible sense of rhythm.

*The music goes round and round, oh oh oh oh oh oh, and it comes out here.*

I record Colette and Mum on my phone as they manage a gentle jive around the coffee table, all three of us singing along with Kenny. Even as I stand watching and recording them dancing and singing, I know this is already an indelible memory, one I will revisit in the months and years to come. Somehow, it captures all the times we have danced together: at dinner dances, weddings, parties, or just for no reason at all. Like this morning. Here we are, dancing and singing together in the living room of Mum's home on this Tuesday morning in the summer of 2020. In this precious moment, cancer does not exist. Covid does not exist. Separation does not exist. All that exists is sheer joy and shared love.

## 16. Terri. Perth. 1st July 2020
### *Sorting out the Shed*

I am recovering from yesterday's dancing and singing. It was such fun and it's good to know I can still jive, even after the radiotherapy. I love the CD Colette made with my favourite songs. Every one of them takes me back to a time in my life long gone. I spent the rest of the day dozing and dreaming of some of those times.

No dancing today. The three of us are in the garden. Maureen and Colette are making great inroads into clearing one of the garden sheds. Well, when I say clearing, I mean sorting. I want to know what's in there. I don't necessarily want to throw anything out. That's why I'm here with a sun hat on my head and a blanket around my knees. I want to keep an eye on what's going on. I would never let any of my sons near the sheds because I know they would throw everything in the dump without telling me. They've done it before!

I told them straight. 'There'll be bandy bendy if that happens again.'

They just laughed. And Barney, who likes to tease me, said, 'Is that better or worse than soapy bubbles, Mum?' Great hilarity. Then he said, more seriously, 'We thought it would be ok. Honestly, we didn't think you'd mind.'

I like to have the last word and I was ready with my reply. 'See what thought did? Planted a cabbage and thought a cauliflower would grow!'

I'm lost in thought when I hear a shriek from inside the shed. Maureen comes out holding up her hands as if she's about to perform major surgery.

'We need gloves! The boxes are sodden and the books are ruined.'

I've no time to answer before she adds, 'Mum, there are books in these boxes I remember packing when you left Skelmorlie fourteen years ago.'

Colette follows her out of the shed. 'I'm not touching them. God knows what beasties are lurking in there!'

There's no answer to that one. But it's not funny that the girls are finding boxes in the shed I've never touched since moving to Perth. Boxes I've never looked through. Boxes I didn't even pack myself before I left. Boxes now ruined. Maureen returns with gloves for herself and Colette, who reluctantly accepts.

'Can I see some of the books?' I ask. 'Can any of them be saved?'

And, despite her fear of the 'beasties', Colette goes back into the shed and reappears with a soggy copy of *Treasure Island*, a *Blue Peter* Annual and an old red book whose title has been obliterated by damp.

'Not in this box, but maybe in some of the others,' she says, but the look on her face tells me she doesn't believe it.

I feel bad. Books are precious. I can't read now and I didn't have much time to read before I retired from the shop. But I love my books. I inherited that from my father. He joined the library in the Gorbals as a boy and read every book he could get his hands on. He often took me with him. We both loved the smell and feel of different books. I still do. Maureen and I visited that library on a trip to the Gorbals a few years ago. The beautiful red sandstone building is still there, but it's now a community centre for deaf people. The new Gorbals library isn't as regal as the old one, yet it's still a hub of activity. I was amazed at the number of school children in front of computers or reading at desks. Imagine having a computer in a library. I wonder what my father would make of it.

It turns out most of the books are beyond redemption. I bought this shed because the one at the top of the garden was already jam-packed after the move. I never got around to sorting either of them. I was driving up and down to the flower shop in Kilmarnock, about 80 miles each way. Then, when I retired, I had cancer. After that, I wasn't strong enough to move boxes or fight my way through the paraphernalia in the sheds. Now, with macular degeneration, I can't see what I'm doing. Maureen's voice interrupts my train of thought. She's probably noticed I'm upset, which I am. She announces that coffee is needed, which it is!

After our coffee break, I'm tired. I don't return to the garden until five o'clock, when the girls tell me the shed is clean and tidy.

'Ready for inspection,' Colette announces.

I'm delighted there's finally some order. They've salvaged two small boxes of books, now drying out in the house. The pile for the dump has grown and I notice bits of carpet and a box of bathroom tiles have been added. I'm happy to let the carpet go, but I'm not so sure about the tiles. You never know, they might be of use to someone. I think it's time for a glass of mead and a few crisps.

### 17. Maureen. Perth. Night of 1st July 2020
#### Much More Than a Shed

Colette is engrossed in her online Scrabble in the big double bed we share in Perth. I'm lying beside her, pondering our afternoon in the garden shed. The conversation is one-sided.

'There were a few challenging moments for Mum today, but overall, I thought she was pleased with our efforts, didn't you?'

'Absolutely."

'We both know how much she hates throwing things out, but we made good progress, don't you think?'

'Absolutely.'

'The boys can't get their heads around why Mum needs two crammed sheds as well as a crammed house. It drives them mad with frustration.'

'Absolutely.'

'I mean, in all honesty, they're not wrong. Let's face it, there's a lot she doesn't need, but very little she doesn't want. Anyway, they're Mum's things. They matter to her. That's all that matters.'

'Absolutely, Maur.'

I give up on the conversation, and think about Mum's most recent story about living in a tent in Skelmorlie. Writing the scene as fiction, from Tina and Alec's point of view, was eye-opening. I felt their despair, their desperation and how it affected each of them differently.

It was also poignant to think of Joe and Terri, our parents, moving to Skelmorlie in 1988. Dad loved 'sea-watching' from the bay window in their top-floor lounge. With a large telescope, he tracked ferries crossing from Wemyss Bay to Rothesay: the *Waverley*, the *Queen Mary*, the *Caledonia*. When he was a boy, Dad's family spent holidays in Rothesay. I wonder if Teresa Coulter was living in a tent in Skelmorlie at the same time Joe Reilly, her future husband, was staying in a boarding house across the water.

During our adult years, when they lived in Skelmorlie, Mum never alluded to her time there as a girl. After she shared the story, I told her I would have loved to visit the camp site with her.

After a pause, she said, 'I wasn't unhappy or anything. But it wasn't anything to shout about either. I suppose I just lived through it, then left it behind.'

After Dad died and Mum moved to Perth to be nearer my brother Barney, downsizing was unavoidable. I'll never forget the words of the exhausted furniture removers:

'Nothin' else'll fit in that hoose, Mrs. We'll have to dump the rest in the garden!'

And that's exactly what they did. The 'rest' consisted of a three-piece suite, two bookcases, a table, six chairs and several boxes of stray belongings, all packed at top speed. It was barely possible to get through the door, let alone live in the house.

I wish I could say I was calm and empathetic as I stood in the garden surveying the chaos. The truth is, I was as exasperated as the removal men and more concerned about what the neighbours thought, than how Mum felt.

And yet, lying here now, I think of Alec and Tina Coulter in 1934, hauling their possessions to Skelmorlie to live in a tent with two children. No home. No job. No future. No choice.

As Colette and I lie in bed, congratulating ourselves, I feel sad for Teresa Coulter, the child. And full of admiration for Terri Reilly, the woman.

## 18. Terri. Perth. 2nd July 2020
### Clean Washing and Dirty Middens

The clearing of the shed was more emotional than physical for me, but none of us feels like tackling the other one today. The girls decide we should relax and have our coffee outside. It may be July, but the weather is far from summer. I am cosied up in several rugs by the open dining room patio door, while Maureen and Colette sit at the garden table under the gazebo erected by Barney for Covid entertaining.

Maureen has sheets on the washing line and it reminds me of when we lived on Coburg Street. The women would pin their clothes to the ropes with wooden pegs and push them high into the air with long poles. It was a great sight, the shapes and colours dancing and snapping in the breeze. On dry days, you had to be up early to grab your spot. In some of the tenements 'round us there was a rota for washday. But if it rained on your day, you might have to wait another week for your turn. Many a *stairheid rammy* (a fight between tenement neighbours) started in the back court at the washing line, and my mother was often in the thick of it.

I'm grateful to have a garden all to myself.

I hear Colette say, 'You're a million miles away, Mum.'

'Not a million, just back in Coburg Street,' I say. 'Thinking about the washing lines attached to the wall of the middens and how I used to watch the clothes flapping in the wind. It also reminds me of dreeping from dyke to dyke.'

Colette laughs. 'Mum, I don't know what you're talking about. Washing lines, I understand, although we don't have them in French apartments. But Middens. Dykes. Dreeping. I haven't a scooby! Maureen, do you understand?'

Maureen looks smug. Of course, she understands, having lived in Garrioch Drive, Maryhill, in a lovely red sandstone tenement before we moved south of the river when she was eight. Colette was only three and too young to remember.

Maureen explains to her sister. 'The middens were the cement sheds at the far end of the communal back garden. The roof was called a dyke and youngsters used to jump from one to another. Not me, I hasten to add. Maybe that's what Mum calls 'dreeping'. We used to put the rubbish into large, galvanised steel bins inside the middens. I remember some of the boys pretending to be Vikings, clashing bin lids. Of course, there was no such thing as recycling in the '60s.'

'That's true,' I agree. 'Everything went into the outside bins. But, unlike the Gorbals, the bins in Garrioch Drive were emptied regularly. And the middens had flat roofs, proper floors and a grill in the ceiling for ventilation. Things weren't as hygienic or organised when I was growing up.'

'You're on a roll, Mum,' Maureen says, always encouraging me to chat about the old days. I keep going.

'We were lucky in Coburg Street. Our middens were brick-built, with makeshift wooden doors. They kept out most of the vermin and kept in most of the smell. People just opened the door, threw the rubbish onto the floor and shut as fast as they could.'

As I talk, I remember more and more. I am definitely on a roll!

'Some tenements around us just threw their rubbish out into the backyard in mounds. Now they really stank. Remember, we had no fridges back then. Food went off and it was thrown in with all the other rubbish. And some folk even emptied their overnight potties onto the pile or into the midden if they had one. During the summer, the smell in the tenement Close was woeful, especially from the toilets on the landing. A sour mix of urine, concrete and cheap disinfectant. To this day, some public toilets remind me of that familiar odour.'

Colette has heard enough about the reality of life in the Gorbals in the 1930s. She puts her fingers in her ears and sings 'La la la la', which is her way of removing herself from the conversation.

Maureen grins and adds, 'Just as well there were no disposable nappies. Can you imagine the smell from the middens!'

Colette throws a garden cushion in her sister's direction.

'Okay, okay, change of subject. What games did you play in the back court, Mum? When it wasn't too smelly!'

Playing in the back court was a big part of my life, especially in Coburg Street. I tell the girls about the games I remember.

'The children from the neighbouring tenements used to congregate there. There was no grass, but we'd collect stones and play shops sitting in the dirt. The stones might represent money or nice things to buy, depending on their size. We would form teams and play Red Rover, or I Sent a Letter to My Love. When the ground was dry, we played with skipping ropes—I was good at doubles. Or we might chalk the pavement and play hopscotch. We called in peever. Sometimes, I played alone outside an old church with steps leading down to a small back door no one ever used. It was my private place. I pretended to be a princess, not from the Gorbals at all.'

Maureen laughs. 'I must be getting old because I remember some of those games from childhood.'

She is instantly teased by Colette. I love how they laugh so easily together. I'm tired and chilly now. It's time to return to the comfort and heat of my sofa.

Once ensconced, I close my eyes, but my mind is still in Coburg Street. I'm thinking of one summer in particular. It was unusually hot and my mother complained all the time about the lack of fresh air. Looking back now, my father was a saint not to point out that when we lived in Skelmorlie, she complained about having too much fresh air!

During that summer, Tina used to open the kitchen window and 'window hing'—lean her elbows on the windowsill and shout over to other 'window hingers' in the neighbouring tenements. I always thought it was very unladylike. My grandmother, Annie Coulter, would never have leaned out of a window, no matter how hot it was inside.

I must have dozed off. I've been dreaming about dreeping from dyke to dyke and from the high wall in the back court onto the dyke. My dress was billowing like a ship's sail and it felt like flying. My brother Alec was only a year younger than me, but he was a scaredy-cat. He used to shout up at me, 'I'm telling on you, Teresa. If you fall, it's your own fault!'

And I would stick out my tongue at him and throw both arms in the air before jumping, just to terrify him.

Happy days!

## 19. Maureen. Perth. 3rd July 2020
*First Love*

Colette is washing her hair, which will keep her occupied for at least an hour. I plan to take advantage of a little time alone with Mum.

I don't want our chats about the past to be the sole focus of our time together, but there's a topic that fascinates me: Mum's love life. She once told me she was engaged to be married three times, the third and final time to my dad, Joseph Reilly. However, I am curious about the other men in her life. She left me in no doubt that anything beyond holding hands meant an engagement ring for Teresa Coulter. There was no 'hanky panky' before marriage. After Colette disappears, I treat us to a second latte, press the record button on my phone and ask the question all girls secretly want to ask their mother, even if they never do.

'Tell me about your first love, Mum.'

'Major,' she says, as if it should be obvious. 'My first love was Major. And it was love at first sight.'

My mug of coffee is halfway to my mouth, which is now gaping. I am completely gobsmacked. Not the answer I was expecting. Major was her childhood dog, not a dashing young man!

Mum laughs. Her face is radiant, her eyes bright, as if lit from somewhere inside.

'If you could describe love on a dog's face, I saw it when Major looked at me. His whole face was full of it. An amazing sight.'

Looking at Mum now, I realise her love for Major is as real as any human love. As she tells the story of the day he came into her life, I understand her surprising response. Mum's human love life will have to wait. And perhaps that is the way she wants it. Daughters may be curious about the men in their mother's life, but that does not mean mothers are always happy to share the information.

## 20. Teresa/Terri. Coburg Street, Gorbals. September 1937
### A 'Major' Influence

Teresa and her brother, Alec, lay in the kitchen bed recess, the curtain drawn round to separate it from the rest of the room. Alec was snoring gently beside her, but Teresa was listening to her mother clattering about in the scullery, muttering to herself in that cranky voice.

She knew better than to ask what was wrong, but would have liked to know how they were supposed to sleep with all that noise. In between the banging of pans, Teresa caught snatches of what her mother was saying.

'Bloody job… late again… starve… good enough for him.'

Suddenly, Tina Coulter screamed. Teresa sat up. Not another mouse! Her mother was terrified of them and her father often had to chase them with the brush while Tina stood trembling on a chair, hands over her eyes. He'd wink at Teresa as he thudded the brush on various parts of the floor, shouting, 'Come out, come out, wherever you are.'

She'd giggle. In those magic moments, it felt like their own special conspiracy.

Teresa waited for her father's reassuring tone and the beginning of a new mouse-catching adventure. But this time, there was no reassurance. No mouse game. Tina's screech was followed by an angry bout of shouting. It was clear she was talking to Dad now, not herself. By this time, her brother was wide awake, with the blanket over his face.

'What do you think has happened?' she whispered, pulling down the cover.

'I don't know and I don't want to find out,' he said, dragging it back over his head.

Now, Teresa could hear every word. The voices were just outside the curtain, so she knew her parents were in the kitchen.

'You can take that thing right back to where it came from, Alec Coulter. As if I don't have enough to do keeping those two out of trouble. The rent man at the door. And you working late every night at that snooker hall.'

Things were never good when Mum used her father's full name. What could he have brought home that frightened her mother and made her so furious? It surely wasn't a mouse!

Teresa hesitated, crept out of bed, peered through the gap in the curtain. And looked straight into a pair of big green eyes.

For a moment, she froze. Then, stretching her hand, she let the big, friendly dog with the most beautiful eyes she had ever seen lick her fingers. It had an intelligent face: black and brown fur, a soft, wet nose, and big sticky-up ears. When it stopped licking, the dog's mouth opened slightly and Teresa could see its long pink tongue. It was smiling. She was sure of it.

'Hello, there,' she said, keeping her voice soft and steady as she stroked its head.

Alec poked his head out from under the blanket and of course, let out a scream when he saw the dog. The spell was broken.

'Jesus Christ, Alec! It's attacked the kids!'

Her father wrenched open the curtain in time to see Teresa kneeling on the bed, her arms wrapped around the dog's neck and her brother shaking under a pile of bedclothes.

'Oh, Daddy! Is he ours? I love him. Is it a boy or a girl? What's its name?'

She couldn't get the words out fast enough. Meanwhile, the dog sat on the floor beside her, tongue lolling to one side, tail thumping.

Her mother's fury boiled over. 'Now see what you've done?' she snarled. 'Back to sleep, the pair of you. It won't be like this in the morning.'

Tina yanked the curtain so hard it nearly came off the runner. 'I'm going to bed, Alec Coulter. You can sleep in the chair beside that beast in case it kills us all in the night. We'll talk about it in the morning. I can't take any more. Oh, and your dinner's burnt!'

Tina's slippers flopped across the floor and the bedroom door banged. Silence.

When Teresa was sure her brother was asleep again, she crept out of bed and crawled under the curtain. Her dad was dozing in the chair by the fire, the big dog lying at his feet. They both stirred as she approached.

'Oh, please, Daddy, don't send him away,' she whispered.

She knew he wouldn't be angry. Teresa had never heard him raise his voice or shout back at her mother. The dog lifted its head but didn't move. Its tail thudded against the floor. Alec reached out to stop the noise in case it disturbed Tina or the neighbours below, then beckoned Teresa to the armchair. She crawled quickly towards it and sat beside the dog, stroking its head and jostling its long ears.

'His name is Major,' her father said. 'He's an Alsatian. Some people call them German Shepherds because they were working dogs in Germany.'

Teresa was concerned. 'Does that mean he only understands German?'

Her dad smiled. 'No. He belonged to a dentist who often brought him into the billiards hall where I work.'

His smile faded. 'He wasn't kind to Major. Kicked him if he whined. Left him for hours without food. Don't know why he had him. He didn't seem to want him.'

'He didn't deserve Major,' Teresa said, moving closer to her new friend. 'And he must understand English, Daddy, because I'm sure he knows we're talking about him.'

She leaned back against her father's chair, legs outstretched. Major's head felt heavy and warm on her lap as she listened intently to the whole story.

'…and then I just told the man he wouldn't be taking the dog home with him that night. Or any night. I said he could call the police if he liked. But of course, he didn't.'

Teresa was in awe. Her dad was so brave. But then a terrible thought struck her.

'What if he changes his mind, Daddy? What if he goes to the police tomorrow?'

She pictured a loud knock, two policemen dragging Major away and her father in jail.

'No, Teresa, he won't.' His voice was firm. 'As I closed the door, I heard him mutter, 'No skin off my nose. I won't have to feed it now."

Teresa resumed stroking Major's silky head, leaning against her father's knee.

'Can we keep him, Daddy? Really?'

She was thinking of her mother's reaction.

'Go back to bed now, darling girl. We'll sort it out in the morning.' He kissed the back of her head.

Teresa gently lifted Major's head from her lap and gave him one last stroke.

'I'll look after him, Daddy. Properly.' She was trying not to cry. 'Please. Please don't send him back to the cruel dentist.'

'It'll be alright,' he said.

But Teresa wasn't so sure.

*He's worried about Mum, not the dentist,* she thought, as she dawdled back to bed. She turned for one last look. Her father was already asleep in the chair. Major lay on the rug, as if he had always lived there. Teresa pulled the cover up to her chin and stared at the ceiling.

'Please, God, let Major stay. I'll be very good, I promise. Please let Mum like him. Please let…'

She must have fallen asleep mid-prayer, because when Teresa woke the next morning, her dream about Major was still vivid. They were running through a field of purple flowers. She wore a yellow frilly dress and white sandals. Her hair was long and blonde like Patricia Kerrigan's in her class and it swished behind her like a white horse's tail. No tall tenements blocked the sun, just fields of purple brushing her legs as she ran and ran with Major at her side.

'If you pair don't get out of that bed, you'll be meeting yourselves coming home!' Her mother's voice echoed in the kitchen, slippers flip-flopping across the floor.

The kettle whistled in the background.

'And you needn't look at me like that,' her mother said from the other side of the curtain.

As Teresa stretched and nudged Alec in the ribs, she wondered if Tina was talking to her father or Major. Teresa slid open the curtain and put on her best smile. 'Good morning, Mum.'

'Don't 'good morning' me, Teresa Coulter. I know you're in cahoots with your father about keeping this species.'

Her mother pointed at Major, who wisely kept his head down, though his ears twitched and his green eyes darted in all directions.

'Oh, Mum. He won't be any trouble, I promise. I'll….'

Alec screamed behind her and was standing on their bed, looking like he'd seen an armed robber. Her brother was such a wimp. Teresa was about to tell him so, but changed her mind.

'He's just a poor dog who needs a home, Alec,' she said in her gentlest voice. 'He's been treated badly. We can look after him. Together.' Then, in her best polite voice, 'If Mum allows it, of course.'

She looked at her mother with what she hoped were pleading eyes. Her dad was still sitting by the fire, pretending to warm his hands. He'd clearly decided there was no more to be said. Tina would make up her mind, one way or the other.

As Teresa walked along Coburg Street and into Norfolk Street, her brother dawdling behind her, she looked up at the grey sky.

'Please, God, let Major be there when I come home. I'll never do anything bad again. Please.'

'You've started talking to yourself,' Alec said with a grin. 'Now, who does that remind you of?'

Then he ran ahead before Teresa could wallop him.

## 21. Maureen. Perth. 3rd July 2020
### Major, Mum, and Me

When Mum and I revisit the day she came home from school to find Major asleep by the fire, she describes the mix of elation and relief she felt.

'My father was at work and I ran straight into Tina's arms. It wasn't how I normally greeted my mother after school, and she was shocked. Tina wasn't much of a hugger, but I believe she was secretly pleased, even if she dismissed my sobs of gratitude. I loved her that day in a way I had never loved her before. She allowed Major to stay and it was the best thing that had ever happened to me.'

I can see tears pooling in Mum's eyes as she talks, but I don't interrupt.

'Right from the start, Major was my dog. He would watch for me coming home from school, his front paws on the window ledge of the top-floor flat. When he spotted me on the street, Major would get so agitated that my mother had to open the door and let him run down the stairs, or he would have leapt right out of the window.'

I smile at Mum. 'That sounds like a scene from the *Lassie* films I used to love.'

She doesn't comment, reliving a scene from her own film of memories.

'You had to put something in his mouth when he ran to greet you,' Mum says, scooping a teaspoon of latte froth, then sitting back with her hands on her lap.

'One day, Tina forgot. When she opened the door, Major raced towards me in the street and tore the entire pocket off my coat. The girls from the McClennan Rubber Works were leaving the factory at the time and they started screaming, thinking I was being attacked.'

Mum laughs at the memory.

'Were you not frightened?' I ask. It seems a logical question. 'He was a huge dog, Mum. And he had just ripped your coat.'

I can hear a tremble in her voice.

Tears trickle down her cheeks, making the powdered blush shimmer and blotch.

'Oh, no! I was never afraid of Major. He was very gentle and he would have protected me with his life. The factory girls soon calmed down. Their screams turned to *oohs and aahs* when I knelt on the pavement and Major licked my face, running around me wagging his tail, with my red pocket in his mouth.'

Mum is staring at something beyond the room. Perhaps she is back on that Glasgow Street with her beloved Major. She picks up the thread of her story.

'Major didn't like men in uniform. One day, we were walking through our tenement Close in Coburg Street. Two policemen were standing outside the ground-floor pawn shop. Major stopped and growled. His lips were open, showing his big teeth. One of the policemen reached for his baton. I was only about eight or nine, but I remember saying, 'I wouldn't do that if I were you. Just put your hand down and I'll take the dog upstairs. He'll be fine.'

When I think about it now, I must have sounded cocky and a bit cheeky, talking to a policeman like that. But he took his hand off the baton and laid it on his trouser leg. Major's lip was still curled and I'd say they were terrified. I just knew if the policeman took out his baton, Major would go for him. He would have seen it as a threat to me. I just said quietly, 'Come on, Major. Let's go home now.' I led him up the stairs and left the two policemen wondering what on earth had just happened!'

'What a story,' I say.

I am genuinely amazed at the daring eight-year-old Teresa Coulter. Yet when I reflect on my mother's behaviour over the years, I should not be surprised.

'Mum, I fancy more coffee and I doubt you'll object to another. Back in two shakes of a lamb's tail.'

In the kitchen, I turn on the kettle and lean back against the worktop. Colette comes through the door—coat on, mask at the ready, on her way to town.

'What's all this? You and Mum aren't still having coffee, are you?' She lifts her shoulders in an exaggerated shrug and throws both arms in the air, singing, *'The never-ending coffee...'* to the tune of *The Never-Ending Story*.

It has become a shared, affectionate joke. This morning, after her loud and uninhibited performance, Colette notices my serious expression.

'Is everything okay, Maur? Is Mum alright? She seemed fine when I was doing her makeup earlier.'

'No. I mean, yes. Sorry, Colette. Mum is in great form. I was miles away. Just thinking of the times Mum wasn't afraid to challenge authority. It makes me realise all over again what an incredible woman she is.'

It doesn't take much for Colette to become tearful. I can see her face preparing to crumple.

'Don't, Colette. Please don't get upset when you're about to go out. Give me an example of Mum challenging authority. That'll cheer you up.'

And it does. She blows her nose and says, 'God, there are so many, Maur. I remember the time she was on the train to England to visit Paul and ended up in a compartment full of football supporters. They were drunk and taunting some passengers. They all stared at their feet, too afraid to say anything in case something kicked off. But not Mum. The bold Terri Reilly got out of her seat and said to the ringleader, 'I was around when your arse was the size of a shirt button, son. And I've dealt with bigger bullies than you.' Mum told me the other passengers cheered and the football supporters behaved themselves for the rest of the journey. I'd say they couldn't believe a wee old lady had stood up to them!'

We erupt into a fit of laughter as we often do together. A voice calls from the living room:

'Have you gone to pick the beans in Brazil, Maureen?'

That sets us off again.

'Right, you say goodbye to Mum while I get these lattes made,' I say.

*'The never-ending coffee,'* Colette sings again as she exits the kitchen.

When she has left for town and peace reigns once more, I regale Mum with Colette's memory of the football supporters.

Mum thinks for a minute while she sips her second latte. 'Sometimes, I just act on instinct. My father called it a gut feeling. I was lucky that time on the train. I could have caused more trouble than it was worth. But I like to think there are times you have to do what you think is right, even if it's not popular. Barney reminded me recently about the time I made an appointment to see his teacher when he was in Primary seven.

I had forgotten about it. The teacher didn't like Barney's handwriting. I met with him and told him my son's writing was perfectly fine and probably better than his own. The next day at school, all the boys were belted because the teacher didn't like any of their handwriting. Barney was the only one who was exempt. I asked him if he felt embarrassed, being singled out like that and he said, "No. I was delighted. I think the other boys were jealous because my mother had complained, but none of theirs had bothered."'

It's a great story and one I had never heard. There are many more, but I return to the subject of Mum's dog.

'What happened to Major?

Mum's face creases with sadness. 'Major was a big dog and in truth, my mother and brother were always afraid of him. It was hard to keep him in a small top-floor tenement flat—not fair to him. My father found a farm for Major. I was heartbroken and he bought me a German Shepherd puppy. I called him Major, just like the real one. But he was knocked down and killed by a car in the street. I never wanted another dog after that. I couldn't handle any more loss.'

I can't help thinking it was his wife and son's fear rather than the dog's size that sealed Major's fate. It must have been a tough decision for Alec Coulter to make.

Mum's beautiful smile returns. 'When we got Heidi, it was a dream come true for me. Not many people get what they want in life. But I got Heidi. I waited a long time, but she made up for losing Major.'

Heidi was the German Shepherd who arrived in my teens, part of the family and loved by all. I remember my son Mark and Mum running together in the park, with Heidi alongside, carrying whatever branch of a tree she could fit into her mouth.

Some memories belong to Mum alone. Others are ours to share. But all are precious.

## 22. Terri. Perth. 5th July 2020
### Reflection: Politics, Covid and WW2

Maureen and I watch Nicola Sturgeon's daily broadcast about the virus. Well, I always watch it. Sometimes, Maureen sits; other times, she flits in and out. Colette likes to watch *Say Yes to The Dress* when she's here. It's a daft TV series about brides buying their wedding dress. Maureen and I prefer to say *No,* but we indulge Colette now and again. We all sit together and watch American brides-to-be having tantrums over dresses they can't afford!

I don't like the SNP as I've mentioned. But Nicola Sturgeon does a good job with her daily midday updates. She's tough, you have to be at times like this. No one likes to be locked up, but it's a small price to pay for staying alive. I'm all for the United Kingdom and I won't even discuss the subject of Scottish Independence. I might be old, but I can still defend my corner and I won't be swayed by the family in Perth. They weren't alive during the war when we fought so hard for the UK. Not for England or Scotland. For us all.

My father was a true socialist. I asked him what that meant when I was a girl and he said, 'Teresa, it means if I have two shirts and you have none and need one, I should give you one of mine.'

It made sense to me at the time. McCarthy would have called him a *commie* in 1950s America. But Alec Coulter's statement was not political. It was about social justice. He had seen so much unemployment and injustice. If people were lucky enough to have work, they had no rights. Trade Unions were badly needed to protect the workers. But Union leaders became too strong. The country was almost paralysed with strikes in the 1970s. Electricity was off as much as it was on. Rubbish overflowed onto the streets, attracting rats.

The whole situation made me angry because the country wasn't being brought to its knees by war. The chaos was caused by people in our own country. What if the same thing happened again? I won't risk voting Labour now. The SNP wants independence and to hell with the consequences. So, I vote Conservative. And that's all that's to it. My father would probably turn in his grave. However, thank God, life is now very different from the Depression years, even with this virus. I want to hang onto what we have, not throw the baby out with the bath water!

Today, Nicola is wearing her blue suit with a short bolero jacket. I must say she's smartened up her appearance and made an effort with her hair since she started the broadcasts.

Maureen pops in carrying a basin of wet towels on her hip. 'Any update?'

'Nicola says we can't have a party yet. Only six people from two households can mix.'

'Well, at least Barney can still come in with the Costa coffee and Bakewell tarts,' she says and disappears again.

Nicola is under pressure from Ruth Davidson, the leader of the Scottish Conservative Party. She's very good and I like her, but I don't think this is the time for party politics. They should all be pulling together, like during the war. But then, Winston Churchill didn't have to give daily bulletins or deal with heckling from the opposition on live TV. And he didn't have people taking photographs of him with a mobile phone and plastering them all over the internet. It's good that things are out in the open, but nothing's sacred any more.

The medical expert has taken over from Nicola now. We had no medical updates during the war. Husbands and sons went off to fight, and families had to wait for letters, or worse, the dreaded telegram. People crowded around the radio, if they had one. And we only knew what we were told, which wasn't much. But it was the way it was. And we didn't know any better.

I have a memory of one night in 1938, when I was about nine years old. My mum and dad were standing at the window of our top-floor flat in Coburg Street. I was sitting with my brother Alec on the edge of the bed in the kitchen recess, but the curtains were still open and we could see their backs. We heard a roar getting louder and louder, like an enormous swarm of bees. We knew it must be the sound of aeroplanes because everyone said the Germans would be coming soon. My brother hid under the covers. My mother sounded frightened. I heard her say to Dad, 'It's happening, Alec. It's happening. We'll all be killed in our beds.'

My father said nothing, but I noticed him handing my mother the cigarette he was smoking. He put his arm around her shoulder. The roaring noise gradually faded into the distance, as if the bees had moved on. Mum took a big puff of the cigarette and handed it back to Dad. Then, she turned to face us, any trace of fear gone.

'Right, you two. School in the morning. Teresa, get into that bed. Now!' And she flung the curtain shut.

That was in 1938, when the Luftwaffe were carrying out reconnaissance flights over European cities, including Glasgow. Of course, we didn't know that at the time. Life went on as normal. Now and again, we would hear the groan of a plane, but see nothing when we looked up. The sound became normal. After a while, no one paid any attention. My mother chain-smoked from that first night of the Luftwaffe fly-over until the day she died.

Later that year, we were all supplied with masks in case one of the German planes dropped gas on us. Come to think of it, the masks worn by doctors and nurses looking after patients with the virus look very similar to ours, only they were black. We had to take them to school with us and sometimes we practiced with them in class. They smelled of rubber and it was hard to breathe with them on. One girl in my class used to scream when anyone tried to help her during drills. I didn't like it either, but I remember thinking it was better than the alternative. Our teacher, Mrs Dixon, told us about the effects of being gassed and her description of people choking on vomit and suffocating was all the encouragement I needed. We were supposed to take our masks everywhere with us, but my mother thought it was a waste of time.

'I'll be working in the chippie until nine o'clock tonight and the only fumes'll be from the fryer,' she'd say when I tried to persuade her to bring it to work. 'Unless Willie Brown comes in. He farts like a trooper!'

And my mother would howl with laughter at her joke. I hated it when she was crude, but it was just her way. I used to turn around and continue packing the school bags. I knew there was no point in saying any more. My father always took his mask with him. And I made sure my wee brother Alec and I were safe. My mother was a law unto herself. Even when war was declared on 3rd September 1939, she refused to take her gas mask when she left the house. She'd say something like, 'If they haven't gassed us yet, they're hardly likely to do it now!'

By the end of that first week in September, women and children were being evacuated from the Scottish cities in droves. Lots of children went alone because their parents had been conscripted or assigned to war-related work. Schools only opened a few days a week and some had fewer teachers and half-empty classrooms. Mum was between jobs at the time and my father encouraged her to take us away from the Gorbals. After a full week of *encouragement,* Mum finally gave in.

'Please, Tina, think of the children.'

'Are you saying I don't think of the children? Don't I spend every night worrying about the children? I'm not going to some Godforsaken place to live with some Godforsaken country family who have Godforsaken cows.' When she was exasperated, Tina would throw in a comment about Skelmorlie. 'I swore when I left that Godforsaken campsite, I'd never set foot in another field.'

*Godforsaken* was her way of trying not to swear! Unlike my mother, Alec and I were thrilled at the idea of living in the country, especially if there were cows.

As soon as Mum agreed, my father organised our evacuation to Ayrshire in case she changed her mind—a real possibility. The day we left, Glasgow Central Station was mobbed with families travelling to rural areas in Scotland. The crowds on the platform jostled us from all sides. It was hard to stay on our feet. A lady in uniform came over and tied a cardboard label on a string around our necks. It didn't go down well with Tina.

'I'm not one of your sodding cows yet,' she said.

The poor woman looked startled. She muttered something about making it easier for families at the other end and scurried off.

I don't remember much about the place we stayed in Ayrshire or the family in the house. They had no cows and I was disappointed. The couple had no children either and the woman was very different from our mother. Her clothes were grey and baggy and she wore her hair in a tight bun, which made her look very stern. My mother complained about everything. The bed was too hard and she couldn't sleep. She missed the sound of traffic. She didn't like the way the woman cooked and refused to eat. The list went on. My brother and I were supposed to go to the local school, but by the time it was organised, Mum said she couldn't stand it anymore. We got the train back to Glasgow. My father was shocked to see us when he came home from work. My mother didn't waste time on pleasantries when she saw him.

'It was bad enough they prayed before every meal, but on Sunday, the two eejits got down on their knees on the stone floor. They had to be joking,' she exploded. 'Bloody Protestants…'

My father ushered us out to play before Tina could go on.

We weren't the only family who came home from their evacuation billet. Lots of evacuees returned to the cities when the anticipated bombing raids didn't materialise. That time was known as the Phoney War. By January 1940, almost half the evacuees in the UK had returned.

Unfortunately, plenty of German bombs fell after that. But what I remember most was the weather that month: the snow, the blizzards, the cold.

## 23. Teresa/Terri. Gorbals, Glasgow. January/February 1940
*Advanced Division*

January was freezing, with blinding blizzards and thick snow. Schools were closed and no one ventured out without good reason. Teresa begged to play with the other children in Coburg Street and eventually her mother relented.

'Get out from under my feet. Take your brother with you. And don't come back here soaking wet or covered in snow!'

The two of them raced for the door, grabbing coats and hats on their way out. They jumped into piles of soft, white ice heaps and threw fistfuls of packed snow at each other. Of course, they came home drenched and dripping all over the scullery floor, but it was worth the rollocking from their mother.

'It was great fun, wasn't it, Alec?' Teresa said to her brother, her teeth chattering as she tucked the bed covers tighter.

He wasn't as enthusiastic as his sister and groaned beside her, 'I'm never going to feel warm again.'

Although schools were closed, their father, who now had a job in the shipyards, had to work every day. He always came home frozen and shivering. Tina fussed over him, which was unusual. That night, Teresa heard her mother say,

'You shouldn't be out in that weather, Alec. Your chest isn't up to this kind of cold.'

She poked her head from the heap of blankets and sat up. She could see through a small gap in the bed recess curtains. Her father looked as white as the snow outside as he flopped into his chair beside the fire. Mum was kneeling in front of him, pulling off his boots. He wasn't usually allowed into the kitchen until he had removed them. That was a surprise.

'It'll only be for another few days. The weather will improve, you'll see. And I can't afford to lose this job, Tina. I'm fine. Honestly. Stop fretting and make me a hot cuppa.'

Teresa watched him put his arm around her mother's waist as she stood up, wet boots in her hand. Another surprise. The scene made

Teresa feel warm inside, but she was still bitterly cold on the outside. She slipped back under the covers before her mother saw her and the atmosphere changed for the worse!

They returned to school after a week and Mrs Dixon, Teresa's teacher, told the class how lucky they had been in Glasgow compared to other parts of the country.

'The River Thames in London froze. Can you imagine that, girls? Frozen! The Thames! I would have liked to witness that spectacle.'

Mrs Dixon's face flushed with dreamy excitement. Some of the girls looked at each other with that *What's she talking about* look they often shared. It was a practiced expression of bored disdain and was supposed to be *cool*. Teresa thought they looked stupid.

'It must have been very cold indeed in London,' Teresa said, attempting to distract from her classmates' rude response.

In unison, they turned their heads, staring at her with that same *what's she talking about* look on their faces. Teresa was now more flushed than Mrs Dixon and it had nothing to do with excitement!

\* \* \*

March was almost upon them. The new baby, Robert, was nearly a year old now and her mother was permanently exhausted. She was still in bed this morning as Teresa helped Alec get ready for school. He meandered out of the kitchen and lifted his coat from the nail on the back of the scullery door, not attempting to take the bag or gas mask from Teresa. He simply followed her downstairs and dilly-dallied along the pavement. They went their separate ways at the gates of St. John's in Portugal Street, Alec to the main Primary School, Teresa to the Advanced Division. She loved school and longed to stay on after she turned fourteen but knew it wasn't an option. She had tried hard to persuade her parents. The headmaster even asked to meet Tina to discuss the idea, but she was having none of it and told him so in no uncertain terms. Teresa still blushed at the memory of that afternoon.

'What good are all your books?' her mother almost spat at him. 'They don't bring in a wage packet. And the sooner Teresa realises that, the better for everyone.'

Teresa had wanted to disappear into one of the cracks in the linoleum floor of his office. Her mother whined all the way home about having better things to do with her time than listen to a load of drivel. Teresa said nothing. There was nothing left to say. She knew her father would have liked her to go to Secondary School. But when Tina ranted about the meeting over dinner, he had just said quietly, 'Your mother is right, Teresa. We can't afford for you to stay on at school.'

He looked so sad. She vowed never to mention it again.

So, here she was in the Advanced Division of St John's, with the girls who had passed the eleven-plus exam and were biding their time until they were old enough to leave and get a job. They were required by law to stay until they turned fourteen and most of them had no interest in learning. Teresa had passed the exam when she was just ten, too young to be considered for Secondary School. She was determined to make the most of it, learning as much as possible while she had the opportunity.

Now seated at her desk, Teresa watched Mrs Dixon preparing for the lesson. She was often the first to arrive at school and relished this special time with her teacher. Mrs Dixon was interesting, unlike some of the other teachers she had encountered. She never shouted, even when Sandra and Gertrude, two of the *cool* girls, talked during the lesson. They were the most fashionable girls in the class and wore their socks folded down neatly, forming a thick ring around their ankles. Teresa thought it looked very stylish but hadn't dared try it herself. They giggled a lot, but it was hard to know what they found funny. Everything, it seemed.

Mrs Dixon was distracted that morning, not lifting her head as she sorted sheets of paper into piles. Teresa knew she had a son in the Air Force and prayed nothing had happened to him. Their neighbour, Mr O'Roarke, had been killed in France and for days they could hear his wife sobbing loudly in the flat below. Teresa was glad her dad had not gone to war. She couldn't imagine him fighting with anyone, even if they were the enemy. She knew his lungs had been damaged from working in the flour mill after he left school at fourteen, the same age she would leave. She frowned, remembering how sick he had been when they were living in Symington. Her mother had said the damp got into his damaged lungs. Teresa couldn't bear the thought of anything happening to her father. She didn't like him being sick, but it was better than worrying about him dying in the war.

A sudden clap of hands snapped her out of her day dream and silenced the animated classroom buzz. Whatever had been troubling her, Mrs Dixon was back to her old self.

'You are women in the Advanced Division. Let's look at how women have advanced since Emmeline Pankhurst.'

Various comments and titters followed Mrs Dixon's statement.

'Who's Emmeline Pankhurst when she's at home?'

'Never heard of her.'

'What a stupid name!'

'Does she live in the Gorbals?'

'My dad says women have got above themselves since the war started,' was Sandra Brady's contribution. 'He says he never gets his tea on time now that Ma works in the factory.'

Gertrude Feeney laughed loudly and punched her pal's shoulder in approval.

Mrs Dixon smiled without showing her large front teeth, meaning she was being tolerant rather than pleased.

'Yes, well, I'm sure your father means well, Sandra.' She cleared her throat and told them a story Teresa would never forget.

'Emmeline Pankhurst founded the Women's Social and Political Union, better known as the Suffragette Movement, in 1903. Those brave women paved the way for the rest of us by fighting, and I mean really fighting, for women's rights.'

'Were they called suffragettes because they suffered at the hands of men?' asked Mary O'Brien, a quiet girl who was accident-prone and often had bruises on her arms.

That's an excellent suggestion, Mary. There's no doubt those women suffered at the hands of the men who jailed them for fighting for their cause. And no man should ever be allowed to inflict violence on a woman. Ever.' She paused, still looking at Mary, then went on. 'But the word *Suffragette* comes from *suffrage*, the right to vote. It was all about giving women the right to vote.'

Then Gertrude piped up, 'So they went to jail just so women could vote for an idiot? That's what Da calls Winston Churchill… and the rest of them,' she added for good measure, to Sandra's delight.

Poor Mrs Dixon. How did she put up with being interrupted all the time? She never reacted, just changed the subject or continued, ignoring the comments. Mrs Dixon told them about some of the things that happened to the suffragettes and how women were first allowed to vote in the UK in 1918. She also shared stories about how they played a vital role in keeping the country functioning during the First World War, stepping into jobs left behind by men.

'Not only will women do the same during this war,' she said, 'but they will have a much more active role in the war itself. There are better opportunities than ever for all of you to…'

Mrs Dixon was mid-sentence when the bell rang, and her class shuffled noisily to their feet and left the room. She stopped. No hint of annoyance.

'See you all tomorrow. Take care out there,' which is what she said every day.

Teresa was first in and last out, as always. 'Thank you, Mrs Dixon. That was very interesting.'

Mrs Dixon smiled her toothy smile at Teresa and told her it was an absolute pleasure. Teresa pondered those beautiful words '…absolute pleasure…' as she walked to meet her brother. She also thought about how wonderful it would have been to march as a suffragette and stand up for women's rights. Teresa wondered if this war would be over before she had a chance to do something exciting and important. Her mother and most of the women in Coburg Street were more worried about having enough rations for tea and cigarettes than contributing to the war effort. There was so much more Teresa wanted to learn. Not for the first time, she had to push down her longing to go to secondary school into the depths of her being.

\* \* \*

**Teresa. April 1940**

After the Easter holidays, all the talk in the Advanced Division was about the war. There was a mix of fear and excitement in the air.

'Why do we have to come to school anyway, when we could be bombed to bits any time?' Sandra said as she carefully folded down her knee-length socks.

Mary O'Brien and Bernadette Campbell looked terrified, but Gertrude eagerly agreed as she slumped into the seat beside Sandra and threw her gas mask onto the desk.

'My Da' says we should all stay in our Close in case the bombs fall when we're out. Mind you, he was on his way out to the pub when he said it.'

Most of the girls laughed. Teresa got the joke but didn't think it was funny. Gertrude was the eldest of seven children. It didn't take a genius to know that her father being in the pub was no help to Mrs Feeney, Gertrude's mother. But she said nothing and tried to smile, keen not to draw attention to herself. Gertrude had everyone's attention now and made the most of it.

'They've built air raid shelters in our back court, but Da' says they're useless and we'll be safer inside the house if we're hit.'

Mrs Dixon entered the room, her arms full of books, as always. She had overheard Gertrude sharing her father's wisdom.

'Well, I'm afraid your father may have been misinformed, Gertrude,' she said calmly.

Teresa couldn't help thinking Mrs Dixon must secretly want to tell Gertrude that her father was a complete idiot. The thought made her smile, genuinely this time.

'Since you are discussing air raid shelters, can any of you tell me the different kinds of shelters available here now?'

Mrs Dixon laid the books on her desk and stood beside it, as if she were midway through a conversation, rather than just through the classroom door. Teresa knew about the Anderson and Morrison Shelters. The Anderson Shelter could only hold six people, so they were not much use for the tenements. Gertrude's family alone would not have fitted into one! Teresa's father told her the shelter was named after John Anderson, who was responsible for Air Raid Precautions. Her uncle John was an ARP warden and helped people to their closest air raid shelter when the siren sounded. He also had to make sure the windows in the area were blackened and could not be seen from the air. Her mother hated the blackouts and told John he should get a 'real' job, but Uncle John just grinned and winked at Teresa.

'There's a chink of light in your curtain, Tina,' he would tease, then add, 'I'd better get going,' and rush out, laughing.

Mrs Dixon was discussing the Morrison Shelter when Teresa re-focused her attention.

'It's rather like a large cage with a strong lid. It can also be used as a table.'

It was too good an opportunity for Gertrude to miss. 'I can just imagine us all having dinner, with Da sleeping it off underneath us in the cage. Safe as houses.'

Great hilarity in the classroom.

'Well, I think it's very serious,' said Mary, who looked proud of herself for speaking up. 'My mammy was visiting her friend one night. Their tenement has a great big wall at the front of the Close called a baffle wall. It's supposed to protect them from bomb blasts and flying debris. Mammy walked straight into it during the blackout.'

'Are you sure it was a Baffle wall yer mammy walked into?' quipped Sandra.

Poor Mary hadn't meant to cause more laughter. Mrs Dixon shot Sandra a look and must have decided it was time to change the subject. Mary's face flushed a blotchy red. Teresa felt like a coward for not defending her. Some suffragette she would have been!

'Right, girls, let's have a practice with the gas masks.'

The laughter was replaced by moans, especially from poor Bernadette Campbell, who was terrified of her mask.

## 24. Teresa/Terri. The Gorbals. 13th March 1941
### The Clydebank Blitz

The siren was blaring. Her mother sat at the kitchen table, drinking her tea. Teresa stood beside her. 'Please, Mum. Can we go? Please!'

She could feel her cheeks heating and her heart pounding. Her brother, Alec, was standing in his pyjamas, hands cupped over his ears and the baby, Robert, was bawling in his cot. Tina continued to sip her tea and smoke her cigarette.

'You're way too anxious about everything, Teresa. How many false alarms have we had at this stage? How many times have I lifted Robert and dragged you all to the Co-op? Then the all-clear sounds twenty minutes later and I have to drag you all back home. I've had a hard shift at the chippie. Now, leave me in peace to finish my tea. Do you know how long I had to queue for it?'

But there was something about tonight's siren that Teresa didn't like. Sharper, more urgent than usual. *It's not possible*, she told herself. *There's only one siren.* She tried to calm down, but the bad feeling refused to shift. It was after nine o'clock, later than usual for the siren. Teresa could not ignore the nervous twisting in her tummy. She continued to needle her mother. It was like prodding a sleeping dog with a stick, something she would not normally risk. But tonight, she went on pleading.

'Please, Mum. Robert's awake anyway and I'll look after him. What harm can it do? It's not raining. Dad's at work. And you'll probably meet some of the neighbours for a chat.'

Teresa knew she was pushing her luck but had to keep trying. She thought about running down to the shelter herself, but how would it feel if she were saved and her family died in a bombing raid? What would her father think of her abandoning them?

Just when Teresa was about to give up, her mother rose from the table and said, 'Well, what are you waiting for? I'm standing here ready to go!'

Teresa grabbed the gas masks and a bag of broken biscuits while Tina changed out of her slippers. Only Teresa's objection stopped her wearing them. She made sure Robert was warm enough and hurried

Alec, who was dithering in the scullery in search of his favourite torch. Teresa led the way.

The Co-op building in Eglinton Street boasted a spacious furniture department in the basement. It was the nearest air raid shelter to Coburg Street. The shelter was swarming with people carrying prams, chairs and even fold-up beds down the steep stairs. An ARP warden stood at the entrance and ushered everyone into the shop and down to the basement. As the number of air raid sirens increased, so too did the volume and range of bits and pieces in the shelter. It became like a home from home and skirmishes often broke out about where people preferred to sit. The ARP warden on duty often had to come down and sort them out.

Thursday. Another weeknight siren. Teresa worried she would be tired at school if they had to stay all night. The shelter was already heaving and noisy. She searched for a quiet corner and a comfortable chair for her mother. Taking Robert from her mother's arms, Teresa set him on the blanket she had grabbed from his cot and handed him the small toy from her coat pocket. The furniture store was familiar to Robert and at nearly two years old, he was accustomed to the bustle and din after so many recent visits to the shelter. Teresa sat with her back against the wall and stretched out her legs. She could feel her heartbeat settling and her jaw muscles relaxing. Her whole body had been tense since the siren blasted, disturbing her homework only an hour ago! Teresa had been so busy ushering them out of the house that she had forgotten her library book. She was reading *Anne of Green Gables,* a novel about a feisty orphan with red hair. Teresa didn't want to have red hair, but she longed to be as adventurous as Anne.

By 11 o'clock, her brothers were both asleep and her mother was chatting to a man who had moved his chair next to hers. Teresa didn't approve of how close he was, but Tina was lapping up the attention and laughing at his jokes. Teresa looked away. She didn't like it when her mother talked in that familiar way to strange men.

With no sign of an all-clear, everyone in the shelter was settling down for the night. Teresa leaned her head back and closed her eyes, thinking about school and wondering if any of the girls would be in class tomorrow. She must have dozed off, because she woke with a start at the sound of shouting from the top of the staircase and then came the sirens from the street. Not an air raid siren. The sharper scream of ambulances or fire engines. Something was wrong. Teresa sat up. Four ARPs were darting around the room with clipboards. Their worried faces had started to cause panic.

'What's happening?'
'Have we been hit?'
'Oh, my God, my son's a volunteer out there.'
'My Billy's at work.'
'My cats are all alone.'

Some women snivelled quietly, others sobbed loudly and hugged their children. Another ARP warden came rushing downstairs, summoned the other four into a huddle, then ran up the stairs again and disappeared. The four wardens approached different family groups, speaking in whispers. It was their turn now. Tina had roused and was drawing deeply on a cigarette.

'Get your things together,' the ARP said. 'Nothing large. Just the bare minimum. We're taking you on a bus to Shawlands. You'll be safe there.'

Of course, her mother had to have her say. 'That's miles away. What's going on?'

The ARP moved on to the next group without responding. A buzz of agitated voices grew louder.

A man shouted, 'There must be a bomb dropped nearby.'

Then another replied jovially, 'Jerry's on his way at last.'

No one else laughed and a woman told him, 'Shut your stupid face.'

The senior warden took control of the situation. Teresa imagined Uncle John doing the same thing somewhere else tonight, telling them all to remain calm and follow directions.

'We're just moving the women and children to be on the safe side,' he said, which still left them clueless. Teresa thought her mother suddenly looked very small and pale, as if the stuffing had been knocked out of her.

'I need another cigarette. I wish your father were here. He'd know what to do.'

Teresa gathered Robert up from the floor and told Alec to take care of their mum. Bewildered at first, he grabbed Tina's coat sleeve as Teresa tried to keep her voice steady.

'Come on, Mum. We don't want to miss the bus.'

She wished Dad were here too, but he wasn't. All she could do was pray he was safe and comply with instructions.

They joined the queue and climbed onto the bus, an ordinary double-decker. Alec and Tina sat on one seat, and Teresa moved in behind them with Robert on her lap. It was hot and stuffy, and the howling of babies and children made it impossible to hold a conversation. Teresa kissed baby Robert's head. He was as good as gold, probably too stunned to add to the decibels. The front of the bus said it was going to Shettleston, wherever that was. Teresa knew it must be serious for them to be on a bus heading for Shawlands instead of its normal route to Shettleston. She didn't know where Shawlands was either, but her mother told her it wasn't far, despite protesting earlier that it was miles away.

As the bus crept along Nelson Street, they witnessed the first clear signs of what had happened. People on the bus gasped. Women started crying again—*greeters*, her mother called them. Teresa wiped a circle on the window with her coat sleeve and was faced with the mangled remains of a tram, hanging like a broken toy from the overhead electricity cables under the Nelson Street Bridge. Small fires flared inside the tram, sparks darting everywhere like fireworks. It dangled and swung precariously, a wreck of tangled metal. Unrecognisable as a tram. Teresa thought she heard screams coming from inside, but with the general noise outside on the street, it was impossible to be sure. She buried her face in Robert's hair and whispered,

*Please, God, let it be my imagination. Please, God, don't let anyone be on the tram. Please, God, keep us safe tonight. Please, God, look after my daddy.*

The window was steaming up again and Teresa vigorously wiped another circle. Her mother was smoking, too stunned to speak. Alec was blubbering and Robert decided to scream along with the others. Teresa glimpsed firemen and ARP wardens racing around in all directions, hoses in hand. Fire trucks and ambulances screeched up and down, sirens wailing. Teresa saw her mother turning Alec's head away from the window. She told Teresa not to look either. But although she pressed Robert's face against her coat, Teresa craned her neck and saw the red-orange glow and thick black smoke of fire at the end of Nelson Street. The road and pavements teemed with people, some in uniform, all running, all yelling. The knot in her stomach tightened and her mouth was so dry she struggled to swallow. Teresa turned her head away from the window as the bus continued down Eglington Street. The chaos of Nelson Street gradually faded into the distance, leaving only the occasional whimper or sob from inside the bus. This was what it felt like. This was war. They had definitely been bombed.

The bus landed at a small school, where hot tea, cold drinks and fresh sandwiches were waiting to welcome the shocked passengers. The ladies who fed them were kind and reassuring. Fold-up beds lined the floor in neat rows, ready for use. A few older women were glad to lie down, but most mothers rocked their children or huddled in groups, smoking cigarettes with their tea.

'Where are we?' Teresa asked one of the kind ladies.

'This is Battlefield Primary School on Victoria Road, my Dear. It's near Shawlands and away from the docks. You will be safe here.'

She patted Teresa's arm and moved on to reassure a sobbing mother. The rest of the night passed quickly. Robert slept and Teresa and Alec lay side by side on a soft rug on the floor under a warm blanket. Tina didn't lie down at all. She just sat with the tea-drinking, smoking women, uncharacteristically quiet. Teresa wondered if her mother was thinking about their father, like she was. The school was more comfortable than the furniture store, but it felt alien and a million miles from the Gorbals.

Teresa didn't hear the familiar sound of the all-clear siren. In the morning, after more tea and sandwiches, the ladies opened the heavy school doors and they were allowed to go home. No waiting bus to take them back to the Gorbals, but one of the kind ladies accompanied them all to the local stop to wait for local transport. They must have looked like a sorry bunch as they staggered off in Eglinton Street. But they were home. And they still had a home. The top of Nelson Street continued to billow smoke from last night's fires. Barriers had been erected at both ends, blocking any view of the damage. An occasional ambulance or fire engine blared past as the Coulters shuffled around the corner into Coburg Street. Out of nowhere, her father came hurtling towards them, nearly knocking his family to the ground. Teresa had never seen him so frantic, his eyes darting from one to the other, as if seeing them for the first time.

'Oh, my God, Tina. Oh, my God. Oh, thank God you're safe. Thank God. Thank God.'

He lifted his wife into the air and Teresa saw her mother throw her arms around her father's neck before pushing him off.

'Of course we're safe, Alec Coulter. Why wouldn't we be? And *God* didn't have much to do with it!'

'When you weren't at home, I went to all the neighbours. No one had seen you. I didn't know what to think. Archie, the ARP, told me all about Clydebank. How badly it had been bombed and…' His voice trailed off.

'Clydebank?' Her mother's voice was quiet now. 'Oh God, Alec. Margaret from the bingo lives there. If Nelson Street's anything to go by, they must have got a right doing!'

Tina hugged him again before gathering herself together.

'Now, I need a proper cuppa. The tea in that place was like dishwater.'

It was an unusual scene and one of the few times Teresa had seen her parents properly embrace. She felt exhausted, but relieved. Her father lifted baby Robert from her arms. He hugged her tightly, then kissed her brothers on the head, much to Robert's delight and Alec's disgust.

'Daaad!' he protested, but he was laughing. They were all laughing. Teresa saw tears glistening on her father's cheeks and leaned in closer to him. He looked at her with such tenderness and said, 'My darling Teresa.'

The family walked together up the stairs of the Close and into their home in Coburg Street. Teresa felt safe at last. What an eventful night it had been!

*25. Terri. Perth. 7th July 2020*
*Reflection: From the Gorbals to Bridgeton*

I still think about that night in 1941. Looking back now, I realise how little we understood at the time. We had no idea it would become known as the first of the two-night Clydebank Blitz.

German bombers were trying to destroy the docks, John Brown's shipbuilding yard and the munitions factories, like the Singer Factory. The industrial areas were badly damaged but not destroyed. Singers was back in action after less than two weeks. That took some doing! People are amazing, you know. They all pulled together to help each other. Most of their houses had no way of cooking and the company supplied hot meals for their workers.

We are enjoying our evening tipple. My first sip of mead slides down easily and warms the cockles of my heart—wherever they are! After eighty years, I still find it upsetting to talk about the Blitz. I suggest to Maureen that another drop of mead might be appropriate. She raises her eyebrows but replenishes my glass. I notice she replenishes her own at the same time. I don't raise my eyebrows or comment. Maureen is talking about a BBC documentary she watched recently.

'They interviewed older people like you who were children during the Clydebank Blitz. Entire families were wiped out over the two nights. Did you know that only eight of the 12,000 houses in the Clydebank area were left undamaged?'

I tell her I didn't know, but that it doesn't surprise me. Then she talks about a story that does surprise me.

'I was just thinking of your memory of the tram, Mum,' she says. 'Apparently, two parachute mines exploded in the Gorbals at about midnight on 13th March. The first exploded in Nelson Street somewhere between a tram and the corner of Centre Street. It was…'

I can't help interrupting, 'That must have been the tram we saw!'

'Absolutely, mum. They say it was so powerful that three French sailors were killed in Broomielaw, on the other side of the river. A couple of stray bombs that did a lot of damage in the Gorbals.'

# Impossible to Fill

I remind Maureen that London and other cities like Birmingham, Liverpool, and Coventry had it much worse than anywhere in Scotland. They were subjected to constant bombing from September 1940 to May 1941.

I tell her, 'I remember my father crying about the London Blitz. They were bombed for fifty-seven nights in a row. It's hard to imagine living through something like that.'

Maureen goes off to the kitchen and I'm glad of the peace. I'm tired now. I don't feel like talking any more. Maybe it's the two glasses of mead! It's not easy to switch off the memories once they are in my head. Now, the past feels like an echo that's always there.

My instinct was right that night in March 1941, even if our tenement didn't take a direct hit. My mother wasn't the only one who thought it was just another false alarm. When we went back to school a few weeks later, Sandra and Mary were absent. They both lived in 101 Nelson Street, one of the tenements bombed that night. The fire in their building had probably been the burning light I could see from the bus.

Mrs Dixon prayed for our two girls and all those killed during the Clydebank Blitz. I remember Gertrude sitting with her head down and her legs stretched out under the desk. Her hair wasn't brushed and her socks weren't folded down. She never laughed or made any comments in class after that. Had her father changed his mind about air raid shelters being a waste of time? Probably not. A building collapsed onto the shelter at 90 Nelson Street. Thankfully, most of the forty-one people were brought out alive. Mrs Dixon told us that eleven people died on the tram we saw on the way to Shawlands. Another twenty were rescued from the wreckage. It made me wonder about the screaming I heard. I used to think about what kind of future Sandra and Mary would have had if they had lived. Lots of children died during the Clydebank Blitz and lots more were never the same afterwards.

My father told me years later that he'd seen the tram on its side and had walked past the bombed tenements in Nelson Street on his way home from his night shift. When he didn't find us at home and no one knew where we were, he went back to Nelson Street and started searching in the rubble along with firemen, wardens and other men from the area. He panicked when he saw a fireman carrying a girl of my age in a yellow dress that looked like mine. Dad said he wept with relief when he realised it wasn't me, then with shame, when he thought of the other distraught father who had lost his daughter. When he told me, I couldn't help wondering if that man was Sandra's father. I was glad I'd never seen her wearing a yellow dress.

Tina didn't want to stay in Coburg Street after the Blitz. She was unpredictable and tended to change her mind, but by July of that year, Dad realised she was serious. I don't think he wanted to move from the Gorbals, but it was easier to agree than argue. A friend of Tina's had told her about tenements with rooms to rent in Bridgeton.

We left Coburg Street and moved to 35 Beechgrove Street in the East End of the city. The area was cleaner and not as congested, but it didn't have the bustling, friendly atmosphere of the Gorbals. The tenement had a nice 'wally' Close, meaning the walls of the Close were tiled up the stairs. But the house wasn't much of an improvement. No inside toilet and I still had to wash in a basin in the scullery. But my mother was happy and that made our lives easier. We didn't see as much of Grandma Coulter or my uncles and aunts in Thistle Street, which made me sad. Although my father never complained, he must have missed them too. On the plus side, Grandma Wilson, Tina's mother, who followed us wherever we moved in the Gorbals, decided the East End was a move too far. So we saw less of her, too.

I had no opportunity to say goodbye or thank you to Mrs Dixon, because we moved during the summer holidays. I would have liked to tell her what a wonderful teacher she was. It wasn't just the lessons that left their mark on me. She made me feel valued in a way I had never experienced before. I think Mrs Dixon wanted to make us feel important, that we mattered.

I started Sacred Heart Junior Secondary School in the autumn of 1941 and left in June 1943. My birthday was on May 2nd, the Sunday after Easter. After a lot of resistance, my mother reluctantly let me stay at school for the summer term, but only because I had a job lined up in Scobie's. If I couldn't stay on at school, I was going to work in a job with prospects. When the Career Advisor told me I could train as a hairdresser, I jumped at the chance. It was an opportunity to learn a skill and escape. I took it.

I'm smiling as I remember telling my mother I wanted a job with training and refusing point blank to work in a factory. I'm not smiling because it was an amusing conversation. Far from it! I'm smiling because, as I sat at the kitchen table with a dry mouth and hammering heart, I thought of the brave suffragettes. I took a deep breath and announced,

'I won't be working in a factory, now or ever. I'm going to be a hairdresser. And I'm going to be very good at it.'

I don't think I even waited for her to respond. My abiding memory of that morning is getting up from the table, walking out of the front door, and feeling as though I had conquered the world. It was a Saturday. I have no idea why I remember that. I jumped up and down on the pavement and danced in circles, not caring who was watching.

I gained inspiration from those suffragettes in the months and years to come. They never let me down. I started work in Scobie's and after a few months, I was offered another chance to go back to school.

## 26. Teresa/Terri. Bridgeton, Glasgow. November 1943
### A Second Chance

Teresa kept her head down as she jumped from the packed tram, one hand clamped onto her hat and the other attempting to keep her coat from flying open in the wind. Icy November rain lashed her bare legs.

'Teresa, is that you?'

She lifted her head, squinting in the dark to see who was calling her. and stared into the smiling face of Mr Douglas, her former headmaster at Sacred Heart Junior Secondary School. Teresa was amazed he recognised her and barely managed to stammer a 'Hello' as she endeavoured to hold onto her flapping clothing and tenuous dignity. Now would be a good time to disappear into the evening mist! Mr Douglas wore his fedora hat low to keep it in place and she could see rain dripping onto the collar of his coat.

'I must look as if I've been dragged through a hedge backwards,' he said and laughed, immediately making her feel more at ease.

Mr Douglas had been so good to her and desperate for her to attend Senior Secondary School. Teresa had told him it would be a flat 'No' from her parents, but he had tried anyway. And just like when she was in the Advanced Division in St. John's in the Gorbals, her mother's meeting with Mr Douglas to discuss the subject had not gone well. Teresa's face flushed with renewed embarrassment at the memory as she stood there in the rain.

'I'm glad I bumped into you, Teresa,' he said. 'How are you doing? Is work going well for you?'

It was difficult to hold a conversation in such an awkward position, especially with the wind competing with every word. As if reading her mind, Mr Douglas added, 'The Premier cafe is just around the corner. Would you like to join me for a cup of tea?'

Teresa did not know how to respond. She still thought of Mr Douglas as her headmaster. In the time it took Teresa to formulate a *No, thank you,* Mr Douglas had started walking, expecting her to follow. So, she did. He was the headmaster, after all.

As they stepped inside the cafe, a warm, greasy atmosphere hit Teresa, thick with the mingling smells of frying food and damp clothing. It was a welcoming sanctuary from the elements. Mr Crolla, the owner, rushed towards them, arms outstretched, ready to take their wet coats and hats. He spoke with an accent familiar in many parts of the city: Italian with more than a hint of a Glasgow twang.

'Come in, come my friends. I think it has been raining like dogs and cats all day, no? I find you a nice place to get warm.'

And with that, he led them to a small corner table and rushed over to the already overburdened wooden coat stand with their soggy clothes and dripping umbrella. They refused his offer of a menu and ordered two cups of tea. Once settled, Mr Douglas wiped his steamed-up glasses with his handkerchief, resuming his conversation from the street. Teresa couldn't help smiling. It was a gesture she recognised from school and its familiarity helped her to sit back and relax.

'How are you, Teresa? How is the job going? Hairdressing, isn't it?'

A harassed-looking waitress dumped their tea on the table, spilling some into the saucers. Mr Douglas gave the girl one of his disapproving stares but said nothing, gently dabbing them with the corner of his handkerchief and folding it carefully before replacing it in his pocket. Teresa sipped the hot tea and finally found her voice, making an effort to sit up straight in her chair.

'It's fine, Mr Douglas. I work in William Scobie's at 38 Bridgeton Cross. It's the largest hairdresser in the area and has an excellent reputation. It caters for both men and women. I'm in the Ladies section and learning a lot.'

Teresa thought she may have sounded a little too keen in extolling the virtues of her workplace. She wanted to let him know she still had ambition, even if she was just training to be a hairdresser. Mr Douglas said nothing, so she took another sip and continued. 'Learning is important to me. Very important. I'm glad I'm not in a factory. Not that there's anything wrong with people who work in factories,' she added quickly, in case Mr Douglas thought she was a snob.

Her mother had said as much when Teresa refused to enrol at the local clothes factory with the other girls.

'I suppose you think factory work is too good for you. Well, as long as you hand in a decent wage, you can do what the hell you like,' her mother had shouted before slamming the door on her way to work as a clippie on the trams.

Teresa should have known Mr Douglas would understand how important learning was to her. They had talked about it often enough when she joined Sacred Heart School after the Blitz.

During their final discussion in his office, the day before she finished school, he'd said, 'You will be wasted in hairdressing, Teresa.'

He was standing at the window looking out at the playground as he spoke, his back turned to her, his voice quiet. Teresa could hear the disappointment in his tone, but there was no hint of annoyance. He was well aware of her mother's views on the subject. Mr Douglas had smoothed a hand over his curly hair and swivelled to face her. He removed his glasses, wiped them with his handkerchief, replaced them and said, 'Good luck, Teresa. You deserve it.'

Teresa remembered walking out of his office, determined not to cry. And determined to do her best, no matter what that meant.

And now, here she was, five months later, sitting across from Mr Douglas, still talking about hairdressing!

'It's a good job, Teresa, but you could do so much more with your life.'

He paused, as if unsure whether to continue. 'Would you like to return to school? I mean… if it were possible, would you like to go?'

Teresa dropped her cup back in the saucer, unconcerned about the liquid spilling down the sides. Raising her voice to counteract the din of the densely packed café, she said, 'Yes' in her most confident voice.

Mr Douglas continued as if he had assumed her answer. 'You could attend Garnet Hill Secondary. You've only missed a term and I know you'll catch up. You could go on to university and study anything you like. You could even study Business and open a hairdressing shop… I mean, salon.' He was smiling now, a big, broad smile that made him look instantly younger. For the first time, she looked at this tall, thin man with curly, greying hair and wondered who he really was.

*Are you married with lots of children? Or are you a bachelor living alone? Maybe you live with your elderly mother?*

Teresa could sense his enthusiasm, even from across the table. Then reality hit, and her smile faded.

'But… how? What about…? It's not…'

Mr Douglas was already gathering his hat and gloves.

'I'll phone Sister Cecelia in Garnet Hill first thing in the morning. Meet me at the tram stop at the same time tomorrow and I will update you on how things stand. But I have a feeling that all will be well.'

Teresa stood outside the café and watched Mr Douglas striding along Main Street, using his umbrella as a stick to propel himself forward. She had abandoned any effort to keep her hat on. Rain dripped from her hair, crawling down the back of her neck, while the wind blew open her coat without resistance. The whole encounter felt unreal, oddly dreamlike. She walked home slowly, replaying every word Mr Douglas had said, over and over in her head, before climbing the three flights of stairs at 35 Beechgrove Street. Teresa was oblivious to her mother's moans about trailing water through the scullery or being late for dinner.

\* \* \*

True to his word, Mr Douglas was waiting when she stepped off the tram after work the following day. Thankfully, it wasn't raining and she'd made sure to look respectable. He wore the same coat and fedora hat and the same animated smile. Teresa knew immediately that she was going back to school. She would soon be in a Garnet Hill uniform, gassing with the other girls, planning their futures together. She imagined how proud and delighted her father would be. She chose to ignore any thoughts about her mother's reaction.

'It's all arranged, Teresa. Your parents only have to make an appointment with Sister Cecelia to sign forms and get a list of the uniform and books.'

Mr Douglas removed his glasses and wiped them in the usual way, trying to cover his awkwardness as he continued, 'I believe there are places to buy these things second-hand and ways to get a little help towards the cost of the uniform.' He replaced his glasses. 'I'm sure Sister Cecelia will have all the details.'

Teresa smiled, grateful for his kindness and his attempt to be discreet. How could she ever thank him? She had a future now, a way out of the Gorbals. She could feel her heart fluttering with excitement inside her chest. 'Thank you, Mr Douglas,' were the only words she could manage past the lump in her throat. 'Thank you.'

\* \* \*

The morning after Mr Douglas shared his news, Teresa took a deep breath and pushed open the door to Scobie's.

Anne, the manageress, was already bustling around with an armful of clean towels.

'Morning, Teresa. Busy day ahead. You can wash hair. I might even let you help me with a bit of styling if you play your cards right!'

Without waiting for a reply, she headed into the back shop for another pile of towels.

'That would be great, Anne,' Teresa shouted after her, with as much enthusiasm as she could drag from the pit of her stomach. She peeled off her coat, trying to push images of yesterday evening's horror from her mind.

She had run home, scaled the stairs two at a time, thrown open the door and blurted her news without taking a breath. Her father sat in his chair beside the fire and said nothing. Her mother said plenty, most of which Teresa couldn't remember. The bits she remembered were predictable:

'It's bad enough you're doing hairdressing when you could be earning much more in any of the factories 'round here. Why do you always have to be so headstrong and selfish? I thought this subject was closed!'

It went on until her mother ran out of steam and went out for the night, banging the door in temper.

Her father just stared at the fire. 'I'm sorry, Teresa,' he said. And she knew he was.

Her mother's parting words rang in her head. 'Your school days are over, Teresa. Get that into your thick head.'

They were in her head, loud and clear, but her head was far from *thick*. She thought about Sr. Cecelia. No doubt she was wondering what had become of her new student. Then she thought of Mr Douglas, disappointed all over again. As she scrubbed the sinks within an inch of their lives, Teresa Coulter vowed to show them all. By hook or by crook, she would succeed. With or without a Business degree.

## 27. Maureen. Edinburgh Airport. 18th July 2020
### First Journey Home

I am sitting in Edinburgh airport, a huge empty shed. Not the busy, bustling environment where excited families prepare for an adventure and tired travellers return to reality. Where business is conducted with open laptops on high stools in coffee shops and passengers chat with strangers or talk loudly into their mobiles.

This eerie silence is unnatural. I turn towards the sound of footsteps echoing on the empty terminal floor. Another solitary traveller. I wonder why they are flying today. Urgent business, important person, family emergency? Not *en route* to a villa abroad or a romantic rendezvous! I have a letter tucked into my passport verifying that my mother is terminally ill and my husband has cancer. It is like having a note to explain a school absence or unsubmitted homework. Two plain-clothed detectives await the arrival of the flight from Nice, ready to ask questions and seek similar documentation. They look intimidating. Has the world gone mad? Is this Orwell's 1984? Are we characters in a Stephen King novel?

God, I wish there were somewhere to get coffee! The only shop open for business in the airport is WH Smith, where the catering is limited to sandwiches and water. I sit back, attach my headphones and try to listen to my audiobook. I am distracted and miss chunks. Abandoning my book, I ponder the reality of life instead of diverting my thoughts with heartwarming fiction.

Somehow, I find it easier to manage worry, stop it escalating, if its source is in the same location. I worried about Martin during my time with Mum and I will worry about Mum when I am home with Martin. Such is life! But worry does not alter outcomes. I read that 85% of the things we stress about never happen. That's a lot of wasted time. The Glasgow expression *you die if you worry and you die if you don't* says much the same thing. I worried Mum would not live until I was able to retire and travel to Scotland—she is still very much alive. I worried Martin would be lost without me in the lead-up to his surgery—he has been just fine. Still, 15% of our worries do come true. Like Clare, my beautiful and special friend of over fifty years. I worried she would die without us seeing each other again—she did. I worried she would die on her own in a hospital ward—she did.

Before heading to the airport today, my brother Barney and I detoured to Helensburgh to visit Clare's grave on the north side of the Firth of Clyde. We stood beside a grassy mound, under which lay my pal. I could find no trace of her. I tried my best but could not visualise her lovely smile or hear her happy laugh. I felt only the pain of loss and the deep sorrow of not saying goodbye to my best friend. She was sixty-four years old, but for me, it was never about counting years. Just a jumble of living, loving memories that will never die.

I shift in my seat and adjust my face mask, as if shifting and adjusting my emotions, wishing just one small coffee shop would open. *Distraction is needed.* I think about leaving Mum, picture her in that long furry waistcoat of hers, me hugging her tiny frame, muttering, 'See you soon, Mum.'

She nods but does not attempt to speak. Then she climbs the stairs to wave from the window, as she always does. It takes a long time for her to arrive there, but I wait until I can see her looking down at me.

*See you soon, Mum*, I whisper again to reassure myself. Then I jump into the car with Barney and watch her waving until the car turns the corner. *Not a great distraction!*

My flight is announced and I gather my bits together. No queue. No chatter. Just a few masked passengers heading towards the gate. As I plonk myself into the seat of an empty row, in an empty aircraft that will take me home to Martin, I allow myself to feel excited. I think about the 85% rule, making an effort to banish unnecessary worries about Martin and Mum. Another familiar Glasgow saying pops into my head: *Life's a bitch and then you die.*

I laugh out loud. No one nearby to hear. I adjust my headphones and settle back with my audiobook.

*I'll be back to hear and write the rest of your story, Mum.*

## RMS *Empress of Australia*

# PART 2
## *GROWING STRONGER*

## 1. Maureen. Belfast City Airport. 15th September 2020
### Leaving on a Jet Plane

Belfast City Airport is much smaller than Edinburgh, which makes it seem as if more passengers are moving around. Perhaps as many as twenty! The departure area is compact and I am thrilled to spot a Starbucks. I nip to the toilet and look forward to settling down with a latte and my audiobook. Unfortunately, although I manage to relieve my bladder, the same cannot be said for my coffee craving. Starbucks is closed when I emerge four minutes later. The young man behind the counter informs me they open for a few hours at a time then close for cleaning. Bloody Covid!

I have been at home in Sligo for nine weeks, during which time Martin has been through his robotic surgery and is recovering well. The consultant believes the tumour was enclosed within the prostate and has been completely removed. However, the cancer cells were aggressive, so the news was not all good. The operation was three weeks ago, but it still feels like abandonment. Love is such a powerful emotion. Sometimes, it pulls me in different directions until I feel overwhelmed and paralysed by the choices I have to make. The edges of my roles as wife and daughter have become blurred, and I find myself weighing up who needs me most at any given time. Of course, I know love is not a cake to be divided into sections, but I cannot physically be in two places at once. I feel as if my love is constantly tested by choice.

The surgery brought its share of practical challenges, but being home with Martin felt good—*safe, calm, reassuring*. I was truly present for him, able to show my love through care, both physical and emotional and watch him grow stronger each day, even if it sometimes meant being a tough nurse instead of a gentle wife. I also felt invigorated and recharged, returning to my writing routine in our cosy lounge with views of countless trees, sprawling fields and craggy mountains. No wonder they talk about the forty shades of green. I can spot most of them from my desk, through windows at both ends of the room.

We have lived in County Sligo in the northwest of Ireland for more than thirty years. Although a city girl until I met Martin, I have fallen in love with its rugged beauty, windswept beaches and unassuming charm. The town is guarded by the unmistakable flat top of Ben Bulben in the north, and Queen Maeve's grave on the summit of Knocknarea to the west.

Even in my Glencar sanctuary, it took time for the words in my head to unravel onto the page. Eventually, I managed to fictionalise the first part of Mum's story and document my recollections of our first weeks together. It was a positive start. As I listened back to the mobile phone recordings of our conversations, I began to hear them differently. Not just the stories themselves, but the way Mum told them—her tone, her interpretation, her comments and asides. It was as if I had found a secret door between her words and the thoughts behind them, like catching a reflection in glass. I did the only thing I could. I wrote them down, and in doing so discovered the third strand of my book: Mum's reflections, pieced together from the spaces between her words..

There is still so much I don't know and want to find out about the woman who is my mum. We have spoken about parts of her life over the years, but I wish I had asked more questions, listened more closely. Now, every conversation carries a sense of finality. I try to fill in the gaps, but it is like holding on to a dream as it fades or trying to photograph a rainbow before it vanishes. We assume we have time. We don't.

I am learning by watching as well as listening. Each morning, I see Mum gather herself, physically and mentally, as she slowly makes her way to the ensuite bathroom. Routine and hygiene have always mattered to her. She no longer has to wash in a basin, but standing at the sink, cloth in hand, she still carries out her thorough top-and-tail wash with no corner left unclean. A long-handled brush helps with her back and a well-placed stool makes it possible to reach her feet.

I don't want to interfere until it becomes necessary. This ritual is about more than hygiene. It is about dignity and independence. A quiet defiance against illness and ageing. And so, I wait outside the bathroom door, just in case and quietly admire my tiny, frail mother, whose determination is unwavering.

Every two days, ablutions include replacing the stoma bag, another quiet testament to her determination. With failing sight, she removes the old bag, cleans the site, and tries to attach the new one before Vesuvius erupts and the whole process must be repeated. Strips of tape for the new bag are pre-cut and laid out in order. The black scented waste bag sits open on the toilet seat, ready for the foul-smelling debris. There is also a solution to unstick the old bag, powder to help attach the new one and several half-moon adhesives to prevent leaks. Yet sometimes, despite her best efforts, there is unexpected seepage later in the day. Pungent, burning and humiliating for a woman whose dignity is so closely linked to cleanliness.

* * *

Once seated on the sparsely occupied aircraft, my thoughts turn to Mum's surgery tomorrow. It is not as serious as Martin's, but it will be traumatic, nonetheless. A cancerous tumour will be removed from her shin. It has been the source of persistent pain over the past few months, causing real distress and adding to her daily struggles. A previous leg tumour was skin-grafted and the graft took over a year to heal. That simply cannot happen this time.

As the short flight begins its descent into Edinburgh, I try to leave Martin and Glencar behind and prepare for the weeks ahead. I find myself looking forward to my mum's beautiful smile. I am ready for the next part of our journey together, whatever it holds. And I look forward to hearing the next chapter in Teresa Coulter's journey in life.

## 2. Terri. Ninewells Hospital, Dundee. 16th September 2020
### More Surgery

We're sitting in the waiting area, me parked in a wheelchair and Maureen beside me. We decided to use the wheelchair so that she was able to come. I could have walked, but that's the way you have to play it with Covid, because relatives are not permitted into hospitals.

A lovely young man comes to tell me what'll happen when I go into the theatre. I don't know if he's a doctor or a nurse, but he's very kind. I had no notion of having any more surgery, but the best-laid plans and all that. This new doctor is easy to talk to and I like the cut of his jib. My leg is very sore now and looks terrible with this big, dirty-looking cancer growing on it. At least they won't take a skin graft from my thigh. The last time, every nurse had a different opinion on how to treat it. Eventually, I asked myself what my father would have done. I cut one leg off my tights and trousers, and exposed the wound to the air. My niece, Lorna, came twice a day to apply and reapply dressings for nighttime. Lo and behold, it worked, thanks to my father's inspiration and Lorna's dedication. The sight of me in my one-legged trousers used to frighten the delivery men, but I just told them I was practising my Irish dancing. That put their gas in a peep!

The handsome young man in the white coat has returned. I can feel my tummy cartwheeling and my ileostomy bag gurgling in sympathy. Maureen helps me out of the wheelchair, and I link arms with my escort and head down the corridor for my theatre date.

'Are you taking me dancing?' I ask and he says, 'Why, are you a good dancer?' And I tell him, 'I am indeed. I do a very good Charleston.'

I'm amazed to find out he has never heard of the dance. I could show him, but I don't think the timing is quite right.

\* \* \*

**17th September 2020. Perth**

It's lovely to have Maureen back with me. She says Martin is doing well after his surgery. I am so pleased. When Maureen is not here, the family rallies round and I can keep in touch with them all with that Face thing. Colette likes to see me when we talk on the phone. She says she knows how I am from looking at my face. But she's always telling me to move the phone up or down because she's looking up my nose or at the ceiling. Imagine if I could have talked like that to my father when I was in Egypt. He never got a chance to travel outside Glasgow, unless you count the campsite in Skelmorlie. When I think of it, I might never have travelled abroad if it hadn't been for my job at Bamber's. I must tell Maureen about how I got that job. It was a very posh hairdressing salon and I'm amazed they took me on at barely 15 years old. I just marched up one Saturday afternoon after finishing work in Scobie's. I told the manager I was the person he was looking for, that I was a quick learner, a good worker and could start straight away. I was angry when I wasn't allowed to go back to school. I made up my mind there and then, I wasn't going to stay in Bridgeton. Scobie's was a good hairdressing salon, but I knew there were better ones in the centre of Glasgow. I wanted the best training. I wanted to make something of myself and Scobie's wasn't going to do that for me. It was time for a change. And I was determined to make it happen.

## 3. Teresa/Terri. Glasgow. June 1944
### *A Cut Above the Rest*

Teresa stood on the pavement gazing at the sign above the shop. *R. Sheldon Bamber, Hairdresser.*

It was hard to believe this was now her place of work. As well as a hairdressing and beauty salon, the shop had a theatrical department, supplying costumes and wigs to local and touring theatre groups. The premises had been owned by the Bamber family for years and was now managed by Mr Skinner. It was spread across three floors, with the main entrance to the left of the large shop window. Inside, a door led into the Ladies' Hairdressing Salon, while a staircase guided male customers down to the Gents' salon in the basement. Another staircase near the entrance rose to the theatrical department. The sign above the window described the hairdressing services and beauty products, while the one above the door read *Fancy Dress*. The four areas of expertise offered upstairs were printed in each corner of the door itself: Wigs, Scenery, Costumes and Masks. The theatrical department was managed by Mr Foster, whom she had met on the day of her interview.

Teresa wiped sweaty palms on her new navy skirt. She wondered if nearby pedestrians, or shoppers coming in and out of Boots the Chemist, could hear her heart pounding like a jackhammer in her chest. She had appeared cocky when she walked through the door two weeks earlier. With so many women in their twenties and thirties—including hairdressers—joining up or being requisitioned for munitions work, Teresa had seen her chance. She stayed on at Scobie's until after her fifteenth birthday last month. Even during a staffing crisis, R. S. Bamber was unlikely to take on a fourteen-year-old apprentice, no matter how confident. But here she was, about to begin a new career in an upmarket salon: thrilled, excited and just a little terrified.

'It's never enough, is it, Teresa?' her mother had said when she told her about Bamber's. 'You always want more. First, you think you're too good for factory work. And now, you think a hairdresser in Bridgeton isn't posh enough. Well, the wages had better be good because you'll have an extra tram fare on top of everything else. And that won't pay the bills here.'

Teresa caught a glimpse of her reflection in a small mirror in the shop window and instinctively patted her hair with both hands. She stared up again, this time noticing a much larger sign next door to Bamber's. Ornate, looping gold letters advertised a dental practice on the first floor. If the sign was anything to go by, it must cost a small fortune just to step inside. Charing Cross Mansions looked every bit as grand as its name and nothing like the crumbling, grey tenements in the Gorbals or Bridgeton.

Mr Skinner agreed to give Teresa a trial in the salon. Her father had accompanied her on a trial run by tram from Bridgeton to Charing Cross, changing at Argyle Street for the number 3 to University. Teresa had carefully timed the journey, determined not to be late on her first day. On the way home, they had stopped at the Gorbals library, one of his favourite places, then visited Grandma Coulter for tea. They found a book about Glasgow architecture and read all about Charing Cross Mansions. Her grandmother was very impressed when Teresa informed her that it had been the very first red sandstone tenement in Glasgow and was considered to be the grandest.

'Your work address will be numbers 12 and 13 Charing Cross Mansions, Teresa. It certainly has a very grand feel to it,' she had said.

'The clock in the centre is so beautiful, Grandma. I read that the two reclining figures holding it up were inspired by a Michaelangelo sculpture. They're meant to represent commerce and industry. Don't you think that's really clever?'

Before Grandma Coulter could answer, her father jumped in with similar enthusiasm.

'Yes. And don't forget the signs of the zodiac around the clock. Not to mention the four figures representing the seasons.'

Her grandmother raised her hands as if surrendering, and said, 'Enough. Enough, you two historians. The tea will be stewed and I had to use the last of this week's rations to procure it.'

The three of them sat in the parlour as her grandmother poured tea from her china cup into her saucer and said, 'Alec, I presume you know that, grand and all as it sounds, your daughter now has a job on the Square Mile of Murder.'

The cup in her father's hand stopped midway to his mouth. He and Teresa stared at each other. There had been no mention of murder in the book about architecture. Annie Coulter blew on her tea, took a sip, then looked up with a wide, toothless grin on her face.

'Of course, that was back in Victorian times. I'm sure it's perfectly safe nowadays. Close your mouth, Alec dear.'

'You never cease to amaze me, mother,' he said.

And they all laughed. It was always special to be with two of her favourite people in the world.

\* \* \*

A tap on the shoulder interrupted Teresa's reverie. She turned to find Mr Foster, the theatrical department manager, standing beside her. He was smiling.

'Good morning, Miss Coulter. Lovely to see you again. Shall we make a start on the day?'

He disappeared inside the shop, holding open the door for her. There was no going back now. Teresa's smart shoes felt too heavy to lift, as if glued to the pavement. She thought of how happy she had been that afternoon with her father and grandmother and how proud they were of her. Then she threw back her shoulders and propelled herself into the shop, and her future.

## 4. Teresa. Charing Cross. November 1944
*Learning the Trade*

The damp chill made Teresa shiver as she stepped off the tram and watched it head towards Glasgow University.

She thought of that wet day a year ago, when she had jumped off the tram in Bridgeton and bumped into Mr Douglas, the headmaster. Was it only a year ago? It felt so much longer. Occasionally, as the tram trundled away from Charing Cross, Teresa wondered what it would feel like to continue to the end of the line and join the other students attending university. But she loved working in Bamber's and was certain it would lead to even better opportunities.

There was so much to learn from watching and listening to knowledgeable and experienced hairdressers. She had started downstairs in the men's department, a completely new experience. Mr Thompson, the most senior member of staff, tried to teach her how to shave faces. She continually burst the practice balloons and eventually he advised her to stick to heads rather than chins.

'Teresa, Teresa, my dear. The skin on a man's face is delicate and must be treated accordingly, as if it were the smooth skin on a baby's bottom.'

The comment made Teresa blush. Mr Thompson had finally deemed her safe to cut men's hair 'to the wood' and shave the back of their necks. She was also permitted to remove the hairs from their ears and noses, not one of her favourite tasks.

Six months on, Teresa breezed through the door, headed across the black and white tiled floor to the back shop, hung up her coat, and slipped into her uniform. The white starched top with blue trim fitted neatly over her blouse and the top of her skirt. A navy belt around the waist made her look much more professional than the baggy smock in Scobie's. Teresa twirled in front of the full-length mirror, pleased with what she saw.

The ladies' salon on the ground floor was the largest area, with two main workstations along opposite walls. One featured individual alcoves for washing, each with a porcelain sink, a hose attachment at the taps, and a shelf for towels and a small mirror. Padded wooden chairs were lined up for customers to lean over the basins, and beside each stood a neat trolley stocked with shampoo, hair tonic, and massage oil. There was no such thing as massage oil in Scobie's. But it was the other wall that truly impressed Teresa. A row of black leather chairs with armrests faced ornate wall-mounted mirrors. The trolleys beside each station held everything needed for modern styling: jars of combs and brushes, bottles of setting lotions, perming solution, and sprays of hair lacquer and fragrance. Each station also stocked pins, grips, scissors, razors and hairnets. The new Bakelite rollers were available, but also traditional metal ones for customers who preferred a weekly shampoo and set. Teresa still felt a rush of anticipation when she came through the door to the salon every day.

'Miss Coulter, you are like an over-excited puppy keen to learn new tricks,' Mr Thompson had said one morning.

His face looked serious, but Teresa knew he was secretly delighted to be teaching such an eager student. Today, he was all business.

'Mrs Patterson is due in for reapplication of perming lotion. It's a tricky procedure. You assisted me last time and now I believe you are ready to work on your own. What sayeth thou?'

Mr Thompson was a keen theatre-goer and often spoke as if he were in a Shakespearean play. Of course, there was only one answer and it wasn't very Shakespearean. 'Yes.' Without further comment, Mr Thompson switched to training mode.

'Have everything at your fingertips before you start. I have allotted an hour and a half for the appointment. Make sure Mrs Patterson wears the protective rubberised cape—she doesn't like it. Don gloves for mixing your solution. It's strong stuff. Remember it contains thioglycolic acid, so be careful. Wear the apron hanging in the back shop.'

He flounced off with a final 'Call me if you require assistance. I shall be attending to Mrs Henrietta Tweedie, may the Lord and his angels help me.'

Teresa ran her hand over the trolley as she checked the essentials: perming lotion and neutraliser, rods and elastic bands, cotton wool. All ready. The sharp scent of the lotion pricked her nostrils. She picked up the brush she would use to apply the solution, then let her eyes skip over the rest of her equipment. She knew the procedure by heart, but this time, Mr Thompson would not be standing beside her. The door opened. The bell jangled.

'Good morning, Mrs Patterson, how are you on this chilly morning? Let's get you a cup of tea before we start.'

* * *

The following day, Mrs Skinner informed Teresa that Mr Thompson never allowed a trainee to perm hair until they had worked in the salon for at least a year. Teresa was thrilled to hear this, especially as the gentleman himself had merely said, 'Mrs Patterson seemed satisfied and therein lies my satisfaction.'

It wasn't a criticism, but it wasn't a compliment either.

Mrs Skinner, the manager's mother, was in charge of beauty products displayed in the glass cabinet under a long countertop near the entrance. A cash register and an appointments book were positioned in the centre of the counter, and Mrs Skinner was the only one permitted to touch them. She was at least eighty and not a great advertisement for beauty products. Another reminder that women of working age were in short supply. Although makeup and cosmetics were not rationed, they were deemed *non-essential* items, and a massive luxury tax made them unaffordable for many women. Teresa had heard intriguing solutions from some of the customers, including beetroot juice for lips and cheeks, and boot polish for eyelashes and brows. She decided to stick to pinching her cheeks for a little colour.

After making her announcement to Teresa, Mrs Skinner shuffled off in her oversized black shoes. She insisted they were 'very comfortable,' but to Teresa, they looked quite the opposite. Poor Mrs Skinner. The war had opened doors for girls like Teresa, but it also meant older women were still working when they should have been relaxing or playing with grandchildren. Teresa was quick to intercept when she noticed Mrs Skinner attempting to lift a heavy box of cold cream jars onto the counter.

'Let me get that for you. Where's Mr Thompson? I thought he was working up here this morning. He said he would show me how to style hair into a Victory Roll today.'

'I expect his wife has a few chores for him to do before he's allowed out of the house,' Mrs Skinner said, with a look that meant so much more. 'She works in an office, doing some sort of important paperwork for the army. She's taken those *Beauty is your Duty* Government slogans a bit too seriously, if you ask me. She won't do housework in case she breaks a nail or ruffles her hair. Have you ever heard the likes? As if looking good is going to win the war for us!'

Teresa was literally saved by the bell, as a loud ting-a-ling announced Mr Thompson's arrival.

'Good morning, thou loveliest of ladies. How are we all this fine day?'

Mrs Skinner threw her eyes to Heaven and continued to unpack her box as Mr Thompson headed into the back shop.

He was tall and skinny with thinning black hair, probably in his forties. He never talked about children, so Teresa assumed he had none. Mind you, he rarely spoke about his wife and he definitely had one of those.

One day, about a month after she started, they were clearing up after a busy morning when Mr Thompson paused mid-sweep, leaned on his brush, and said: 'Teresa, do not tread the same boards or make the same mistakes as yours truly. I should have loved every bugger and married none.'

Message delivered, he continued sweeping. Teresa was stunned, but relieved no reply seemed expected. When they had finished, he disappeared into the back-shop, rummaged in his bag and thrust a tin box into her hands. She knew it contained the sandwiches his wife made for him every day.

'Enjoy. I think they're cheese. They usually are. I'm off to the local watering hole for sustenance.'

And away he went, leaving Teresa with a box of sandwiches and no idea what to do with them. Eventually, she decided that the polite thing to do was to eat them. It wasn't right to waste food with all the rationing. And that's how it was most days after that.

Mr Thompson did not wear a uniform, but he looked smart in black trousers, a black shirt and a white tie. Somehow, it suited his personality. He always addressed her formally in front of customers.

'Now, Miss Coulter, the Marcel Wave was the basis of hair styling in the 1920s, but pins and rolls are the order of the day now. If you master these, you can start calling yourself a hairdresser.'

It was exciting to watch Mr Thompson work. He was as comfortable with ladies' complex hairstyling as with men's short, back and sides. He said the war and staff shortages had made him versatile. Teresa thought he was being modest.

This morning, Teresa stood beside Mr Thompson as he chatted easily to Marjorie Mead, who worked in a munitions factory and was desperate for a Victory Roll.

'They're all the rage, Mr Thompson. V for Victory, like the sign the pilots make after a raid. We women have to do our bit, isn't that right, Miss...'

'Coulter. Teresa Coulter. Teresa.' She glanced at Mr Thompson for approval. Marjorie Mead was only slightly older than her, after all. He didn't react, just continued laying out the required pins

'Absolutely. Yes. Quite right. We should all look our best,' Teresa said, although she tended to agree with Mrs Skinner that hair and makeup were pretty poor weapons against Hitler. As if reading her mind, Marjorie Mead added,

'I read that Hitler has set up a Fashion Board to force women in Germany to wear plain clothes, have natural hair and use no makeup or perfume. The man's insane. So let's stick it to Mr Hitler and be as glamorous as we can, I say.'

She held up two fingers. 'V for Victory. Let's do this, Mr Thompson.'

Mr Thompson carefully sectioned Marjorie's hair, twisting each strand into a neat curl and pinning it flat against her head until it was crowned with a mass of coils. Then he wheeled over the large hairdryer, lowered the hood and switched it on. Within minutes, Marjorie had nodded off, chin on her chest, a sight that made both Teresa and Mr Thompson grin conspiratorially.

When the dryer bell rang and Marjorie roused from her nap, Mr Thompson set to work again, brushing and shaping the curls into two perfect Victory Rolls. He smoothed each side upward from a centre parting, pinning the rolls high at her temples, then gathered the rest of her hair into a soft roll at the nape of her neck. A generous spray of lacquer fixed everything in place. A classic style with a touch of Bamber's polish.

The result was stunning and Miss Mead was thrilled. Admiring the rolls in the mirror, she patted the high curl on top and declared, 'That's sticking it to Hitler. Right, Mr Thompson?'

Mr Thompson beamed approval. Neither he nor Marjorie Mead noticed Mrs Skinner sitting at her counter, head in her hands in quiet disgust. No wonder she wasn't busy.

## 5. Terri. Perth. 13th October 2020
### *Talking and Remembering*

I'm sitting with my leg up as instructed by Maureen. After nearly four weeks, it seems to be healing well.

Maureen has gone for her walk. It's important that she has some time to herself. One of the positive things about being at home here so much is that we've been able to talk. Really talk. And that helps me remember parts of my life I thought I had forgotten. Normally, I am too busy just living every day to dwell on the past, but I must say I'm enjoying our chats about events from long ago. This morning, we discussed Bamber's. What a great time that was. I haven't thought about Mr Thompson, Mr Foster, or Mrs Skinner for years.

I forgot to tell Maureen about the incident with old Mrs Skinner. I can't remember how the conversation started, but one day she started talking and I thought I would never get back to work. Maybe she was trying to warn me about the dangers of men, because lots of girls were 'caught out' by handsome lads in uniform going off to war. Anyway, I can still visualise Mrs Skinner sitting at her cosmetics counter, elbow on the glass top and chin in her hand. That's how she always sat when she wasn't busy, which was most of the time.

I was cleaning the sink in the nearby washing station when she announced, 'We already had two boys when I discovered I was pregnant again.'

I hadn't the faintest idea what to say. Mrs Skinner wasn't usually a talker.

'Times were hard. I didn't know how we would manage with a baby to look after and another mouth to feed. I didn't tell Mr Skinner, senior. There was no point in us both worrying. Then I decided to do something about the pregnancy myself.'

Of course, I had no clue what she meant by 'do something about the pregnancy.' I continued to listen and she continued to talk.

'I had heard of a few things you could do. I tried them all, but nothing worked. I got into a very hot bath. I drank a lot of gin one night and jumped off the kitchen table.'

Now I was shocked and horrified. Why would Mrs Skinner drink gin and jump off a table? It didn't make sense. She wasn't a drinker. I can't remember exactly how I responded. It was a very long time ago. But I think I managed to ask something obvious, like, 'Why did you jump off the table? Did you hurt yourself?'

Mrs Skinner took her elbow off the glass top and laid a hand on each knee. Isn't it strange that I can recall certain details? I also remember how empty her eyes looked.

She said something like, 'The baby, Teresa. I was trying to get rid of the baby. But it didn't work. I'm ashamed of what I did now. But I felt so alone and hopeless at the time.'

Just when I thought she might cry, Mrs Skinner's face lit up with the biggest smile I'd seen since I started at Bamber's.

'Thank God, it didn't work, Teresa. Because now I have my wonderful daughter, Elizabeth. She is the joy in my life and the only one of my three children who looks after me. The boys are men now and have their own busy lives, like my eldest son, who runs this shop. But Elizabeth is always there for me. I have never felt hopeless or alone since the day she was born. Don't they say God works in mysterious ways?'

And with that, Mrs Skinner got up and shuffled across the floor into the back shop to put the kettle on. I stood, cloth in hand, a million confusing thoughts in my head. I was fifteen and had no idea about men, sex, or pregnancy. And I certainly had no idea about abortion.

Years later, Mrs Skinner's words came back to me when I was pregnant with Joe, the youngest of my five children. He's fifty-six now. We had four children at the time and my husband, also Joe, had decided to leave his secure job and set up his own flower shop. It was a big decision. The stakes were high and money was tight. I watched from the window of our new home in Fernleigh Road, Newlands, as Joe walked the big Silver Cross pram to the nearby convent. Ironically, we wanted to give it to someone less fortunate than ourselves. I knew the pram would be needed in less than seven months. We would have to buy a new one, which we couldn't afford. I just didn't have the heart to tell Joe that day. As I stood there feeling helpless and hopeless, I thought of Mrs Skinner. How she smiled as she described the joy her daughter, Elizabeth, had brought into her life. At that very moment, I realised it would all be fine. And it was. When I look at young Joe now, I cannot imagine our lives without him. As Mrs Skinner said all those years ago, God works in mysterious ways.

Maureen is back from her walk. She's in the kitchen making lunch. I can't eat much these days, but we're having grilled halloumi cheese, which is salty and tasty. Waiting for lunch reminds me of another story to tell her. I loved my job at Bamber's, but my mother was right about the wages. I was an apprentice, not earning as much as in a factory. I had to do something about it. Bamber's closed at lunchtime on Saturdays. One afternoon, I took a tram to Eglinton Street, where I'd heard they were looking for staff in the Colosseum Department Store. Sure enough, I was interviewed by Mr Murphy, a small red-haired man, who said I could start the following week.

I was in charge of selling stockings on the ground floor. The job was fun and I was quite good at sales. Every Saturday, I raced from Charing Cross to Eglinton Street and worked for the afternoon in the Colosseum. One Saturday, I had been working for about half an hour when Mr Murphy called me into his office. I can still remember my hands sweating and the saliva in my mouth evaporating as I waited outside.

'When do you have your lunch, Miss Coulter?' he asked.

I didn't understand why he was asking, but my dry mouth managed to stammer that I usually took my break at three o'clock and ate my lunch then..

'That can't happen anymore, Miss Coulter,' he said. 'You will go to the canteen as soon as you arrive and have something to eat before starting work.'

He looked up from his desk and smiled. 'Go and have something now. We can't have you fainting on the job.'

It was an act of kindness I never forgot. And I worked twice as hard after that.

Lunch has arrived. Unfortunately, I won't be full of energy afterwards like in the old days at the Colosseum. I already feel my eyes getting heavy and hope I can stay awake long enough to eat. I want to tell Maureen about Mrs Skinner's wisdom and Mr Murphy's kindness, but we have plenty of time. Another thought occurs to me

'Maureen, did I tell you I went camping in Aberfoyle at weekends?

## 6. Maureen. Perth. October 2020
### *Living and Loving*

Mum lives in a cosy courtyard of fourteen terraced houses facing each other and separated by a large rectangle of artificial grass. On the outskirts of the courtyard, numerous pathways meander through neighbouring small estates and along the river towards the centre. Although the Fair City of Perth is larger and more urban than Sligo, they share a kindred spirit, both shaped by nature and a strong sense of the past. I feel at home here, which makes it easier to be away from the peaceful Glencar Valley. Located on the banks of the River Tay, Perth is within easy reach of both the Highlands and the historic town of St. Andrews, where I have walked the beach and dipped in the North Sea with my brother Barney and his wife, Lorna.

A daily walk has become part of my routine. I listen to my audiobook, ponder life, or simply allow myself to marvel at the wonder of nature. Today, the surrounding gardens are less colourful than last month, but flashes of red and orange dahlias still peek from foliage. Nature is preparing for the end of another year, just as I am preparing for the end of another life, my mum's. I cannot begin to guess how to do that. I love our time together, especially in the mornings when Mum is bright and alert, and we chat about the past and the present, and laugh for no reason. It all seems very normal. But normality will come to an end. Covid-19 restrictions allow us to live in support bubbles, where two households behave as one family unit. I am also living in a time bubble with Mum and its fragile transience feels like the kind of bubble blown by a child who waits for it to burst or disappear into the sky.

My current audiobook has been a comfort during recent walks. It is called *Dear Life, a Memoir* by Rachael Clarke, a Hospice consultant in England. She talks about managing the living rather than the dying. It is life-affirming, not depressing, and reading it is timely. Maybe the only way to prepare for death is to keep living. And loving. It might sound clichéd, yet it still feels true. I worry about managing Mum's needs as her health declines. Focusing on living and loving one day at a time makes the fear feel less intimidating.

I turn my face to the sky and absorb the warmth of this burst of late October sunshine. Having finished the current chapter of the book, I remove my headphones and tune in to the rhythmic rush of the river and the chatter of birds. I pause to admire the wild red crocosmia scattered along the riverbank and greet dog walkers with a casual, 'Hello there.' Most people remove their masks now when out walking and it feels good to give and receive a smile. The small pleasures in life are the sweetest.

As I climb the stairs away from the river and join the road that forms the homeward circuit, I consider Mum's story about hiking after finishing her two Saturday jobs. My first thought is that, in her shoes, I would have rushed home to put my feet up, not get on a bus to Aberfoyle. My second thought is that I have never associated Mum with hiking. I know she walked the Great Wall of China with the Soroptimists, but even then, she wore heels, because trainers did not match her outfit. Mum cannot remember the name of her hiking friend from the Colosseum, only that she worked in the glove department. She giggled at the memory of the short kilt she wore during their hikes. I'll bet she wasn't wearing trainers (known as plimsolls) with her kilt.

I return from my walk, refreshed and content.

'Hello, Mum. I'm back. You should see the dahlias in the garden round the corner.'

When I open the living room door, the TV is blaring and Mum is asleep.

## 7. Teresa/Terri. Bamber's. September 1946
### *Style and Fashion*

After more than two years at Bamber's, Teresa had earned Mr Thompson's trust and now had her own steady stream of clients. Though still with much to learn, she embraced every opportunity to strengthen her skills and broaden her experience.

Teresa also enjoyed working with Mr Foster in the theatrical department. The large room had an atmosphere of organised chaos, giving it a certain theatrical vibrancy. Lavish costumes hung from a long rail, head statues wore an assortment of coloured wigs and boxes of theatre props were piled on the floor. A distinctive waxy smell mingled with the faint flowery fragrance of face paint. Traces of camphor or eucalyptus also lingered, along with the subtle scent of old powder puffs and faded perfume clinging to the costumes and wigs.

Mr Foster liked nothing better than talking about all things theatrical and Teresa liked nothing better than soaking up every detail.

On her first day with him, he'd said: 'In summary, my dear, you are imbibing the delightful aroma of the theatre in all its glory.'

Today, they were on the roof garden of the third floor of Bamber's, cleaning wigs and costumes recently returned from the Empire Theatre. It was a tedious process and learning about the theatre was the main reason Teresa volunteered to help. The wigs had to be brushed, then sluiced in petrol, dried and re-brushed before styling. Mr Foster never showed any signs of boredom. He loved every aspect of theatre. He was often given tickets for upcoming productions at the King's, the Royal, or the Empire and sometimes passed them on to Teresa. She would sit in the Gods, the highest and cheapest seats, mesmerised from curtain up to final applause. Now that she knew a little about costumes and makeup, she tried to pay attention to detail, but it was hard when the stage was so far away.

'Did you ever think about becoming an actor, Mr Foster?' Teresa asked, blowing a stray curl from across her left eye. The smell of the petrol in her bucket made her nose twitch and tickle. She was desperate to sneeze but didn't want to take off her gloves to blow her nose. It was a struggle to get them on.

'Good God, no. I leave that to the professionals. Although I did take part in a school production of the Pirates of Penzance once.'

He stopped sluicing, lifted his head and laughed loudly, unlike him.

'I was a complete disaster. Awful. The worst! After that, I stuck to backstage work. And that's how I ended up here.'

They sluiced in silence for a while, but Teresa guessed he would have more to say in a few minutes. She was right.

'Twenty shades of blusher, Teresa. Twenty! That's how precise the colour has to be to match skin tone. Makeup is an art as well as a science. When used on stage, it's as important as costumes. If not more so. The audience must believe they're looking at real people, not actors. Too pale and they look like ghosts. Too dark and they look like caricatures. Too red and they look like clowns.'

Teresa had heard Mr Foster's mantra about the art and science of makeup during his evening classes at Glasgow College of Art. She assisted him every Tuesday, handing over tubes of greasepaint and tubs of powder as needed. Every week after work, they walked together from Charing Cross to the top of Sauchiehall Street. The beautiful building, designed by Charles Rennie Mackintosh, felt more like a gallery than a school. Teresa loved standing on the ground floor with her eyes closed, basking in the soft light streaming through its ornate windows.

She was jolted back to the present when Mr Foster said, 'Teresa, don't swish that wig with such vehemence or you'll have petrol all over the pavement down below.'

Teresa lifted her right arm from the bucket and rubbed her nose gently, careful not to get any petrol fumes in her eyes or drips on the floor. Her father had been shocked when she told him how they cleaned the wigs.

'What if there's a fire, Teresa? How can it be safe to be up to your elbows in petrol? Can't they just use soap and water?'

'No, Dad. It's how we keep the wigs looking like real hair. And they don't smell of petrol by the time we're finished. Anyway, we're out in the fresh air of the rooftop garden. The view is lovely. And thankfully, Mr Foster doesn't smoke.' she'd said, half-joking to lighten the mood.

Her father wasn't convinced, but he let it go.

'Sorry, Mr Foster,' she said now. 'I was just thinking about blushers and how good it is that women are starting to buy real makeup again.'

Mr Foster, happily distracted from her overzealous sluicing and nose-rubbing, returned to his favourite topic.

'I agree, Teresa. But the women of Glasgow have a lot to learn about selecting and applying the right shade for their skin tone and hair colour. Poudre Leichner has been described as an opalescent bloom that lends a new radiance to the complexion.'

Teresa thought of her mother and the other women on Beechgrove Street. They weren't ready for opalescent bloom. Most of them relied on cold cream and hope.

In her two years at Bamber's, Teresa had absorbed a wealth of knowledge, not just about hair and wigs, but also makeup and style. Mr Foster often told his students there was no such thing as fashion, a claim that always sparked a flurry of questions. He would raise a hand to quiet the room and declare, 'You must dress according to your shape, not magazine trends or film stars. Look at the shape of your legs, then decide on your skirt length.'

The first time she'd heard it, Teresa glanced down at her own legs. Her skirt failed the test. But she never forgot the advice.

Mr Foster clapped his hands. 'Now, let's get these wigs out of the petrol and ready for their next production.'

He always sounded so dramatic. Teresa still thought he would have made a credible actor.

## 8. Teresa. Charing Cross. November 1946
### The Recruitment Office

Teresa was in the back shop having lunch when Mr Thompson came in, quietly closing the door behind him. He was frowning, something she rarely saw and his expression was unusually serious.

'Teresa, that Army Recruitment Officer from Sauchiehall Street is in the salon and wants you to do her hair.'

Teresa was relieved. Not serious after all. He was hovering, hesitant.

'Are you ok, Mr Thompson?' she asked, walking towards the sink with her dishes.

'First, it was Miss de la Fuente and now it's the Recruitment Officer. I don't know what I'm doing here anymore. There. I've said it.'

Before she could think of a response, he had disappeared into the salon, leaving Teresa with her mouth open and a half-washed cup in her hand.

Gita de la Fuente was an Italian opera singer with the Carl Rosa Company. She was beautiful and talented, yet gracious and unpretentious. It was true. She had come in a couple of times while the Company was in Glasgow to have her long black hair washed, trimmed and styled. Miss de la Fuente liked the way Teresa rolled and loosely pinned it, and yesterday she had asked for the same again. Teresa had been delighted but thought no more about it. Until now. What on earth was wrong with Mr Thompson? Hadn't she learned everything she knew about hairstyling from him? Maybe he and his wife were having problems again. Either way, Teresa didn't have time to worry about him. She was keen to get out front and impress Sergeant Nugent, the army recruitment officer.

The sergeant had been coming in every Friday for the past six weeks, since taking over the office in Sauchiehall Street. At first, she had helped Mr Thompson wash and pin-curl her bob, but now Teresa wanted to be available herself. Since their first conversation about army life, Teresa had wanted to know more. It sounded so exciting: meeting new people, training, maybe even working abroad. This could be her way out of Glasgow. A chance to see the world.

Teresa smoothed her overall, checked her hair and makeup in the back-shop mirror and marched out, hoping she would pass muster, as they said in the army. Mr Thompson was washing Margaret Doyle's hair and hearing about her 'man', who liked to have one pint too many on a Saturday night. His expression was politely blank, the look of a man who had heard it all before. He simply interjected a salutary 'Well, I never.' or 'Really?' at appropriate intervals. Teresa smiled as she passed the sink. He chose to ignore her.

'That is unspeakable, Mrs Doyle.' he said louder than was necessary.

Sergeant Nugent was already seated in her army uniform with her cap in her lap.

'Teresa, it's good to see you,' she said, then added in a whisper, 'I hope you don't mind me asking for you. Mr Thompson is very nice, but he still thinks we should all be in Marcel Waves or Victory Rolls. You're much more up to date with the modern shorter styles.'

She winked conspiratorially at Teresa. Poor Mr Thompson.

After washing Sergeant Nugent's hair and starting to comb it ready for styling, Teresa steered the conversation towards army life, pretty much all she wanted to talk about these days. She mentioned her plan to join the army at home one evening after the sergeant's third visit to the salon. They were at dinner and Teresa had been bubbling with excitement. Her father had been encouraging.

'It's a great idea, Teresa. The war's over, which means you shouldn't be in any danger. I think army life would suit you. And they pay well.'

The mention of pay was probably for Tina's benefit and she loved him for it. Then came her mother's response, which felt like a bucket of ice water in her face.

'You always have such grand notions, Teresa. Haven't you got a decent job here? A job manys a girl would give their eye teeth for. Can't you just settle for once?'

And that was the end of the discussion. Her mother dismissed the idea in one fell swoop and went on to regale them with the story of a man who had jumped onto her tram and tried to get off without paying.

But Teresa had not given up on her dream. As she carefully separated the strands of Sergeant Nugent's hair and twirled them into tight curls, she said, 'I wish I'd been old enough to join the ATS during the war.'

It wasn't the most subtle approach. The sergeant's silence did not deter her.

'I read there were over a hundred roles for women in the Auxiliary Territorial Service. That's incredible. Women like you made such a difference.'

The flattery worked.

'Yes, well, don't forget the women in the WAAF and the WRNS, not to mention the Land Army, the factory workers and all the volunteers. But yes, women made a colossal difference. And still do.'

Teresa jumped in. 'Thank you for seeing me in your office and giving me the forms. I filled them in like you told me. Did your secretary tell you? She said I should hear soon, but there's been no word. Do you decide who gets in, or is it a Major or someone like that? I want to do something while there's still time.'

Sergeant Nugent shifted in her seat. Teresa thought she looked more awkward than uncomfortable.

After a pause, she said, 'Don't be impatient, Teresa. You're still very young. Not even eighteen. You have your whole life ahead of you. There's no rush. These things take time. It's a lot to consider. And anyway, who would do my hair if you left?'

She laughed, but it wasn't her normal laugh. Again, Teresa thought she seemed awkward. Sergeant Nugent changed the subject and began talking about her upcoming holiday at home in Leeds. That was the end of the discussion about recruitment.

'I'm sorry about today, Mr Thompson,' Teresa said, shutting the front door and turning the sign to *Closed*. They had been busy all day, especially as Mrs Skinner was at home after a fall. Probably those stupid shoes. Teresa and Mr Thompson sat in neighbouring salon chairs, as if waiting for a haircut.

'I just feel old, Teresa. I have been a hairdresser for too many years. Maybe I should just hang up my scissors and leave, like Mrs Skinner.'

Teresa was shocked. 'Oh, please, Mr Thompson, don't do that. Where better to try new products than R. Sheldon Bamber? Permanent waves are becoming very popular and long curls are on the way back using large rollers.'

Mr Thompson's mood wasn't that easy to shift. 'You are a quick learner, Teresa, and a gifted hairdresser. I think it will be you teaching me soon. When you return from the army, of course.'

He lifted his head and looked at her with sad eyes. It was his first comment about her joining up. And now, she understood the problem.

'But I'll be back, Mr Thompson. And I'll work here whenever I'm on leave. You have taught me so much and I'm very happy here. My plan wouldn't have been possible without you. And anyway, they mightn't want me. I haven't been accepted yet.'

He jumped to his feet, animated and energised. 'Then get out there and make it happen. I never saw you run away from a challenge, Teresa Coulter. And they would be as mad as poor Lady Macbeth not to allow the best young hairdresser in Glasgow into their bloody army!'

Teresa was speechless. Mr Thompson had never paid her such a huge compliment. And she had never heard him swear either. His hand shot to his mouth and then he laughed, relieving the tension and making them both feel better.

'Didn't I hear your recruitment officer say she was going home for a holiday? Get into that office and find your forms. I was listening and got the distinct impression she wants you as a hairdresser more than a recruit. But that's her problem. Now, let's get out of here or it will be time to open up again.'

'When Mr Thompson finished double locking the outside door, Teresa threw her arms around him in a clumsy hug before racing off to catch her tram. He was probably as surprised as she was.

\* \* \*

On Monday lunchtime, Teresa visited the Army Recruitment Office on Sauchiehall Street. The officer covering Sergeant Nugent's holiday was a friendly girl of about twenty. She quickly found Teresa's forms and declared everything to be in order.

'All you need now are your parents' signatures. They both have to sign, seeing as you're only seventeen. Then it should be all systems go. You'll receive a letter about attending Training Camp in Guildford.'

Teresa clutched the forms in their official brown envelope as she sat on the two trams home to Bridgeton. Questions danced in her head: *How will I persuade Mum to sign these forms? What makes me think she'll agree when she's against me joining the army? Will Dad be able to sway her? Is this the end of another dream?* As she entered the Close and made her way up the three flights of stairs, Teresa remembered Mr Thompson's words about her never running away from a challenge. She would find a way.

## 9. Maureen. Perth. 22nd October 2020
### Stories Coming to Life

It is the day before I have to return to Sligo. We are talking about how Mum joined the ATS, a story she never tires of telling. It was a turning point in her life, a step into something bigger. Today, she is reliving the night her parents signed the army recruitment forms, allowing her to become a member of the Auxiliary Territorial Service for two years.

'When I took the forms out of the brown envelope and laid them on the kitchen table, my mother signed them without a word. No objections. No snide remarks. She even signed before my father. I couldn't believe it.'

I am sitting beside Mum's bed with my morning cuppa while she tackles breakfast. She has managed half an orange and a handful of dry Rice Krispies and is now making a valiant effort with a potato scone and butter. I thought a bit of chat might distract her from the eating process. It does. I am genuinely intrigued by how Tina could have been so opposed to Teresa joining the army, yet signed the forms without a fight.

Mum takes a sip of hot water, then says, 'That was my mother. She changed her mind faster than you could say Jack Robinson.'

'It was a major turnaround,' I say.

Mum pauses before answering. 'I never found out what changed her mind, you know. But I've always suspected my father had something to do with it. He probably highlighted the significant financial benefits. Tina was heading out to bingo that night and as soon as the door closed behind her, my father told me to run to the post office.

'Don't wait until the morning,' he said, thrusting a stamp at me. 'She could come home later and change her mind again. Once it's in the box, there's nothing she can do.'

And I did just that. I ran to the box outside the post office and thrust my brown envelope inside the slit as if it were on fire. Thankfully, the temporary recruitment officer didn't write on the envelope, which meant I could use it to post the forms. Otherwise, I would have had to wait until the next day to buy a new one. And who knows, the story might not have had a happy ending.'

Another question nags at me. 'What about Sergeant Nugent, Mum? Did you see her again after her holiday, or had you already left Bamber's by then?'

Mum smiles. 'She came into the salon once, just before I left for Guildford. I must admit I was a bit nervous. But she was very pleasant and wished me well. Said I'd make a great army hairdresser. Mr Thompson insisted she'd tried to stall the application to stop me from leaving. But like the letter in the post box, once the wheels were in motion, there was nothing she could do.'

I can see Mum is weary now. I suggest a snooze before getting up and she looks pleased. I lift the tray and turn on the radio.

'I'll just catch up on the latest news on Radio 4,' she says, and is asleep before I reach the door.

As I pack the dishwasher, my thoughts return to the story. Mum always speaks fondly of her time at Bamber's, yet she was willing to walk away from it all to join the army. She truly was an ambitious teenager.

While Mum sleeps, I sit at my 'suitcase and tray' desk, trying to capture the details and context of our chat. I have lots to do before the journey to Ireland, but my writing matters too. I stare out at the trees in the garden, searching for inspiration. Today, I'm in Guildford, stepping into Teresa's footsteps and the excitement of her new beginning. The words flow until I hear a voice calling from the bedroom. Reluctantly, I let go of the past and return to the present. Barney and Lorna are on their way with coffee and Bakewell tarts. I had better get a move on.

'Coming, Mum.'

## 10. Teresa/Terri. Bridgeton, Glasgow. 27th December 1946
### A Warning about Drink's Demons

The scullery was bitterly cold. Teresa's fingers were stiff and numb as she polished her brown shoes. She had bought a new pair but wanted to be prepared and organised. Her bag had been packed almost as soon as the recruitment forms were posted, but she kept it out of sight, keen to avoid a confrontation with her mother.

Only eight days remained before she left for Guildford. Trains were still packed with troops returning from Christmas leave and she hoped hers would not be delayed or cancelled. It was a long journey: first to London Euston, where her aunt Emma would meet her, then on to Guildford from Waterloo. Emma worked in service at one of London's big houses, and since it was her day off, she had organised permission for Teresa to stay overnight in her room.

The sound of a key in the lock interrupted her thoughts. Her father came through the door and hung his cap on the nail he always used.

He turned towards her and without any preamble, said, 'Let's go for a drink before you go.'

Teresa stopped, brush in one hand, shoe in the other. 'Erm, yes. Ok, Dad. Lovely.'

Alec Coulter didn't drink and she had never tasted alcohol. Why did he want to take her for a drink now? Did he have something serious to say to her?

Her father noticed her puzzled expression. 'Don't look so worried, Teresa. It's only a drink.'

His smile alleviated some of her anxiety. She was still confused, but whatever the reason, it would be good to spend some time together before training camp. She finished shining her shoes with a cloth and left the scullery, while her father filled the basin and washed in readiness for their outing.

\* \* \*

A group of festive revellers hung around the entrance to The Seven Ways bar. Teresa could feel her heart quicken at the thought of pushing past them, until her father led the way to another entrance further along the pavement. The upper panel of the dark wooden door was made of thick, textured glass with the words *The Snug* etched in the centre. Inside, a blast of heat and the chatter of couples at small round tables greeted them. Teresa felt her nerves settling as she was engulfed in the friendly atmosphere. The bar was cosy, not how she had imagined it at all. More like a sitting room than the kind of place men staggered home from on a Saturday night. The crackling fire in the large, green-tiled fireplace provided a perfect background for the low hum of voices. Walls lined with wooden beams, decorated for Christmas, added to the intimate, homely atmosphere.

'Here we are, Teresa,' her father said, pointing to a small booth along the side wall. 'One of the few bars around Bridgeton Cross with a proper Ladies' Lounge,' he added, clearly chuffed with himself.

Teresa pulled off her hat and gloves and slid onto the upholstered wooden bench. Her father had done his research, as usual. Anxiety dispelled, they sat opposite each other in their booth. Alec stretched his arms across the table and grasped her hands in his.

'I'm so pleased you're getting away from here, Teresa,' he said, eyes bright with enthusiasm. 'Adventure is good for the soul, and travel is the best way to learn about different cultures and people. I know it's only England, but that's just the first step for you.' He paused, as if unsure whether to continue. 'As long as you don't forget where home is and ...'

She tightened her grip on Alec's hands before he could finish. 'I love you, Dad. I'll miss you so much, no matter where I am in the world. And I will always, always come home to you.'

Teresa noticed the slight tremble in her father's lip, but he quickly composed himself and rose from the table, rubbing his palms together, a gesture she knew well. He often did it to change the subject when her mother was on a rant.

'Now, let's get those drinks. What'll you have?'

Teresa had no idea what to say. She thought of Grandma Coulter, who always drank a *small sherry* at Christmas.

'Sherry,' she said. 'I'll have a small sherry.'

Her father seemed happy with the answer and left her to make his way to the bar. As Teresa watched him walk away—back straight, head held high in his well-worn suit—she knew she would miss him more than anyone or anything. Alec Coulter had never had the chance to escape, to travel, or to chase adventure. Teresa had no intention of wasting her opportunity. She had read about ATS girls being recruited for overseas service and that was where she planned to be. Abroad. Away. Adventuring.

Teresa took a closer look around while waiting for her sherry. The decor was simple. An ornate mirror hung above the fireplace, flanked by a brass coal scuttle and a set of fireside tools. A few prints of Bridgeton Cross and the well-known 'Umbrella' were dotted around the walls. She had been mortified that first day at Sacred Heart school, fresh from the Gorbals, when she assumed the teacher was talking about an actual umbrella, not the much-loved dome-shaped meeting spot. A customer at Scobie's had told her it was designed to resemble a Victorian bandstand and as she looked at the picture above her, she had to agree.

Her dad reappeared at the table and placed a small, thin glass of sherry in front of her, though it looked darker than the sherry she remembered in Grandma Coulter's glass.

'Cheers! I'm raising a glass of shandy to celebrate my girl joining up.' He lifted the glass to his lips, but as Teresa was about to sip from her glass, Alec held up his hand. 'Stop!'

Teresa almost dropped her drink. Gone was her father's jovial smile of celebration.

'How do you know what's in that glass?'

Teresa was confused and bewildered. She could feel her face flushing. 'Because...because I asked for sherry?' she said, unsure if this was the right answer.

'Yes, but how do you know I put sherry and not something else into your glass? Did you see it poured? Did you watch me at the bar?'

Teresa slowly lowered her glass onto the table. She could feel the sting of imminent tears and tried to keep her hands steady, her breathing even. 'Well, no, I...'

'Exactly,' said her father.

He leaned across the table and although he was smiling again, his tone was solemn. 'Never assume the liquid in your glass is what you ordered, or that it's safe at all,' he said. 'I'm sorry if I frightened you, but you must never accept a drink unless you see it poured with your own eyes. That's why I brought you here. I know you'll be offered alcohol now that you're joining the army. What you drink and how often is entirely up to you. This isn't a sermon about the dangers of alcohol, darling girl. It's about the hidden danger of unscrupulous men. You need to be aware that something could be added to a drink without your knowledge. Something that could harm you, Teresa. I want you to know how to protect yourself.'

She was relieved, if more than a little surprised. But her father's words made sense and forewarned was always forearmed. It was just like him to teach her a lesson by showing, not telling. But there were still practical issues to iron out.

'So, what will I do with it? The drink I didn't see poured?'

'Empty it into a plant. Or into your shoe if you have to. Just get rid of it.'

Alec was laughing, but when he sat forward and looked at her, he looked serious.

'Do whatever you have to, Teresa. Just don't drink anything if you haven't seen it poured. Now, see what you think of that sherry? It's a bit of an old lady's tipple, but you might enjoy it. I think I'll stick to shandy.'

'Well, since I didn't see the drink being poured, I think I'll throw it into that plant over there and join you in a glass of shandy. But only if I can come to the bar with you this time.'

They laughed so loudly that the couple at a neighbouring table tutted, which only fuelled their laughter.

## 11. Terri. Perth. 26th October 2020
### Reflection: Good Times

As I sit here with my morning latte in front of me, I can still see that glass of sherry on the table and my father's face across from me. He was such a wise man. Ahead of his time.

I didn't drink much in the army and certainly nothing I hadn't seen poured from the bottle. I never had to water the nearby plants with unwanted alcohol, but occasionally, I had to come up with creative ways to avoid drinking it. I have often regaled my children and grandchildren with that story, in the hope they will heed my father's message. Girls are better informed and more aware of the dangers than we were back then. Maureen says you can even be injected in the leg with a drug that has the same effect. My husband, Joe, used to say, 'There are no new sins.' But the longer I live, the more I realise there are always new ways to commit them.

Like the changing of the guard, Maureen left on Friday and Colette arrived yesterday. I can hear her clattering around the kitchen. She is washing down the cupboards. Maureen is a global cleaner who likes to take frequent breaks and chat, but Colette is more like me—well, the old me. She notices the details, preferring to get on rather than have coffee. I have to remind her when it's time to sit and relax.

Telling Maureen about my ATS training was fun and I was amazed how many names I remembered. As a rule, I don't believe in overthinking. But our discussion got me wondering what became of all those girls in Guildford. I kept in touch with some of them by letter for a few years but we eventually lost contact. I suppose life became too busy. Although they're either very old or dead now, I still picture their faces and hear their voices as clearly as the day we arrived at Stoughton Barracks. They say when you get old, you can remember what happened fifty years ago, but not what you had for breakfast. Fortunately, I can also remember what I had for breakfast and even dinner last night. I don't always feel like eating it, but I remember what was put on the table. I may have cancer in my bladder and a hole in my leg where the tumour was removed, but I still know how many beans make five.

'Colette, your coffee's getting cold.'

## 12. Teresa/Terri. Guildford. 5th January 1947
## ATS Training Camp

'Shove up.'

The voice startled Teresa, scattering her thoughts about that final farewell at Glasgow Central. Her father had told her how proud he was, as he often did. She had boarded the train and waved through the open window. His body stood erect, but his face was blank, one hand raised and the other dangling by his side. As the steam closed around him, Alec Coulter gave one lonely wave and Teresa's heart ached.

ATS training camp in Guildford was only four weeks long, but it marked the beginning of a whole new life. They both knew things would never be the same.

'You look like you're… *Going My Way*.' The tall girl sang the last three words with a dramatic lilt, mimicking Bing Crosby from *The Bells of Saint Mary's*. She towered over Teresa, grinning broadly. Not quite Crosby, but full of personality. Then came a big, warm and unfiltered laugh, soon to become an unmistakable trait. She heaved her kit bag onto the rack and extended a hand.

'Mae Brown, Army Territorial Service rookie, at your service,' she said, with an enthusiastic salute, earning a few sniggers from the other girls in the carriage. 'Glasgow born and bred,' she added and plonked herself into the adjacent seat.

Teresa felt her cheeks flush. She didn't like being singled out so enthusiastically. But neither did she like snooty girls who looked down their noses. Composing herself, she straightened up in the seat and turned to the smiling girl beside her.

'Teresa Coulter. ATS. Army hairdresser-to-be. Also Glasgow born and bred.'

There were more sniggers from the snooty girls. And that was it. She and Mae Brown, both from Glasgow, were training camp buddies.

Trains were still delayed or rerouted due to troop movements, though not as often now, and a few hours later, they slowed and a platform came into view. Mae was on her feet, head craning out of the window before the train even stopped.

'Guildford, here we come,' she announced to the whole carriage, grabbing her kit bag.

'Come on, Coulter. We don't want to be last off the train and be in the NCO's bad books on our first day.'

Teresa, accustomed to doing what she was told, quickly lifted her kit bag and followed Mae. She was right. It wouldn't do to draw attention to herself on their very first day in the army. The recruits spilled out of the train in a less-than-orderly fashion and were shepherded onto two waiting buses. The air was sharper than in Glasgow and Teresa wondered if the clothes she had packed would see her through army barracks in winter.

As soon as the buses stopped, a voice outside shouted, 'Line up. Line up.'

The command was repeated until both vehicles had discharged their cargo. They shuffled into three wavering rows, suitcases at their feet: twenty-four rookies, eager to find out if they had what it took to be in the Auxiliary Territorial Service. The voice revealed its owner. A petite, austere-looking woman of maybe thirty, maybe forty, or even just twenty-five, stood before them. Teresa tried to take a closer look from her place next to Mae in the middle row, but all she could see was a meticulous uniform and a cap worn so low it almost covered the woman's eyes. She was about to turn and ask Mae to guess her age when another command blasted from the open mouth of their future NCO.

'By the leeeeeeeft!'

It was deep and posh, and louder than any sound Teresa had ever heard from a woman. The way she stretched out *leeeeeeft* was hilarious. Teresa burst out laughing, assuming it was some sort of welcoming, ice-breaking joke. That is, until she realised no one else was laughing and the formidable woman in uniform was staring straight at her.

'Was there some confusion about my order, Private...?'

She glanced down at her clipboard, but the rows in front of her were not in any order, so Teresa interjected, 'Coulter.' She could hear the tremor in her voice and saw a small cloud of breath hit the cold air.

'Do you know your left from your right, Coulter?' This time, the voice was calm and quiet, but just as deafening in its contrast.

'Yes... erm, Sergeant,' Teresa said, praying she had used the correct title and that the scary NCO wasn't a captain or a major. The letter had said they would report to a Non-Commissioned Officer on arrival, but it hadn't explained how to address her. Thankfully, there was no further discussion.

The NCO turned and marched away, clipboard gripped tightly under one arm. 'By the leeeeeeeeft!'

The lines of recruits lifted their suitcases and followed the striding sergeant to the quarters that would be their home for the next month. They were assigned billets and bunks, dismissed, and instructed to unpack before dinner. Teresa sat on the edge of her bunk and thanked God she had not been sent home for insubordination. She couldn't believe she had laughed like that. It wasn't as if she had ever been the class comedian or a bag of laughs at the salon. Mae Brown sat on the bed beside her, just as she had on the train.

'Now, that's what I call an entrance, Coulter.'

She mimicked the NCO's voice as she said her name, laughing as if it were the funniest thing she had ever heard. Teresa did not find it amusing. Mae didn't know her. Didn't know she hated drawing attention to herself. Didn't know how much she wanted to do well here. Didn't know how important it was to her. However, her new friend obviously noticed the expression on Teresa's face and stopped laughing. She embraced her in a spontaneous hug and when Mae spoke, her voice had lost its bantering brashness.

'It'll be fine, Teresa. I've no doubt the NCOs heard a lot worse in her day. She'll have forgotten all about it already. And you've got a whole month to show her what we Glasgow gals are made of.'

Teresa smiled, despite herself. Mae was right. And now that she thought about it, the sniggering girls from the train had patted her on the back on the way into the hut, as if she had done something admirable. It was an ill wind…

\* \* \*

Teresa snapped awake. Physically and emotionally exhausted from the journey, she had drifted off almost immediately. It was still dark and the hut was cold but not freezing. The soft snoring from neighbouring bunks was shattered by a shrill bugle call. It must be six o'clock. Day 1 was under way.

After breakfast, the recruits were measured for ATS uniforms, having been instructed to bring thick stockings and brown leather shoes from home. Amanda Peterson, or Mandy, as she liked to be called, was unimpressed with the colour. She had been one of the sniggering girls from the train, but turned out to be nicer than Teresa had imagined. She had joined the ATS because she was fed up with the life of a debutante —whatever that was—and wanted to do something useful.

'Khaki? I defy any woman to look attractive in bloody khaki.' she moaned, stretching on her bunk and attempting, unsuccessfully, to bounce on the hard mattress.

'I mean to say, the WRNS wear navy and the girls in the WAAF have a nice shade of slate blue.'

'So why did you join the ATS?' asked a girl who'd introduced herself as Peggy Grimshaw.

If she was being sarcastic, she hid it well. Mandy didn't appear offended.

'Well, it wasn't for the uniform, Darling.'

She tucked her hands behind her head and stared up at the roof, as if talking to herself more than to Peggy.

'I wanted a bit of excitement before I have to go off and get married. My brothers are always talking about the great girls they met in the ATS during the war. They could strip down any vehicle and put it back together as competently as any man. And drive tanks, motorcycles, ambulances. That's what I want to do.'

That shut them all up. Mandy sat up in bed and started reading from the list of uniform items they had been handed.

'Full panelled khaki skirt, belted tunic, khaki shirt with separate collar and tie, service jacket and...'

'What colour is the service jacket, Peterson?' someone shouted.

Everyone laughed and Teresa started to relax. She didn't just want to do well in Guildford. She wanted to have some fun. And this bunch looked like they did, too.

Mandy stood on top of her bunk and read aloud with theatrical flair: 'Sturdy brown leather shoes, three pairs of thick khaki Lisle stockings to match the stylish shoes and two suspender belts... which may or may not be... yes, you've guessed it... khaki.'

General hilarity broke out as some of the girls joined in.

'Ooooh.' they squealed, pulling up their skirts to show a flash of leg.

'Two pairs of knickers and two pairs of wool pants,' Mandy continued.

'…which may or may not be khaki,' chimed her fellow actors in unison, as the hut full of strangers roared with laughter.

'She's coming.' shouted Peggy, who had stationed herself at the window.

Mandy leapt down and they all stood more or less at attention as the sombre NCO from the previous day walked through the door. She stepped into the middle of the room and spoke in a less formal tone this time.

'Welcome to Guilford. You have arrived at No. 7 ATS Training Centre, Stoughton Barracks. I am Staff Sergeant Mathews and I will be overseeing your general training here. Hopefully, you will all make it through.' She paused for effect. 'But this is by no means guaranteed. You should pay attention, work hard and obey every command from your superior officers… which, in your case, is everyone.'

Teresa thought she saw a flicker of a smile, a faint softening at the corners of the NCO's mouth. Perhaps Staff Sergeant Mathews wasn't quite as serious as she had first appeared. Teresa couldn't wait to get started. She wanted to learn everything.

'I will now formally introduce you to the Navy, Army and Air Force Institute, known as the NAAFI. It's where you had dinner last night and breakfast this morning. All meals are served in the NAAFI. It is also the venue for camp social activities… not that you will have much time for the latter.'

Another flicker, more noticeable this time. 'This evening, you'll be welcomed by Major Harcourt, who likes to personally introduce herself to all new recruits.'

Her tone snapped back to military formality. 'The real work starts tomorrow morning at 0600 hours sharp. Fall in and follow me.'

A few girls smirked, mimicking their NCO as she marched out of the hut. Teresa was not one of them. She was sticking firmly to the rules from now on.

## 13. Teresa. Guildford. January 1947
### Training Routine

**Day 1**

Teresa made her bed as neatly as possible before inspection. Official bed-making instruction would follow later this morning, but she wanted to be a step ahead.

'Teresa, I have a problem.' Mae Brown stood at the end of Teresa's bunk looking uncharacteristically solemn.

'What's wrong, Mae? Has something happened? Are you ill?'

'Not yet. But I will be if I don't find a pair of proper brown leather shoes before we get our uniforms tomorrow.'

She held up a pair of well-worn brown suede shoes, more suitable for dancing than army drills.

'I couldn't afford a pair of leather shoes and stupidly thought these would do the trick. Well... I mean... at least they're brown. Honest to God, it would sicken your dickie and make yer tie squeak.'

They looked at each other, then laughed in unison.

'Never fear, Coulter's here,' Teresa said, opening her locker and removing her brand-new brown leather shoes.

'I have a spare pair. You can have these.'

Mae stared at her, momentarily stunned. Teresa saw the glisten in her friend's eyes and didn't give her a chance to speak. She understood exactly what it felt like to be short of money.

'Right, these will be too small for you, so let's run a bath of cold water and you can walk up and down until the shoes adjust to your feet. Leather will stretch, you know. I learned that from Mr Foster.'

Mae recovered her composure. 'Do what? Who?'

'Well, he... oh, never mind. Just take my word for it. Now, let's get going before someone wants a bath or the NCO appears at the door.'

Mae thanked Teresa every 20 seconds for at least three minutes before they headed to the bathroom for *Operation Shoe Stretch*.

'In the name of the wee man, Teresa, I have to get them on my big banana feet before I can walk up and down in the flamin' bath.'

The two girls pushed, pulled, giggled and eventually squished Mae's feet into Teresa's shoes.

'Ok… now, lean on my shoulder and put one leg over the bath into the water. Great! And the other… Now walk.' Teresa struggled under the awkward weight of her friend.

'We must look a right sight,' said Mae through grunts, giggles and gritted teeth. 'Me waddling up and down in a bath of cold water like an enormous duck. And you, trotting alongside like a human walking stick.'

After twenty minutes of splashing and laughter, Mae was able to let go of Teresa's shoulder. The pair declared *Operation Shoe Stretch* a success. Mae was thrilled. She wore Teresa's new leather shoes with pride and great aplomb, as if they had been made for her.

\* \* \*

The next morning, Teresa was making final adjustments to her bunk when Mae, who was standing at the window, shouted, "Teresa, come quick. Look at this. You have to have a gander at the goings-on out here.'

The window was fogged with heavy condensation. Mae had cleared a circle in the centre and was amused by whatever she was watching.

'You ought to see these rookies, Teresa. Just off the buses. They look like frightened rabbits.'

Mae's distinctive laugh echoed throughout the hut and attracted everyone's attention. A group of girls huddled around her, craning for a view.

'Mae, we've only been here for two days,' Teresa said, not moving from her bunk.

'Aren't we still rookies ourselves? After all, we're still in mufti. Without our ATS uniform, we look the same as them.'

But Mae was having none of it. 'Weren't we here before them? So they're rookies compared to us. That's the way it works.'

Mandy Peterson joined in. 'Besides, we never looked like frightened rabbits. Isn't that right, Coulter?' And they all laughed, even Peggy Grimshaw, who already had a reputation for being the most serious girl in their hut.

\* \* \*

## Day 8

After a week, they were all in uniform and beginning to look like army personnel. Teresa had demonstrated how to wear the ATS caps without disturbing their hair. Mr Thompson had gifted her a good pair of scissors when she left Bamber's, and she had already been cutting and styling within the group. In return, Mandy had given her the end of a Yardley Victory-Red lipstick, released to celebrate VE Day. Teresa was looking forward to her role as an ATS hairdresser and was curious about where she'd be stationed. That information would have to wait until after the Passing Out Parade, presumably in case they didn't make it that far.

By 0900 hours, inspection was over and the recruits had assembled on the parade ground for drills. After a sprinkling of overnight snow, the area had been cleared, ready for marching practice. It was known as square-bashing due to the shape of the parade ground and was one of Teresa's favourite activities. The sense of order and energy invigorated her, everyone moving in complete unison. The rigid routine made her feel included, accepted, at home somehow. She belonged to a group of disciplined women with whom she had something in common. Teresa was now used to the NCO's barked orders—clear, uncomplicated, succinct. She did not have to think on the parade ground, just listen carefully and follow instructions. It felt good and she was good at it, which felt even better. There had been no further mention of her first-day reaction to army commands. In fact, Staff Sergeant Mathews had singled her out for praise after the previous morning's drill. Teresa had smiled discreetly and blushed, but her heart was dancing and fluttering with delight.

*　*　*

## Day 16

As the days slipped by, temperatures gradually fell and light snow flurries came and went, though never enough to disrupt the camp routine. Pre-breakfast fitness classes and cross-country runs continued as normal. Teresa's hiking experience in Scotland had kept her fitter than some of the others. Exercising made her feel alive in a way that surprised her. Their open mouths resembled chimneys puffing smoke from a Glasgow tenement as they breathed hard in the icy air.

Sometimes, it was difficult to make out the face of the girl standing beside her. Mae struggled but was determined to keep up and became fitter every day. Mandy and some of her cronies were new to the concept of strenuous exercise, especially in intense cold weather. They complained every single morning:

'I swear I'll have hypothermia before this month is up.'

'I'm going to have a heart attack and then what'll they tell my parents?'

'I think my toes have gangrene.'

'What's exercise got to do with fixing engines or driving a motorcycle?'

No one bothered to respond any more, apart from the odd, 'Oh, shut up!' hurled by a fellow rookie, but it was usually said in good-humoured ribbing. However, when it came to stripping a Land Rover engine or driving on rough terrain, Mandy was in her element and had no problem wearing thin overalls in draughty garages. There had been talk of outdoor rifle practice, but weather conditions meant training had to be postponed until their first posting. Teresa was relieved as she had no desire to handle a weapon. Hairdressing scissors were lethal enough for her.

There was plenty to learn in the classroom. Mae, confident and quick, was a great help to Teresa, for whom it was all new. Mae understood record-keeping, communications and army administration. Fieldcraft was new to everyone and included navigation, map reading, and survival skills, which they practised on each other in the hut after class. There were also lessons in military etiquette and structure, and the recruits were surprised to learn that army discipline did not distinguish between men and women.

They were learning about the history of the ATS today. Everyone was on their best behaviour, even Mandy, who muttered as they filed in:

'I hope this won't be a complete bore. I'd much rather be fixing a greasy engine or flying round on a 633cc Norton.'

Mae, sitting behind her, leaned in and whispered to the back of the head, 'Careful, Peterson. That sounds like dissension in the ranks to me. You'll land in the Brig.'

Mandy turned, ready to retort, but the NCO shouted, '...'ttention!' and they all jumped to their feet.

Major Crawford introduced herself and launched into the story of the ATS. Teresa and her father had visited the library before she left Glasgow, but the major's confident delivery breathed new life into the facts. From Dame Helen Gwynne-Vaughan's wartime service to official recognition of the ATS in 1938, the message was clear: women had earned their place.

'We gained full military status in 1941,' the major said. 'That's when the Government…that is to say, men…realised they couldn't do it without us.'

The recruits burst into spontaneous applause. Teresa thought of the poster in the Sauchiehall Street window that had first caught her eye: *They can't get on without us*, it had said. *Join me in the New ATS*. And she had done just that.

Back in their billet, the girls chatted while filing nails, writing letters, or just flopping on bunks.

'Rather fun that I'll be doing the same job as Princess Elizabeth,' said Mandy. 'Imagine… the future Queen passing out as a qualified ATS driver.'

'She obviously didn't mind the khaki,' came a voice from the next bunk.

Mandy hurled a pillow in reply.

'At least the uniforms have improved, thanks to Jean Knox,' said Peggy.

'Yes. And I'm glad we've got a hard peak on the cap,' added Teresa. 'Much easier to manage with waves or curly hair.'

Mandy still wasn't happy. 'Shame about the stockings. They make my legs look like tree trunks.'

Mae had the final word. 'At least we've got stockings. I used to go through stacks of pencils, drawing lines up the backs of mine.'

They were still laughing when Peggy shouted, 'Lights out. She's on her way.'

## 14. Teresa. Guildford. January 1947
## The Big Snow

**Night of January 23rd**

It had been a busy day and bedtime chatter in the hut quickly gave way to gentle snoring. But sleep was short-lived, brutally interrupted by the fierce blizzard that slammed into Stoughton Barracks just after midnight.

The wind vented its fury, rattling the corrugated iron walls and hurling snow at the hut like a weapon. For a moment, Teresa was five again, lying beside her dad, listening to the flapping canvas of their tent during a storm in Skelmorlie. But there was no father-figure to comfort her tonight. She pulled the rough grey blankets tighter around her shoulders. The din outside was rivalled by the shrieks inside, as girls dived into each other's beds or disappeared under the covers.

'Is it just me or are we about to be catapulted into space? Mae called from the next bunk. 'Sounds like the boiler's about to blow at the steamie.'

Teresa smiled.

'The boiler at the *what?*' Mandy shouted back. 'Assuming it's a car, Brown, that's the head gasket you're thinking of.'

Mae and Teresa caught each other's eye and giggled. Teresa wondered if she should enlighten Mandy: it was a public washhouse, a place to meet and gossip as much as to scrub clothes, nicknamed for the thick steam and chatter that filled the air. As she opened her mouth, Peggy cleared her throat, raising her voice just loud enough to be heard.

'Well, I'm not thinking about steamies or cars. I'm imagining how it must have felt to be bombed in army camps like this during the war.'

The ATS recruits fell silent. Outside, the wind roared like an angry bear, snow thudded onto the roof, and the door and windows whined in sympathy.

Fuelled by their reaction, Peggy added, 'And, by the way, Peterson, a steamie is the only way Scottish women can get their washing done.'

This time, Mae and Teresa were helpless with laughter. No point contradicting Peggy. Their giggling soon spread through the hut, breaking the tension.

\* \* \*

In the days that followed the storm, weather dominated life in the camp. After the initial blizzard, snow continued to pour in a thick white waterfall. No swirling, no drifting, just steady and relentless. They woke every morning to an eerie silence, as if nature had thrown a huge blanket over the world. Even in the freezing temperatures, bright morning light burst through the flimsy curtains and streaked across the floor, giving a false impression of summer warmth.

'It's like Glasgow in a downpour,' Mae announced one morning from under the covers, the sleeve of her greatcoat wrapped round her neck. 'Chucking it down… only white and cold enough to freeze the you-know-whats off a brass monkey.'

Only Teresa was familiar with the expression, but the recruits didn't have to be Glaswegians to understand Mae. Puffs of white breath steamed from every bunk as they laughed. Even the stove in the middle of the floor puffed in agreement.

Walls of snow made movement outside almost impossible. The parade ground vanished and it was treacherous just walking to the NAAFI or nearby classrooms. No sooner were the paths cleared than fresh snow covered them. Word spread that snow and freezing temperatures were causing chaos across the UK, with transport halted, businesses closed, and widespread food shortages. Experienced ATS drivers were sent to deliver supplies near local HQs.

The ablutions hut was particularly challenging. Teresa had often washed in cold water, but with pipes frozen, the metal basins had to be filled from another source. Most mornings, they had to break the ice first, resulting in gasps, screams and swearing from many of the girls. Their Passing Out Parade would now be held in the NAAFI, if they could keep the paths clear long enough. It felt like an anti-climax. They had worked hard and wanted their moment of glory.

'It's just not fair,' said Mae.

'I know,' agreed Peggy, flapping her arms to keep warm.

'Why did the snowstorms have to arrive now, just in time to ruin our parade?'

'Oh, I couldn't care less about the stupid parade,' snapped Mandy. 'I just want to be out there with the other ATS drivers doing something exciting.'

They fell into a moody silence. Mae sat on the bed beside Teresa.

'Are you disappointed, Coulter? You love all that marching on the Parade Ground.'

She was right. Teresa was disappointed, but it couldn't be helped. They were lucky compared to so many people across the country. One girl in D Hut received a letter saying temperatures had dropped to minus ten or lower. Teresa prayed her family in Glasgow were safe.

The door flew open and in walked Staff Sergeant Mathews, followed by Major Cosgrove and a flurry of snow. They kicked the snow from their boots and shook their caps, tucking them under one arm. The dusting of fresh snow on their shoulders made them look like they'd been in a snowball fight—unlikely, but the image made Teresa grin.

'Did you hear that, Coulter?' Mae beamed at her. 'We all passed.'

The major was smiling and Staff Sergeant Mathews looked around the room, clearly delighted.

'Well done, everyone. It has not been an easy road for you recruits, but it's onwards and upwards from now on. I'm proud to call you all members of the Auxiliary Territorial Service.'

They forgot about army etiquette and began cheering and hugging. No one noticed the major and NCO slipping out. The snow continued to batter their hut, but as Teresa danced in a circle with Mae Brown, she couldn't recall ever feeling this happy.

## 15. Teresa. Edinburgh. March 1947
### First Posting as an Army Hairdresser

Teresa did not think it was possible to feel colder than in Stoughton Barracks, but Edinburgh proved her wrong. It may have been early March, but this winter still held the country in its grip. The icy wind took her breath away and made her eyes sting and water. Even with her woolly pants, thick stockings, skirt, jacket and greatcoat, the Easterly wind found its way into every gap with a biting sharpness beyond anything she had known during her leave in Glasgow.

After tearful farewells, Teresa had been grateful that Mae, also from Glasgow, had travelled with her all the way home. Their journey from Guildford had been arduous and hazardous in equal measures: three days of freezing stations, broken connections, long delays, and packed train carriages with no heating. And now it was time to embark on her first posting as a fully-fledged member of the ATS. She pulled her cap down over her forehead and crunched through the snow until she reached the Administration Block in the centre of Broomfield camp. At eight o'clock, the building was already bustling. Personnel of various ranks and uniforms moved in and out of offices, the clatter of typewriters escaping each time a door swung open. After kicking off loose snow from her shoes at the front door, Teresa followed the signs to the NCO's office on the second floor. Inside, a young clerk looked up from his typewriter.

'Name?' he asked, already reaching for a form. Teresa provided her name and rank, and he nodded towards a wooden bench. 'Wait there.' A few minutes later, he rapped twice on the NCO's door and summoned her.

The NCO was a heavy-set woman in her mid-forties with a stern face, but a smile that suggested a warm heart. She stood up from behind her desk and grabbed Teresa's hand in a firm handshake.

'Sergeant Maud Platt. Very pleased to have you with us, Coulter. We haven't had a barber here in so long, the men have started tying their hair up into buns.'

The sudden, snorting laugh that followed took Teresa by surprise. She stood in front of the desk, feeling awkward. Was she allowed to laugh at an NCO's joke? Sergeant Platt didn't seem to notice her quandary.

'Let's get you over to the Laundry Hut. The sooner you start, the sooner all that unruly hair will be dealt with.'

Another snort, then she pulled on her cap and great coat and led a very puzzled Teresa back down the stairs into the snow. What was she going to be doing in the laundry? Distracted by the thought, Teresa almost lost her footing on the slippery path.

'Careful, Coulter. You will be issued with overshoes to keep your shoes dry and your feet on the ground. Damn this snow. Never known a winter like it. Arrived in January and looks like it'll be spring before it disappears. Maybe even summer at the rate it's going.'

Yet another snort. 'Edinburgh is renowned for being chilly, but I'm from Kent myself and we've had it bad there this year too. I think the whole blasted country has been under snow. Our ATS girls have been delivering mail and food parcels as well as rescuing people stranded in their homes. But don't worry, Coulter, we need a barber too much to allow you to speed off on a motorcycle.'

That word again—barber. Teresa wondered if the NCO was known as a joker and if the habitual snorting would eventually drive her mad.

They stopped in front of a standard green Nissen hut, much like the ones in Guildford, only larger. All army camps looked more or less the same and during training, they had been told why: the curved design was practical, easy to assemble and built to withstand harsh weather. Mandy Peterson had once remarked on the lack of imagination. Staff Sergeant Mathews had not been amused.

'If it's imagination you're after, Peterson, book into the Ritz,' she'd snapped.

At the time, Teresa had thought that, without those curved roofs, their billets in Stoughton would have collapsed under the sheer weight of snow.

One half of this hut was empty, and the other half buzzed with noise, chatter and a haze of hot steam. That is, until Sergeant Platt and the newbie entered. Four women stood to attention.

'At ease, ladies. This is Coulter. She will be making good use of the other half of your hut as our resident hairdresser.'

Teresa let out a sigh of relief. Hairdresser—she was the hairdresser, not the barber after all. Sergeant Platt's announcement was met with whoops of delight.

'Welcome to the Royal Corps of Signals, Coulter,' Sergeant Platt said and Teresa finally relaxed, allowing herself to smile sincerely.

It felt like a place where she could belong and she couldn't wait to get started. But as she looked around the empty half of the hut, Teresa wondered how she was supposed to turn it into a hairdressing salon.

As if reading her mind, Sergeant Platt said, 'I have drafted a strapping young soldier with a van to accompany you on *Mission Hairdo*. He will help you purchase whatever you need for your shop and transport it back here to base.'

Another joke and another snort, but Teresa liked this woman, her boss for the foreseeable future. She thought they would get along just fine, snort or no snort.

\* \* \*

The next morning, as promised, a young soldier appeared in front of Teresa's billet, blowing the horn of his large army truck. She peered in at him.

'Are you looking for me?'

'Well, that all depends on who you are, Ducks?' he said with a broad smile and thick Cockney accent. 'If you are the delectable Private Teresa Coulter, here to give us all a chicker, then I'm your man. Hop in.'

Without knowing what a 'chicker' was, Teresa jumped into the passenger seat.

Her face must have betrayed her, because her cockney driver ruffled his curly hair and said, 'A haircut, Coulter. A bleedin' haircut. And you'll probably want to give us a short back and sides, army style, even though it's brass monkeys out there.'

The truck roared into action within seconds. Her driver introduced himself as 'Digger Dunne. Private... and confidential. Royal Corps of Signals, at your service.'

He was about the same age as Teresa and said he had it on good authority that they were the two youngest recruits in the camp. She had to admit, he was easy company and she suspected their mission to set up the new salon would not be uneventful. Teresa couldn't help wondering if everyone in Broomfield was a comedian.

'Where to, m'lady?' Digger asked as he drove into Edinburgh, ignoring warning signs of ice and snow on the roads.

*Think Teresa, think. Where did Bamber's source their supplies for the salon?*

'Ogee's,' she blurted, startling her young chauffeur. 'Ogee's has a branch in Edinburgh,' she said with tentative confidence. 'I would like to go to Ogee's, Mr Dunne.'

Her statement sent the driver into a fit of giggles.

'Mr Dunne!' he spluttered. 'Mr Dunne is me old pot and pan. You can't call me Mr Dunne. We're the same bleedin' age, remember. Digger. Call me Digger.' Then, when he had collected himself, he added, 'Never fear, Digger's here… Miss Coulter.' She ignored his wink. 'We'll stop for a cuppa and I'll give my pal Reggie, a Rip Van Winkle on the eau de cologne. If the shop's in Edinburgh, he'll know it.'

Once again, Teresa had no idea what he was talking about, but for some reason, she trusted Digger Dunne. If Ogee's was in Edinburgh, he would find it. She wouldn't worry about plan B until plan A failed.

A coffee, a sandwich and a phone call later, they screeched to a halt outside Osborne, Garrett & Co Ltd, better known as Ogee's. She climbed down from the truck. It was time for some more of that bravado if she was to buy the necessary equipment and supplies with some credibility. She was only seventeen, but Teresa Coulter closed her eyes and imagined she was back in Bamber's. What do you see? she asked herself. Just think of all the things you need to work effectively and efficiently. That's all you have to do. Then buy it.

She swallowed hard and said, 'Let's go, Digger. There's a lot to buy.'

It was like entering Aladdin's Cave for hairdressers. A fizz of anticipation swept through Teresa, banishing any remaining nerves or uncertainty.

'I want to start with the chair,' she said, as she pictured the luxurious seating in Bamber's. 'I want a comfortable, leather upholstered chair for my customers. Oh… and a large ornate mirror.'

Teresa wasn't convinced beauty was a feature of army life, but if she had a blank chequebook, now was the time to use it.

'I like the sound of that chair,' said Digger. 'Sign me up for the short back and sides. At least I'll get a good rest while I'm there.'

By mid-afternoon, the truck was packed with everything from sinks and dryers to scissors, razors, and combs. After Ogee's, they stopped at a few other shops sourced by Digger in advance. Teresa selected the items and Digger did the lifting and carrying. At one stage, he was holding so many towels that the pile covered his eyes and he nearly stepped off the pavement. Teresa grabbed him just in time. He started laughing as soon as he regained his balance.

'Any excuse to grab hold of me chalk farm, Teresa Coulter.'

Although struggling with Digger's Cockney slang, she got the gist.

'That's quite enough of that, Private Dunne... Digger. And it's Private Coulter to you.' But she was smiling and so was he.

They found another cafe, ordered more coffee and swapped stories of how they came to be in the army.

'Any chance of a date next Saturday night, Coulter? There's a do on in the NAAFI,' Digger asked, after unloading the truck into her half of the laundry hut.

'No, Digger. No chance at all. No point in leading you up the garden path. I have plans and they don't include dating.'

He looked forlorn until she added, 'But I'll give you a dance if I see you on Saturday night. I'm pretty good at swing.'

'A good barber *and* a good dancer? You're on.' And he jumped back into the truck, whistling a Glenn Miller tune.

Teresa was surprised at her boldness. But hadn't she just spent a small fortune on her very own hairdressing salon, courtesy of the army? Life was good and getting better every day. She was going to make this new venture a success, if hard work and determination had anything to do with it.

Three days later, Teresa stood in the middle of what now looked like a hairdressing shop rather than a redundant half-hut. It was small, but as a one-woman enterprise, it only had to accommodate one member of staff. Mr Thompson would have been horrified. On the other hand, there was no one to tell Teresa what to do. She would have *carte blanche* —whatever that meant in the army. She had no illusions that it involved experimenting with daring new styles, but as she surveyed her new salon, Teresa Coulter could not have been more pleased.

## 16. Terri. Perth. 9*th* November 2020
### *Remembering Edinburgh*

Maureen lived in Edinburgh for five or six years before moving to Ireland. I went back and forth from Glasgow when the flower shop wasn't too busy. I loved being back in the city, although Broomfield Camp was in Davidsons Mains, nowhere near Maureen's home in Duddingston. It felt good to be close to the place where I had fun at an important time in my life.

I had forgotten how bad that winter of 1947 was and how long it lasted. We got used to seeing piles of frozen snow everywhere. I think the thaw began in the middle of March, and then, of course, there was the slush and the floods. Once the weather settled, I used to meander around the city centre when I had a day off from hairdressing and ATS duties, soaking up the atmosphere. To this day, I watch the Edinburgh Tattoo on television every year and I always become emotional when the military bands march in that wonderful castle quadrangle. I suppose it's the idea of the thing.

Yesterday's Remembrance Sunday felt especially meaningful. My son Paul played the bagpipes right here in The Falconry, St. Boswell's Place. I sat outside my house at No. 25, while neighbours stood at their doors or in the courtyard as a mark of respect for all those lost in wars. So many now. Fraser from No. 23 wore his green beret and medals from the Marines and he marched alongside Kyle, a lovely young cadet wearing his smart Black Watch uniform. They walked perfectly in step. It reminded me of how much I loved square bashing. Fraser laid a wreath at our memorial, the carved falcon standing on its wooden pedestal in the centre of the courtyard. After the minute's silence at eleven o'clock, Paul lifted his bagpipes and played *The Last Post*. Somehow, it felt like he was playing for me, too—not that I deserve to be counted among all those brave men and women. But it was precious. And I think Paul also felt it.

Last night, I dreamt I was back in Broomfield. I was with Frankie, Isa, Sandra and Jimmy Gambol. Names I hadn't thought of in years. It was the day when the Princess Royal, Commander-in-Chief of the Royal

Corps of Signals, visited the camp. About a month after I arrived, rumours were flying that she was planning a tour of Scotland. The weather was so harsh we all assumed the visit would be cancelled. Then one morning, there was an unmistakable buzz in the camp. Officers rushed from hut to hut issuing orders, while soldiers scurried about with buckets of cleaning supplies. The Princess was determined to boost morale, ice and snow or not. A real trooper.

'Just go about your business as normal,' our NCO told us, then added,. 'Of course, I expect you all to be on your best behaviour.'

Imagine my shock when the door of the salon opened and in walked Her Royal Highness, Princess Mary, followed by a swarm of senior brass. I was doing Private Jackson's hair at the time. I only remember her name because I still have the newspaper clipping upstairs. We both jumped to attention, only to be told, 'Carry on, Privates.' So we did.

I remember praying the Princess hadn't noticed the shake in my hands. She asked what it was like to be the only hairdresser or barber in the camp. I told her it was quite a busy job, with 100 men and 60 women to attend to. But I can't remember how she replied. I was too nervous.

I often thought it was just as well it wasn't a man in the seat on the day of the Royal visit. The recruits cried like babies when they had to have their precious hair cut into an army-style short back and sides. Those were the good old days, when I was only responsible for myself and no one was responsible for me.

## 17. Teresa/Terri. Edinburgh. July 1948
### The Rifle Training Captain

Teresa's time in Broomfield was a balance of hard work and lots of fun. Once the hairdressing hut was up and running, her salon was popular with men and women of all ranks in the camp. She made new friends and travelled back to Glasgow during her leave to see the family and catch up with the staff in Bamber's. Life was good.

During the summer of 1948, the rifle training captain came to Broomfield and Teresa joined his class as training had not been possible in Guildford. The sun was warm on her shoulders as she lay flat on the ground, steadying her breath, cheek pressed to the wooden stock of the Lee-Enfield. She had become accustomed to the rifle's kick and now her shots were hitting the target board with satisfying consistency. She was aware of him. Captain Warr stood behind her, silent but watchful. His presence sharpened her focus, not with nerves exactly, but something close.

'You are very good at this, Coulter,' he said. 'I would go as far as to say you are the star student in this class. Have you ever fired a gun before?'

Teresa waited for the heat in her cheeks to fade before sitting up from her crouched position and turning to face the instructor. Captain Terence Warr stood with his cap tucked under his arm, clipboard and pen in his hand. He was tall and broad-shouldered, with dark, slicked-back hair and a neatly trimmed moustache that added to the warmth of his smile. To Teresa, he looked every inch the handsome army officer. As soon as she glanced at him, her face flushed again and her heart thudded. She tried to steady herself. Yes, every inch the kind of handsome officer to be avoided at all costs.

'No, Sir. There's not much call for it in hairdressing.'

Captain Warr laughed at her response and she instantly panicked.

'Even hairdressers in *No Mean City*?' the soldier lying adjacent to her quipped.

Captain Warr looked puzzled, but without hesitating, said, 'If I want your opinion, I will ask for it, Harrison. You are a lousy shot, so I would keep practising if I were you. In case Coulter aims in your direction. She won't miss, which is more than can be said for you.'

His reprimand was met with laughter and a few claps from the others, except Harrison, who now looked very sheepish. Teresa was used to his sarky comments about Glasgow. Still, Captain Warr had stood up for her in front of everyone. She sneaked another glimpse. Gosh, he was handsome.

'Class dismissed,' Captain Warr announced in a clipped military tone.

They all stood, dismantled their rifles and went off to change into uniform before dinner. Teresa got to her feet as elegantly as she could. The captain was wearing cologne with a distinctive scent. It was sweet and discreet, unlike some of the men in camp, who believed the way to a woman's heart was through their nose.

'I am sorry about that, Coulter. Unfortunately, not all men in the British Army are gentlemen. Do you mind my asking what he meant by '*No Mean City*'? His tone remained formal, yet gentle. 'I can hear from your accent that you are Scottish, but not any more than that. I'm afraid I am from Cambridge and very ignorant of accents north of the border.'

They were now facing each other.

'I... I don't mind, sir. I pay no attention to the remarks anymore,' she said. She held his gaze, trying to banish the image of her tomato-red face. *Don't look at his brown eyes,* she told herself. But she was doing exactly that—staring straight into them.

'I'm from Glasgow, Sir. There's a well-known book called *No Mean City.*' Her voice was steadier now. 'Lots of people think we're all razor-wielding gang members like in the book. They believe that's how we all live.'

She decided to omit that she had been born in the Gorbals, like the gangs in *No Mean City* . If Captain Terence Warr noticed her blushing cheeks or trembling voice, he gave no indication.

'Well, it is quite obvious you have no association with any such gangs, Coulter. But thank you for your explanation. I don't want you to get cold out here. Or worse, to miss dinner. I suppose I had better let you go.'

They both laughed easily this time. Teresa would happily have missed dinner for a few more minutes in his company. As she walked away,

Captain Warr added, 'I look forward to seeing you tomorrow for our final session, Private Teresa Coulter, from *No Mean City*.'

Teresa kept walking. She did not acknowledge the remark or turn her head, but she was aware of a surprising lightness in her step. Her skin tingled, as if touched by invisible finger tips. She embraced the unexpected warmth of attraction, savouring the moment and flurry of unexpected anticipation.

\* \* \*

From the first day of rifle training in the classroom, when he had introduced himself and smiled at them all, Teresa had felt drawn to the captain. She had been careful not to share this with any of the girls in the hut. They were all swooning over the handsome officer. Quips flew around the hut like flies.

'He's so dishy…'

'He can shoot me any time…'

'I'm going to ask for a few private lessons…'

They had two days in class before being allowed onto the firing range. During that time, Teresa watched Captain Warr intently while he spoke and more discreetly when he was silent. Over the past week, she had tried to make sense of her growing attraction and after today's exchange, she was more confused than ever. Several good-looking men had asked her for a date since joining up, including officers, and she had never been tempted. So what made this one different? Her head screamed: *You're here to learn, Teresa. You're here to make the most of every day, not swoon over some army captain who pays you a little attention.* Unfortunately, her heart was struggling to listen.

\* \* \*

After a restless night and a mental tug of war, Teresa spent more time on her appearance than normal the following morning, careful not to make it obvious. Captain Warr did not approach her during the training session and the feeling of disappointment surprised her. She gave herself a firm talking-to and tried to focus on hitting the targets. As she gathered her equipment after the final session, Teresa heard his voice behind her. She froze, the spark of excitement rising before she could stop it.

'So that's that,' he said. 'Another rifle training course done and dusted. It will be my last for a while. I'm being posted to Nairobi in the New Year. A fresh start. Rather exciting. A complete change of scenery and a little adventure.'

He was smiling, but she sensed a slight hesitation in his voice. She let him continue without commenting.

'I am due some leave before I go.' He paused. 'A little bird told me you were also heading off on leave.'

Teresa looked at him, any hope of resolve melting. 'Yes,' was all she could stammer. Then she straightened her shoulders and lifted her chin, because that's how you looked confident—at least, that's what Mr Foster told his Fashion Students.

'I'd like to be heading off abroad like you. I've joined up for a further eighteen months now that the ATS is transitioning to the WRAC and I'm hoping for a posting in Egypt. So, yes, I'm now entitled to a month's leave. I'll be heading back to *No Mean City*.'

She felt her confidence growing. Captain Warr laughed, a warm, genuine laugh that caught her slightly off guard. It was he who was looking into her eyes now, maybe even into her heart.

'*Touché*, Coulter. Do you think you could be persuaded to join me for dinner before you travel home? I've some commitments in Edinburgh, then I'll be travelling to Cambridge for a few days to prepare for Nairobi. You can tell me more about this *No Mean City* of yours and your plans, and I can tell you about my new posting. What do you think?'

And as if it were perfectly normal for a Private to accept a dinner invitation from a visiting captain, Teresa Coulter replied without a moment's hesitation,

'That would be lovely.'

## 18. Maureen. Sligo. 10th November 2020
### The Work Ethic

I have been at home in Sligo for more than two weeks. After seven days of strict isolation, I escaped the confines of the bedroom and ventured into the sanctuary of our upstairs lounge, with the stove glowing and inspiring views of Glencar valley. This was my second arrival in Ireland since Covid. A homecoming should mean sinking into the embrace of loved ones. It was achingly hard not to reach for that comfort, making do instead with a face mask and a handshake from my husband of forty years. Martin is still recovering from surgery and it was important to be vigilant after travelling. On the positive side, Isolation gave me time to adjust to being away from Mum, sift through notes and analyse my thoughts. Even so, I was thrilled and relieved when the two weeks ended. Free at last to hug Martin.

For some reason, we are all familiar with the name, Terence Warr. We know he was the man mum ditched for Joe Reilly, our dad and hero, so that's fine with us. But it was fascinating to hear how the two of them met, and I am curious to hear how their relationship developed. However, today I am pondering the importance of work in my mother's life.

Even now, when Mum talks about Bamber's or her role as a hairdresser in the army, her face lights up. The years between then and now dissolve. The fatigue that dominates her life is given temporary respite, and her voice, often thin and frail, becomes vibrant and assured, as if gaining strength from the memories. Watching this transformation lifts my spirits as well as Mum's. Sometimes, I repeat questions to which I already know the answer, just to maintain the momentum, prolong the connection, hold onto the moment. And yet, I did not always admire or understand my mother's passion for work.

There were five of us. I was born in 1956 and my youngest brother arrived eight and a half years later. As was traditional, Mum did not work outside the home during those years. I have happy early memories of my dad going to work and Mum being home: making dinners, cleaning the house, walking with us to the park. We moved from our two-bedroomed flat in the West End of Glasgow, albeit a beautiful top-floor tenement overlooking the Botanic Gardens, to a three-bedroomed semi-detached house in the suburban South Side. I was eight and Mum was pregnant with Joe, the youngest. It was exciting to have an upstairs and our very own garden. However, on reflection, it was far from fun for Mum. The new house was in need of repair, with sparse furniture, no proper heating and only bare, splintered floorboards underfoot. She also had four children, an imminent fifth and a husband hanging on to his mental health by his fingernails. Dad suffered from severe anxiety, with recurrent panic attacks and other signs of overwhelming stress. We were oblivious to these realities at the time, but he talked about them later in his life.

'When I was driving to work, the traffic lights had to be green.'

'But what if they weren't?' My brother, Paul, asked.

'A red light meant I had to stop. I would sit there with my heart thundering along like a train. I could hear it and feel it in my chest. My hands would get hot and sweaty, and sometimes I struggled to breathe.'

'Wow, Dad! That must have been terrifying.'

And it was. He was prescribed diazepam, a sedative, to make him feel calm. He never took even one of them, but he carried that little bottle in his jacket pocket for the rest of his life, never leaving home without it, transferring it from suit to suit.

The catalyst for Dad's anxiety was his job. At the time, he was the Flower Manager for a large company with over 50 fruit and flower retail outlets in Scotland. Unfortunately, Joe Reilly did not share their ethos but was trapped by his responsibility as husband and father. It was Mum who offered him an escape route. He often talked about how she was the driving force behind his decision to quit the job he hated and open his own flower shop. She had a calm, unshakeable strength and total belief in her husband, thus encouraging him to believe in himself. I know how this conversation went because he told me several times, always with gratitude and love.

'Leave, Joe. Just leave. We'll manage. You're a talented florist and you're wasted in that place. You're a florist, not a *yes man* or a staff manager. You learned about business from them, but now it's time to go it alone. I know you can run your own successful business.'

And he did. 'Joseph Reilly, Artistry in Flowers' opened its doors in 1964, the same year we moved house and welcomed my brother, Joe. It must have been an enormous burden of care for my mother to take on, testing her resilience to its limit. The following year, she started working in the shop on Saturdays, as income was insufficient to pay staff weekend rates. Terri Reilly never returned to hairdressing, though she continued to cut hair and provide styling advice within the family, whether we wanted it or not. She was a shrewd businesswoman as well as a talented hair stylist and quickly became a vital cog in the flower business wheel. The energy and determination that had propelled Teresa Coulter in her formative years never dwindled.

As the eldest in the family, I took on parenting duties as Mum became indispensable in the increasingly busy shop. On Saturdays, I looked after the children, made dinner and tidied the house. I don't remember ever feeling aggrieved. However, occasionally, Mum decided to take Saturday afternoon off, promising mother-daughter time in town. Something would turn up: a customer walked into the shop, the delivery driver needed help, the bride's mother wanted advice, or the phone was ringing off the hook. I bitterly resented our time together being usurped by the machine that was the shop. On reflection, and with the wisdom of hindsight and empathy, I marvel at how Mum coped. Survived. My dad was a wonderful man, but far from domesticated. He could make French toast, but had no idea how to use the washing machine or change a nappy. Never do I recall my mother complaining, suggesting he was capable of learning, or arguing about who did what in the house. As children, we simply accepted this was life in our house, a happy house. But when Teresa Coulter—Terri Reilly—went to work, it was all-encompassing. Whatever the task, she gave it everything. Or, as she liked to say, she 'gave it the gun,' one of her favourite expressions.

During a final chat before leaving Perth, I asked Mum, 'What was it about working that you loved so much? After all, you only retired at seventy-eight because you had no choice. Did you not want to do other things or fancy taking it easy for a few years?'

She thought for a few seconds and said, 'It's important to have a work ethic. Work gives you status and that's important too.'

She did not explain why a work ethic or status matter, just that they do. But in her stories, I am able to peel back and understand the layers of emotional truth she cannot express in words.

## 19. Teresa/Terri. Liverpool. 7th January 1949
## Last Man Standing

Teresa had imagined this day for so long. Now that it had arrived, she could hardly take it in. She was about to embark on the adventure of a lifetime, bound for the Middle East: Egypt, Port Said, Ismailia. Dots on a map in the library would become real places where she, Teresa Coulter, would be living a real life. The idea made her heart somersault.

There were times she had doubted it would ever happen. Having filled in the application forms for an overseas post, reassured they needed army personnel with her experience, Sergeant Platt had delayed signing off on the transfer.

'Good soldiers are hard to find, Coulter. And good army hairdressers are even harder to find. Stay another while and then I'll let you go. Anyway, why on earth would you want to venture out there to be boiled alive, bitten to death and catch some wretched foreign disease?'

She had laughed, snorted and dismissed Teresa. However, after her third application was rejected, Sergeant Platt's mother became ill and she had to take leave. Teresa seized the opportunity, reapplied and was selected for overseas duty in Egypt. It struck Teresa as oddly reminiscent of the situation with the recruitment officer in Bamber's, who had tried to block her joining the ATS. Both officers had tried to hold her back, but their mothers had other ideas. She also believed her Guardian Angel had a hand in it.

Teresa was booked on board the next available sailing to Port Said. She had welcomed the New Year with her family in Beechgrove Street, and her father accompanied her to Central Station early that morning. He had waved her off to Guildford, Edinburgh and now Egypt. She didn't want him to come to Liverpool. It was one thing to wave goodbye at Central Station, but quite another to have him standing on the dock, watching her sail away on a massive troop ship. This was a journey she had to make, a chance she had to take, an adventure she had dreamt about. Even so, parting was no easier.

As Teresa pushed through the crowds of service personnel strewn across Liverpool Docks, the butterflies in her tummy were steadily growing into giant seagulls. Hundreds of people were milling around or clustered in circles, with hardly an inch of space to be found anywhere. Families huddled together: mothers, wives, children and sweethearts, all clutching their loved ones. Loud sobs occasionally broke through the general hubbub, while groups in uniform were in fine fettle, laughing and looking forward to whatever lay ahead.

The thrill of anticipation twisted into a knot of apprehension as Teresa caught sight of the enormous ship in the harbour. She hadn't given much thought to the actual journey. The closest she had come to sailing was watching the ferries come and go from Wemyss Bay when she was five years old. Her heart was clattering like boots on a metal staircase and her tongue felt like cardboard. Just when she contemplated running in the opposite direction, Teresa thought she heard a familiar voice. There it was again, calling her name.

'Teresa, this way. Over here.'

She desperately tried to follow the sound.

'Coulter. Teresa Coulter!'

Like the parting of the Red Sea, the crowds cleared and Teresa spotted Mandy Peterson, waving frantically, an enormous smile lighting up her face.

'Mandy Peterson...' was all Teresa could say before her friend from training camp in Guildford hurtled towards her, arms outstretched for a robust embrace.

'Oh, Coulter, it's so good to see you again. I never thought I would meet anyone I knew here. I can't tell you how happy and relieved I feel. I was seriously thinking about changing my mind, you know. They asked me to travel at the last minute and I said 'Yes' before I had time to think things through. Experienced drivers are badly needed and believe it or not, that's me.'

Teresa decided not to admit she, too, had thought of fleeing. Instead, she smiled.

'I'm delighted you're here too, Mandy. It truly is lovely to see a friendly face. You look fabulous, by the way. I love the new hairdo. Do you have family here to see you off?'

Mandy patted her hair. 'Thanks, Coulter. Just had enough time to visit my hairdresser. One never knows when another will turn up... unless, of course, *you* happen to be stationed nearby.'

Her laughter tapered off, her expression serious now. 'Mother and father are in France for the winter and they're not best pleased with me anyway. They think it's bad enough to have a daughter who drives a truck, without her running off to the Middle East to mix with foreigners.'

Their conversation was interrupted by an announcement over the loudspeaker:

*'Attention, all military personnel: please proceed to the dockside and prepare to board. Stand with your regiment and await further instructions.'*

This was repeated several times and greeted with howling from the family groups and whoops of delight from the *fine fettle brigade*. Teresa grabbed Mandy's arm. Her fear had vanished and though her heart still pounded, it was with exhilaration rather than anxiety.

'This is it, Peterson. Let's go and find ourselves some adventure.'

'And a handsome man.' Her friend winked, slinging her kitbag over one shoulder. 'Come on, Coulter. We don't want to miss the boat. Whoever boards first must wait for the other near the railings at… '

Mandy's voice was lost in the tide of uniforms surging towards the waiting vessel.

A passing soldier overheard her. 'Don't worry, girls. The Empress of Australia won't leave without two gorgeous passengers like yourselves.'

And Teresa laughed, even as the seagulls swooped back into her tummy.

Each regiment had its own area marked out on the dock where a staff officer held a sign aloft to guide the appropriate units. Before long, the dock became a huge parade ground with hundreds of military personnel standing to attention. Family and friends applauded as the various regiments and divisions were called to board. Teresa found the designated zone for the Royal Corps of Signals, taking her place among the others, kitbag at her feet, a riot of thoughts in her head. This had been her dream since she was old enough to think for herself. As she waited for her name to be called, Teresa wondered if she would ever return to her life in Glasgow. The memory of that final hug with her father at the station brought a fresh clutch of anxiety and self-doubt. She straightened her shoulders, lifted her chin and forced thoughts of home firmly to the back of her mind.

Each regiment was called by rank and surname. As soon as they were summoned, the troops marched in a steady single stream up the ship's ramp, turning left or right at the top depending on gender. The Royal Army Service Corps (RASC) was announced over the loudspeaker. Teresa watched Mandy Peterson amble towards the *Empress* and grasp the handrail, hips swaying as if the ramp were a catwalk. Typical Peterson, thought Teresa, grinning as her friend made the most of her moment, relishing the whistling and banter from the men already aboard ship. Then came the turn of the Royal Corps of Signals. Teresa held her breath and lifted her head high, trying to look as confident as possible, at least on the outside. Every muscle was taut and she had to concentrate on breathing. She repeated the rhyme from her childhood. It helped when she was nervous.

*One two three four, Jenny at the cottage door.*
*Five six seven eight, Jenny at the cottage gate.*
Breathe, Teresa, breathe.
*One two three four, Jenny at the cottage door.*
*Five six seven eight, Jenny at the cottage gate.*
'Bailey... Black... Bradley... Cameron... Cuthbertson... Davidson... Dudley...'

*Wait a minute. Where's Coulter? Why has my name not been called? Did I miss it? Am I not on the list? Oh God, what's going on?*

No one else seemed to share her panic, stepping forward without question when they heard their name.

*What should I do? Will I just stand here?*

Soon, all personnel from the Royal Corps of Signals had boarded. Except Private Teresa Coulter. By now, her brain had frozen. A vast canvas of military uniforms had shrunk to a few small patches of impatient stragglers. The Women's Royal Naval Service (the Wrens) were now marching aboard, two by two, swinging their arms with grace and confidence. Easy enough when someone carried your kitbag, tennis racket included.

Teresa had been distracted watching the Wrens, but now they were all aboard. A few latecomers were still making their way up the ramp. And then, horror of horrors, there was no one left. She was standing completely alone. Every thudding beat of her heart echoed in her ears and her chest. This was not excitement, anxiety, or even fear. This was ice-cold terror. She could feel the blood draining from her face, pooling in her fingers and feet.

*What if I faint in front of an entire ship full of troops? No. I can't let that happen. I just can't. Pull yourself together, Teresa.*

She tried to ignore the raucous din coming from the troops draped along the side of the ship. They were all staring down at her as she stood to attention—the only soldier left on the Liverpool dock. An assortment of good-natured jibes rang out from the otherwise dignified *Empress*:

'Come on, love, we won't bite.'
'Get yourself up that ramp or we'll all be late.'
'Waiting for a personal invite, Darlin'?'
'Was it something I said?'
*One two three four, Jenny at the cottage door.*
*Five six seven eight, Jenny at the cottage gate.*
Breathe, Teresa, breathe.
*One two three four, Jenny at the cottage door.*
*Five six seven eight, Jenny at the cottage gate.*

Raised arms beckoned her on board, hands clapped in unison as if the restless troops were attending a football match. The strains of the popular song *Slow Boat to China* grew steadily louder. Teresa wondered if it was possible to die of embarrassment. She kept her arms at her side and her eyes facing front, but her mind had defrosted and was racing again.

*My mother must have changed her mind and done something to ruin my plans. The army decided they didn't need a hairdresser after all. No adventure. It's over. Liverpool Dock is the most exotic place I'm going to see.*

The Tannoy crackled to life. An announcement. Just for her.
*'Royal Corps of Signals. Coulter.'*

Roars and cheers from the ship were joined by whoops and applause from the crowds behind. It took every ounce of self-control and determination Teresa possessed to lift her kitbag, march across the empty dock, and climb the ramp to board the magnificent *Empress of Australia*.

*Nothing that happens in Egypt could be more nerve-racking than this,* she thought. *No one will ever believe me.*

Mandy Peterson barged through the throngs on the deck and enveloped Teresa in a bear hug. 'Now, that's what I call an entrance, Coulter.'

## 20. Maureen. Belfast City Airport. 17*th* November 2020
### *Navigating Covid*

Belfast City Airport is busier than it was in August. Travellers are still predominantly business types, with earbuds in place, facemasks askew, muttering into phones or hunched over laptops. But there are more strays like me now, each with their own reason for risking a flight. Starbucks is open and I hurry over in case it closes without warning, as it did on my last trip to Scotland. I find a socially distanced seat—plenty to choose from—and wonder if yellow hazard signs or the large X on every other chair will become the norm post-Covid, if there is a post-Covid.'

I unload my rucksack and drop into an unmarked seat. Visiting sick relatives is one of the few non-business reasons to fly. Sad eyes glance over masks, staring into space, yet we are islands. Covid has forced us into solitude as well as isolation. We no longer engage with others. We avoid them. The simple act of talking to strangers, of sharing our stories, has been stolen by the virus. We hide behind masks and the invisible barriers erected by fear.

As someone who regularly travels between Scotland and Ireland, I've seen how differently each government handles Covid-19. For example, I have to quarantine for two weeks when I return to Ireland, but not when arriving in Scotland. Northern Ireland is part of the UK, but because of the Common Travel Area, a long-standing agreement with the Republic of Ireland, people can still move fairly freely across the border. During this trip home, we took advantage of that agreement, spending three nights in Northern Ireland at the Lough Erne Resort, just an hour from Sligo. The family organised the treat to mark our 40th wedding anniversary, which we spent apart in September.

Masks were mandatory inside the hotel, but we bundled into coats and walked the winding paths around the golf course, fringed by majestic woodland and imposing forest. Distance is not always about geography, and as we strolled and chatted, the emotional space between us gently closed. I don't remember what we talked about, only that death, cancer and Covid had no voice. It was the perfect antidote to the separate lives we have been living.

I am leaving Ireland, now in a six-week lockdown until 1st December. The hope is that this will lower Covid cases enough to ease restrictions over Christmas and allow families to come together. In contrast, Scotland's new five-tier Strategic Framework comes into effect today. A tier system is based on registered Covid cases in each of the 32 local authorities. Perth & Kinross, where Mum lives, is in Tier 3. I am travelling in the right direction—away from lockdown and towards freedom.

We have become numb to statistics that would have horrified us six months ago. I watched Sky News over my porridge this morning. Nearly 11,000 Covid deaths were reported globally in the past 24 hours. That's 11,000 people with lives, with families, with jobs, with talents. I did not cry or gasp. I finished eating, packed the dishwasher and went upstairs to prepare for my flight. However, sitting in this quiet departure area with my latte and a sandwich, I think about the other statistics I chose not to absorb. As of today: 53.7 million confirmed cases, 1.3 million deaths. I stare at the giant poster of Northern Ireland on the wall in front of me, focusing on every detail to stop my burning eyes from leaking. Not numb after all.

I take a breath and begin to wonder what freedom might look like for Mum and me. Broadly speaking, Tier 3 means restaurants and cafés will open during the day, but alcohol is not permitted either indoors or outside. I presume this is because alcohol and social distancing are unlikely bedfellows. I glance at my empty latte cup and picture Mum and I sitting opposite each other, shopping bags at our feet and frothy coffees in our hands. I cannot fix the world, but I can make it a little better for my mum. The thought makes me smile and I feel a whoosh of longing to be with her.

The Shielding Programme in Scotland, designed to protect vulnerable people like Mum, was paused at the beginning of August. Public transport is still for essential journeys only, which means our first real taste of freedom will depend on access to a car. I will be back here in just three weeks, then two weeks of quarantine before Christmas. I want to make the most of this time with Mum.

I am so busy dreaming and scheming, I miss the Edinburgh flight announcement. It's only when I look up and realise my fellow travellers have disappeared that I am jolted back to the present.

## 21. Maureen. Perth. November 2020
### *Back in the Saddle and the Driving Seat*

**17th November 2020**

Barney, my brother and long-suffering chauffeur, drops me at the house and goes off to collect their second car: a black Ford Fiesta, usually driven by one of his daughters.

'Of course. No problem,' he said, as soon as I suggested borrowing it for a few weeks.

Mum is waiting at the front door, impeccably dressed, makeup applied, hair curled. She looks so vibrant, I have to remind myself she is terminally ill. Her trademark floor-length fur waistcoat hangs over navy trousers, a yellow blouse with a large bow tied under her chin and a bright orange cardigan. I drop my rucksack and bend to hug her tiny frame, thinner than when I left, but still strong enough to wrap both arms around me in a blanket of love. I feel that reassuring release of tension I now associate with arriving home with Mum or with Martin, just as predictable as the tightening in my chest when I have to leave either one of them.

'It's so good to see you, Mum. You look great.'

'It's so good to have you back,' she says.

I hear her unsteady voice and see her struggle to suppress tears.

We walk into the kitchen, by which time she is smiling again.

'The kettle's boiled. We have time for a coffee before we leave.'

Looking at the three mugs laid out on the counter, Mum realises there are only two of us.

'Where's Barney? I thought he was going to take us to my appointment with the optician.' she says and when I explain we will now have our own transport, I am rewarded with another smile—well, more of a beam.

True to his word, Barney arrives with the car and Gus, their Lucas Terrier. He accepts a cup of tea and a chocolate ginger, while Gus settles for his usual tea biscuit. Fed and watered, the two of them head off on foot. I am apprehensive about driving. Late-onset Stargardt's

Disease has affected my central vision. I am unable to read easily, but can still drive short distances—for now. Long may it continue.

*　*　*

## 19th November 2020

It is my sister's birthday and the day starts with a video call to Colette. Mum shows off her glasses with zany new multicoloured frames purchased yesterday. They complement her animated personality and bright smile. Colette admires them, we chat for a while and sing *Happy Birthday* to her—badly.

I am fine driving around Perth, but baulk at tackling *The Road and the Miles to Dundee,* as the song says. Thankfully, Barney rearranges his work schedule and chauffeurs us to Ninewells Hospital for Mum's post-surgery review. The consultant is pleased with the wound's progress and provides her with a thick support stocking, which Mum accepts as if she has been handed a soiled nappy.

I do a quick relationship repair and say something like, 'It's great to be at this stage. Thank you so much. I'll help Mum with the stocking. They can be tricky.'

I push the hospital chair out of the narrow cubicle and into the corridor. After three or four visits, I have mastered the art of pulling, but not pushing. Somehow, I manage to steer her into the lift and downstairs to wait for Barney.

'I'd like to buy the nurses a few sweeties, Maureen. Here's the shop. Just get a nice selection and we can take them back upstairs.'

I am now puffing from the effort of manoeuvring the chair, patches of hot sweat spreading under my arms. *You must be bloody joking,* I think, but clamp my jaw shut in case the thought sneaks out. Mum wants to show her appreciation to the hardworking staff, and that has to be a good thing, even if it feels like a workout too far for her daughter.

Barney's daughter, Grace, is studying Medicine in Dundee and returns with us to Perth. We stop for lunch in Glendoick Garden Centre, and it feels both normal and exhilarating. We have not eaten in a restaurant since June. As I watch Mum and Grace chatting and laughing, my heart feels full. Once again, I commit to cherishing every moment we have together. We will take our little car and escape the house whenever Mum feels well enough. *Bring it on.*

## 22. Maureen. Perth. 23rd November 2020
### Let the Shopping Begin

We leave the car in our usual spot in the multi-storey car park in Perth city centre. Wrapped in winter coats, we link arms and cross the road, heads down against the raw November wind.

'Thank goodness for my rainmate,' Mum says. 'My hair would be an absolute site otherwise.'

Mum looks frail, yet elegant, as we walk in tandem, clinging to each other for balance. She chose the long, army-style navy coat this morning (she loves anything with brass buttons) and insisted on wearing it with a matching cap, gloves, and coordinated scarf. The look is topped off with what appears to be a clear plastic bag worn over her hat and tied under her chin. One of Terri Reilly's trusty 'rainmates' stashed in every coat pocket and handbag ready for emergencies. Like today. She also has a black one for evenings. And being Mum, she wears this small black bin bag on her head with such panache, it might as well be the latest must-have fashion accessory.

'Ain't that the truth, Mum,' I say now.

My mum extols the virtues of her rainmate every time she wears it and I have endorsed its effectiveness numerous times over many years. Today, this predictable banter instills a feeling of giddy happiness. I cannot believe we are out and about together. I want to remember every single ordinary detail.

We walk through Boots the chemist onto Main Street. It is the route we always take, but we are like children let loose in a sweetie shop as we stand there, surveying the store-lined street and shopping centre across the road. Too much choice.

'Where to first?' I ask. 'Do you fancy Primark, or will we start with a coffee?'

'*Echie or ochie*,' says Mum, then adds, 'Six and half a dozen really', which means the same thing. She is pretending to be non-committal, but I see her eying up Primark. It has always been one of her regular shopping haunts. Decision made. We join a short queue outside the shop and are greeted at the door by a pleasant lady with a clipboard.

'Have you been in since we opened up again, Ladies?' she asks.

A resounding, 'No,' in unison.

She moves swiftly into instruction mode. 'Okay. Use the hand gel provided inside. Maintain social distancing. Use the baskets from this pile.'

She points to a heap of net baskets. 'Then leave the used one in the pile beside the checkouts.' She takes a breath. 'It's a one-way system, so you can't come out this way. You have to exit through the shopping centre at the other end.'

Finally, we answer a list of tick-box questions about whether we have been in contact with Covid or have any symptoms ourselves. Another resounding 'No.' Then and only then are we granted access.

I am not a lover of shopping like my mum and sister, preferring books to clothes. However, having been deprived of retail therapy for many months, I feel the buzz of that first purchase. I buy underwear, socks, a nightdress and a blouse. Mum decides on a green coat, two cardigans, pyjamas and a variety of miscellaneous items which cannot be lived without. I contemplate mentioning the wardrobes already filled to bursting and drawers crammed with similar bits that could not be lived without. But she looks happy and that's good enough for me.

Instead, I say, 'Fill your boots, Mum.'

And she does. I suggest a coffee break, but she has a different idea. It feels like every other shopping expedition: me craving coffee and Mum keen to visit a few more shops before sitting. I usually complain loudly before giving in. Today, I want to relish every minute, saving the details in my mind's freezer. I will document our outing in my journal tonight, because memories can fade even as we make them. The freezer in our head is not nearly as reliable as the one in the kitchen.

'Just the pound shop. And maybe a quick look in my favourite card shop. Then I'll be done,' Mum says. 'I have to make hay while the sun shines. 'When I sit down, I may not be able to get up again.'

I love Mum's laugh—distinctive and hearty, without being loud or annoying. Funny how you start to notice the way a person looks and talks, how they smile and laugh, or frown and cry, when time is finite. I am ambushed by a swell of emotion as I look at my Mum, lost inside her heavy coat, a large handbag over her arm. Laughing and living.

Of course, the truth is that life has not returned to normal. People are wary of each other. Shops are open for business, but warning notices are displayed on windows and doors:

*Maintain a safe distance. Follow the yellow markings on the floor. Do not touch items unless for purchase.*

Mum has Macular Degeneration, and her poor vision means proximity to everything and everyone is essential. I spend my time in the smaller shops issuing additional warnings. She does her best, but it is not easy for her or anyone in a similar situation. I also think of those who have a hearing impairment or who lip-read. A face mask is more than a barrier against Covid. It is a communication barrier.

By the time we sit down for badly needed respite and sustenance, my arms throb from carrying bags in one hand and holding onto Mum with the other. We settle at a table in the shopping centre café where we can watch the world go by. Mum looks pale and weary but maintains her Terri Reilly 'shop 'til you drop' attitude. Since my return to Perth, we have had no time to revisit the past. As we tuck into our toasted cheese, I test the waters. I have become shamelessly opportunistic.

'Do you remember when I went to India in 1979 and you told me that black tea was better than a cold drink for hydration. You said it was a lesson you'd learned in Egypt. I was twenty-three and didn't have a clue when I set off. I still can't believe you were only eighteen, in a foreign country halfway across the world. Ismailia, wasn't it?'

And that is enough of a prompt. I see the spark in Mum's eyes as she sips her cappuccino and begins to tell me about her time in the Middle East. I lay my phone on the table and sit back, enthralled for the next forty minutes, until our discussion ends abruptly when Mum announces,

'Maureen, if I don't get to a toilet very soon, there will be an accident. Do you know what I mean by that?'

And I do.

## 23. Teresa/Terri. Ismailia, Egypt. 20*th* January 1949
## At Last!

The perspiration is already gathering at Teresa's hairline, trickling down the sides of her face and clinging to her skin. After ten days at sea, she has been in Ismailia for an additional two, long enough to complete the arrival formalities: registration, a quick briefing, and a few restless nights in temporary camp accommodation. Damp patches have formed under her arms and she is relieved she won't have to salute Lieutenant Compton. At least the lieutenant can't see the sweat pooling at the top of her thick stockings, threatening to run down her legs.

The detachment commander behind the large oak desk is nothing like Sergeant Platt in Edinburgh. No jokes, no snorting and certainly no warm welcome. She is an attractive woman in her late twenties or early thirties, with a polished English accent that Teresa can't place. A crisp efficiency sharpens Lieutenant Compton's sculpted features, making her look stern. Teresa can feel the lieutenant's eyes scanning her up and down. She nods at Teresa's heavy great coat.

'You will be issued with two uniforms suitable for life in Egypt. It's a wonder you haven't overheated under the weight of your current one. The uniform here is known as Khaki Drill, or KD. It looks much the same, but is made from lighter material: an aertex shirt, no tie and a soft cap. You may also wear soft khaki ankle socks, but are advised to cover your legs during the hot summer months. Damned mosquitoes will eat you otherwise.'

The lieutenant proceeds to deliver a lecture on how to wear the uniform and the dangers of the sun. Teresa is astonished to learn that sunburn and sunstroke are punishable offences.

'It's not currently warm by Egyptian standards, but it will get hotter. Much hotter. Always wear a hat, even when you are off duty. I'm sure you don't want to end up in the brig like some young recruits.'

This is said with a little too much relish, and is followed by another lecture, this time about hydration.

'Drink water, but not cold water. Make sure you know its source and never have ice, especially if you are off base. Have black tea as opposed to fizzy drinks. They will never quench your thirst for more than a few seconds. Oh… and if you eat street food, you will end up with ghastly diarrhoea. It's called a gippy tummy for a reason..'

If the last comment had been made by Sergeant Platt, Teresa would have known it was a joke, but nothing on the lieutenant's face gave her that impression. Teresa hoped 'gippy' tummy was not a disciplinary offence.

Lieutenant Compton scratches notes on the paper in front of her. Without lifting her head, she says, 'Dismissed, Coulter. Welcome to Ismailia,' then, as an afterthought, 'Speak to Sergeant Mathews about your uniform. She will also direct you to your workplace. You may rest today and start in the morning.'

Teresa is relieved to have the remainder of the day to recover from the journey and acclimatise a little. The lieutenant may not have thought it was warm, but it was much hotter than aboard ship or at home.

\* \* \*

Teresa's first night at Moascar Camp had been far from restful. The accommodation for new arrivals offered little comfort and they had been warned it could take time to adjust from sleeping on a moving ship to dry land. As Teresa walked away from the lieutenant's office, she reflected on the journey, her first sea crossing and one she would never forget. There was an instant sense of camaraderie on board. They had to attend talks about Egypt but also had time to relax and watch the changing landscape. Liverpool faded and the grey chill of home was gradually replaced by blue skies and increasing warmth. The taste of salt spray from the deck as the majestic *Empress of Australia* sliced through the water reminded her of the tangy breeze in Skelmorlie.

The sessions about the ship's history had fascinated Teresa. It was hard to believe the ship weighed over 21,000 tonnes. It moved so effortlessly.

'She's a German-built ship, seized by the British in 1919,' the CO had informed them. 'Helped rescue victims of the Kanto earthquake in Japan, 1923. Yes indeed, a vital role for the old girl.'

She grinned when the ship was referred to as female, until the soldier beside her whispered, 'All ships are a *she*.'

'And she was utilised as the Royal Yacht for a Canadian tour in 1939,' the CO continued, as if discussing a guest of honour.

Teresa had jotted it all down to include in her first letter home. She pictured her father reading it and absorbing every detail. The thought made her feel happy and unexpectedly sad. Her first bout of homesickness.

Days aboard the ship blurred together. They passed the tip of Cornwall and headed for Gibraltar. It seemed odd to think of Gibraltar as a British Overseas Territory when it lay twelve hundred miles from the mainland. A colourful flotilla of trading boats met the *Empress* in Valletta, Malta's sun-baked harbour. Her senses were flooded with sights she'd only dreamed of or read about: ochre buildings rising against a dazzling blue sea and the air thick with the scent of unfamiliar spices.

From there, the *Empress* sailed to Cyprus, where she had to drop anchor a mile offshore as she was too large to dock in Famagusta. And then finally, Port Said, the last leg of the journey. Teresa felt the thrill of a world unfolding before her, full of possibilities to be explored. Several large personnel trucks met them at the dock in Port Said. Either by accident or design, her name was the first of twenty to be called for Ismailia. She had been informed that the boarding delay in Liverpool was due to a clerical mix-up. A member of the Military Police (MP) was mistakenly listed as male and clearly wasn't. Typical, she thought, wondering what gender hairdressers were supposed to be. She made a mental note to tell Mr Thompson when they next met. He'd enjoy the absurdity.

As she sauntered towards her billet on her first day in Egypt, Private Teresa Coulter hummed the well-known song that had welcomed her aboard the *Empress of Australia*:

*I'm gonna get you on a slow boat to China,*
*All to myself alone…*

Give or take a shaky start, she had made it. She was here.

## 24. Teresa. Ismailia. May 1949
### *A New Way of Life*

Four months after her arrival in Moascar Camp, Teresa breathed in the distinctive mix of parched earth and distant cooking fires. She had been assigned a room in cool whitewashed barracks, very different from the huts in Guildford and Edinburgh, but necessary to deflect the intense summer heat.

Neat rows of tents and an occasional hut were scattered around the camp, each with its own function. She relished her early morning walks to the salon, the cool night air giving way to the first warmth of sunlight. Soldiers chatted and smoked in clusters before the day's work, and an occasional truck rumbled past, its canvas-covered back filled with men heading to the depot. As Teresa walked past the mess hall, the clatter of enamel mugs and murmur of morning chatter spilled into the open air.

Swaying date trees ringed the camp. Beyond its edge, the land opened into a vast desert, scattered with small local villages of mud-brick houses and flat roofs. As Teresa veered off the main path towards her shop, Egyptian workers passed in flowing galabeyas, their donkeys laden with supplies. The working day started early here, before the heat of the sun made its presence felt. Kicking the dust from her shoes, she climbed the stairs of *Chez Elizabeth*, grateful for the welcoming shade of its spacious veranda.

Teresa surveyed her Egyptian salon, pleased with what she saw—a far cry from the half hut in Edinburgh. Thankfully, the shop had already been set up as a hairdresser and barbers before she arrived. No need to start from scratch, sourcing and buying equipment. Of course, she had added a few touches to make it more stylish and efficient. It was important to put her stamp on the place. With a name like *Chez Elizabeth*, Teresa assumed the salon had been named after Princess Elizabeth, once a member of the ATS and now happily married to Philip.

Teresa smiled at the memory of her first day in the salon, although it seemed like a lifetime ago now. She had been surprised to find an

Egyptian man squatting on the veranda. He grinned, pointed to himself and proudly announced, 'Mohamed.' Then, with a hand on his heart and a slight nod, he said, 'As-salamu alaykum.'

They had learned aboard ship that this meant *Peace be with you*. These days, she and Mohamed greeted each other with the simpler *Salam*.

Mohamed lived in a nearby village with his wife, Aya and son, Annan. Teresa guessed he was somewhere between thirty and fifty—hard to gauge because leathery skin hung on his frame like an old coat. He was small and wiry, with a gentle face and bright eyes, and when he smiled, which was often, his teeth were stained red from chewing betel nut. Mohamed always wore white and covered his head with a folded *keffiyeh* to guard against dust and sun. Over time, the two of them had settled into an easy rhythm and quiet understanding she had come to value. Mohamed kept the place spotlessly clean and made sure she stayed hydrated, offering regular cups of chai.

Later that first day, after Mohamed had introduced himself, he pointed to the midday sky, swayed his head from side to side and said, 'No. No.'

Then he unrolled his mat and slept for over an hour, waking with renewed energy. Teresa was accustomed to his ways now and had learned to read his body language—or rather, his head language. A gentle sway from side to side meant agreement or acknowledgement. A tilt to one side was a question. A vigorous shake, often with raised hands, signalled a firm objection.

\* \* \*

Teresa felt alive in this new world, soaking up the dramatic landscape and unfamiliar rhythm of life. The temperature climbed higher each day and she was glad to have adapted gradually. By day, she worked as a busy hairdresser, and by night, she was involved with the Ismailia General Headquarters (GHQ) theatre company. Lessons from Mr Foster often came to the forefront, though she wished she had retained more of his wisdom. She applied stage makeup, supervised wigs and helped with costumes. Entertainment was seen as vital for troops overseas, and they had an enviable supply of props and outfits: everything needed to put on a professional show. Mr Foster would have been in his element.

Though not an officer, Teresa's role as camp hairdresser set her apart from the other women in the Royal Corps of Signals. She could mingle more freely and stay out later, privileges she appreciated but never abused. She also had a room to herself. The privacy suited her, though at times, she missed companionship and fun.

It was Tuesday, and the salon would soon erupt with activity as new recruits arrived for haircuts and styling. Teresa had to leave promptly after work as GHQ was midway through a production of *Othello*. She was mulling over her schedule and preparing trolleys of products and equipment when Mohamed appeared, standing aside dramatically to reveal an attractive girl of around Teresa's age.

'I'm so sorry. I thought you were open for business, but I suppose it's still a bit early. I'm Janey... Janey Dodds... Private Janey Dodds. I arrived last night and look like I've been wrestling with a bush... and lost. I'm desperate. Can you save my life... and my hair? I've been told you're rather good. And I'll never tame this mop in the heat without help.'

Teresa could see no evidence of bush-wrestling. Janey did not appear to have a single hair out of place under her cap. Tall, with the figure of a model, she had dark brown eyes and long auburn hair pinned neatly into waves. Her open, genuine smile revealed perfect teeth, but it was the warmth behind her smile that most impressed Teresa. She realised she had been staring.

'Terri... Terri Coulter,' she blurted. Encouraged by Janey's obvious confidence, she added, 'I enlisted as Teresa, but decided it was time for a change. So now I go by Terri.'

The name felt new in her mouth, like trying on someone else's shoes. Most of the military personnel in Moascar and at GHQ had never even heard the name Teresa. Terri felt right. And the timing felt right, too. She decided to leave Teresa somewhere between Edinburgh and Egypt. Yes, Private Terri Coulter had a distinctive ring to it.

'Well, Terri Coulter, my real name is Anne. I never liked it and changed it to Janey when I joined up. Just don't tell my mother if you ever meet her. She'd kill me. I know we've just met, but it feels like you and I are going to get along just fine.'

And Teresa—Terri—had to agree with Janey Dodds.

'I can't imagine my mother ever addressing me as Terri,' she admitted. 'Let's just call it our Middle Eastern secret. The freedom to be who we want to be in Egypt. Now, let's have a look at that mop of yours before my first real customer comes through the door.'

\* \* \*

Two weeks later, Terri stood in front of Lieutenant Compton, who had become less intimidating since her regular visits to Chez Elizabeth.

'Are you sure about this, Coulter? Single quarters are hard to come by and highly sought after.'

'It'll be fine, Ma'am. Honestly. There's plenty of space for two beds and I'm out most evenings anyway... working with GHQ productions.'

'Very well, Coulter. As you wish. But don't come running to me if it doesn't work out. I will not be revoking the change.'

Terri couldn't wait to tell her new friend. Although Janey Dodds was beautiful and came across as confident, she had opened up about her own self-doubt..

One evening after dinner, they had been sitting on Terri's bunk when Janey said, 'It was expected I'd join the army as an officer, but I wasn't "officer material." They informed me I lacked leadership skills... among other things.'

She gave a small shrug. 'My father's a major. My parents just assumed I'd follow that path. I must be a huge disappointment.'

Janey's head dropped and her voice quivered, but she took a breath and steadied herself. Her usual brightness returned. 'I hope to make the grade after a few months here. And I think you can help me, Terri Coulter.'

'Me?' Terri jumped off the bunk. 'I was born in the Gorbals, Janey. Ever heard of *No Mean City*? How am I going to help you become an officer? Are you mad?'

Janey shook her head. 'But you're different, Terri. You know what you want and where you're going. I'd love to be more like you. I don't fit in with the other girls and they know it. That's why the shared hut was so difficult. But I don't fit in with the officers either. And I have no idea how to fix it. There's no pretence with you. You're just who you are and I admire that... I really do. I don't think I've ever known who I am. Oh, I knew I'd have to join up because of my father... and I'll probably end up an army wife like my mother. But beyond that... nothing.'

Terri liked Janey. But it was clear they came from very different backgrounds. She couldn't imagine how her friend would handle a tenement without an indoor toilet. Still, Janey's life had difficulties and demands, even if they weren't as obvious. She settled herself back down beside Janey on the bed.

'You say I know what I want and where I'm going,', 'But that's not exactly true. I just know what I *don't* want... where I *don't* want to be. I'm always learning because I had to leave school at fourteen. I try to make up for it now by paying attention to everything. I work hard. Every day's a school day for me.'

Janey listened attentively. Terri realised she had never voiced those feelings aloud to anyone. But the serious mood didn't last long. Janey lifted a pillow and launched it in Terri's direction.

'Every day doesn't have to be a school day. I'd like to become an officer... eventually. But I want to have some fun first. What do you say, Terri Coulter? You help me become *officer material,* and I'll help you have more fun.'

Terri retrieved the pillow from where it had landed in the middle of the floor and hurled it back at Janey, who was now sitting demurely on the edge of the bed. Her aim was better and it hit Janey squarely in the face.

'Are you implying I don't know how to have fun, Janey Dodds... or is it Anne? I forget.'

Quick to recover, Janey cuddled the pillow to her chest, a beautiful, broad smile on her face. 'Does that mean you're up for a little fun in the middle of all this learning, Terri Coulter... or is it Teresa? I forget.'

At that moment, two Egyptian porters appeared. A quick knock barely registered before they barged in, a bed hoisted on their shoulders. The girls collapsed in fits of laughter, while the men exchanged confused looks, obviously wondering what the two ladies found so funny.

## 25. Terri. Perth. 24ᵗʰ November 2020
### Reflection: The Middle East

Maureen is upstairs writing. I like to leave her in peace to get on with it, but I pop in whenever I go upstairs to the toilet. I wish she had a proper desk, but she tells me everything is fine, so I leave it at that.

I'm sitting in my own office—well, on my chair with the last two weeks' post beside me in a pile. I know I should sort through it, but I can't find the energy. I have a large shredder and like to put any paper with my address on it through the machine. You never know who's watching these days. I didn't have the heart to tackle it while Maureen was away. She says we might do it together tomorrow. I'm happy just to sit here and doze today. The BBC News is on in the background, but it's just more charts and figures about the virus. I feel tired and fall asleep more often now. Maureen says it's because we've had such a busy time. I suppose she's right. I seem to be full of beans one day and can't keep my eyes open the next. We had a lovely day yesterday. I can't believe the last time I went out shopping was seven months ago. Me, who was in town at least once or twice every week. But I got used to being at home and the family have all been so good at coming to see me.

I must have drifted off again. I'm not sure if Maureen is still upstairs or out for a walk. The house is quiet and I've no idea what time it is. I was thinking about Egypt, or maybe I was dreaming. It doesn't matter. We chatted a lot about the Middle East yesterday. It was cold and wintry outside, but when I remembered Ismailia, I could feel the heat and smell the desert air.

I told Maureen about how Mohamed was waiting to greet me on that first day in *Chez Elizabeth*. To say I was shocked when he started to undress is an understatement.

'I thought I was in over my head and had started planning ways to defend myself, fight him off. And then he hung his galabeya on the washing line and started sweeping the floor.

'Poor Mohamed,' Maureen said. 'You could have done him a mischief with any number of sharp objects from the salon.'

We had a good laugh about it, but I felt bad at the time. I had a lot to learn about Egyptian ways. It was the custom for men to remove the outer garment—their galabeya—before any kind of manual work. Mohamed and I didn't speak the same language, yet eventually, we understood each other very well. He was a good worker, but never rushed, even when we had a queue of customers waiting. One of the girls in the camp taught me to say *Igjri 'alā, tūūshi 'alā*, which means something like 'move quickly,' or as we'd say, 'get a move on'. I used that Arabic phrase many times with the family over the years. It was never any more effective with them than it was with Mohamed.

I forgot to tell Maureen that Ian Bannen, the well-known Scottish actor, was a corporal in the army and involved in GHQ theatre productions when I did hair and makeup. He was from Airdrie and we used to chat about life in Scotland. He was a good actor, a very nice man and handsome too. I particularly remember his performance in *Othello* in 1949. We were busy that year, with *Pygmalion* in the summer and *Othello* in October. I'd finish work, grab a bite to eat, then a driver would take me to the GHQ Theatre Club or to one of the larger bases in Ismailia, where they had a hall big enough to put on a show. If anyone from the camp was in the production, we'd borrow a Land Rover and travel together. I still have some programmes somewhere, with *Coiffeur: Terri Coulter* written inside. I always thought *coiffeur* had more panache than 'Hair and Makeup.' They were great days: busy, varied and never a dull moment. I always said I lived a whole lifetime in the army. And I did.

I hear Maureen on the move. The door opens and she arrives with a tray. I'm not sure if it's lunch or dinner time. I tell her I've been snoozing and dreaming about Egypt. Maureen says she has been doing research and is interested in the history of that time. It turns out to be a late lunch. I'm quite hungry and I like French toast, so that's good. We chat while we eat.

'Was there any trouble when you were there, Mum? I mean, wasn't that when Egyptians wanted the British out?'

It was a fair question. 'Well, we knew there was tension. I remember seeing government buildings in Ismailia with smashed windows. The truth is, I didn't think much of it then. I was busy with the salon and the GHQ theatre. But sometimes you could feel it. And there were always rumours in the NAAFI. I suppose we were all just trying to get on with day-to-day life.'

Maureen clears away the dishes. I should have told her…

I've been asleep again. What on earth is wrong with me? There's music on the television, and I was dreaming of one night when Janey and I went dancing. There were lots of dances in the NAAFI, but I was usually too busy to go. That night, with no GHQ productions in the pipeline, we put on our glad rags and headed out. I used a bit of makeup from my theatre box, styled our hair and off we went. I remember we giggled a lot because I'd borrowed a pair of Janey's slingbacks, but they were too big and kept slipping off my feet. I was a good dancer and never short of a partner. I taught Janey how to jive and if memory serves, that's where she met Peter, her husband. She became an army wife after all.

I haven't thought about Egypt in years but it's like I'm back there. I feel happy. I feel young. Not that I feel old—I don't. Not in my head anyway. I've had to let one or two doctors know that being old doesn't make you deaf. Or stupid. One time, I went to the Glasgow Royal Infirmary about my skin cancer and the doctor said, 'You have a little thing on your nose. We'll just whip it off for you.'

He didn't even look up from his notes when I came in and sat down in front of him. I wanted to tell him, *You may be a big man, but a wee shirt'd fit you*, but I thought that might be going a bit far. Instead, I sat up straight in the chair and said, in my best business voice, 'Do you mean a basal cell carcinoma? Or is it a squamous cell? I've had both. And I would like to discuss my treatment options with Mr Taggart, the consultant. Please tell him Mrs Reilly is here to see him.'

He lifted his head after that.

## 26. Terri. Egypt. Early September 1949
### The Holiday with Friends

'Just think, Terri... a whole week. We're going to have the best time.'

There was no stopping Janey once she was on a roll. Her enthusiasm was infectious and Terri had to admit she was looking forward to visiting Cairo, Alexandria, and Famagusta. Her army leave had always been spent working. When the members of the ATS were invited to join the newly formed Women's Royal Army Corps (the WRAC) in the summer of 1948, Terri jumped at the chance. It allowed her an extra eighteen months of service and greatly increased the likelihood of an overseas posting. It also earned her a month's leave, most of which she spent providing holiday cover in Bamber's. Like many in the ATS, she sent a chunk of her pay home, and the extra pocket money had been welcome. This would be her first proper holiday. She wished Terence was coming with them. He felt the same and said so in his recent letter. She couldn't wait for them to spend time together.

'Did I tell you Peter's bringing his friend, Dickie? You two will get on like a house on fire.'

Janey, perched on the end of her bunk, concentrated on painting her toenails, deliberately avoiding eye contact with Teresa. When her comment was met with silence, she stopped and raised her head.

'OK, I see your face, Coulter. I don't mean like that. I know what you're like. But it'll be fun... I promise. Peter's hiring a car. We'll drive to Cairo and Alex, then catch a lift on naval transport to Cyprus. A perfect balance of culture and sandy beaches, don't you think?'

Terri was standing at the mirror adjusting her soft cap. Although the WRAC women wore olive green, the Khaki drill uniform was still preferred in hot climates. They only wore the green beret on more formal occasions.

'As long as this Dickie character knows I'm spoken for, Dodds. Terence and I are getting closer and more serious, even if it is by letter. There'll be no chance of hanky-panky. Do you know what I mean by that?'

'You and your wacky Glasgow expressions. I get the gist alright. Anyway, I'm beginning to think this Terence chap is a figment of your imagination. You just use him as a way of fending off dates with real men.'

'Good try, but you're still not reading my letters. Anyway, I suppose another passenger is better than playing gooseberry to you and Peter for a week.'

Terri knew her comment would provoke a reaction. Janey really liked Peter, but their relationship was strictly platonic. The three of them often spent their free time together, exploring the area. Peter was a real theatre buff and attended all GHQ productions. He and Teresa often swapped opinions.

'As if!' Janey sighed, lifting her long legs and fanning her toes in the air.

'Just wait till you're the poster girl for the WRAC campaign. Peter won't get a look in,' Terri teased, mimicking her friend's well practiced pose on the poster, before making a final adjustment to her cap and heading for the door.

'Don't spend all day on those nails. It's hardly *officer material* behaviour… even for a pin-up girl.'

Terri dodged out of the room before anything could be thrown her way.

\* \* \*

Two days later, the four of them set off in a jeep. The girls in the back tried not to look down at the sheer drop as Peter navigated the Ismailia Desert Road to Cairo for their first stopover. When the boys realised Janey and Terri had never been on a camel, there was no way out. It had to be done. They would find accommodation in Cairo and organise a camel excursion before heading to Alexandria.

If they thought the Desert Road was dangerous—and it was—the traffic in Cairo was lethal in a different way, even if it barely moved. The biggest city in Egypt lived up to its reputation: a vibrant cacophony of mayhem and activity. Dickie knew of a cheap hotel and Peter weaved through the chaos until they jolted to a stop in a side street off the main thoroughfare. They unloaded the bags and booked into two small rooms. No wonder the hotel was cheap. The air inside was thick with stale heat and the furniture was dusty, but at least the bedclothes were clean.

'There's no fan,' moaned Janey, throwing herself onto one of the small beds.

Terri tried to sound reassuring as she forced open the creaking shutters. 'We're only here for the night. And anyway, we'll be off early in the morning for our camel ride.'

'You're right as always, Coulter. Let's get out of here and find a nice restaurant. Dickie says there's a good one nearby.'

Terri pulled the only dress she had packed from her suitcase.

'Well, I hope his taste in restaurants is better than his choice of hotel,' she said, and even Janie had to laugh.

Soon, they were giggling like teenagers.

The restaurant was certainly a step up. Soothing music played in the background and ceiling fans turned lazily overhead. Well-dressed diners sipped cocktails at round tables, laid with starched white cloths, candles, and an array of gleaming glassware and cutlery. A waiter wearing a long apron and a stony expression led them to a table. Terri instantly felt out of her depth. She looked down at her place setting: three knives, three forks, two spoons, three crystal glasses and a linen napkin neatly folded inside an ornate silver ring. Her heart sank. Who did she think she was? What was she supposed to do now? Her name wasn't Terri. She was plain old Teresa Coulter from the Gorbals, whose mother preferred fish and chips out of a newspaper to any meal requiring a single knife and fork, never mind three.

Peter and Janey were deep in conversation, but Dickie must have noticed the panic in her eyes.

'I think they put all this cutlery on the table just so they can charge us extra for washing up.' He was grinning, his expression soft and kind.

He discreetly explained how to use each piece of cutlery, without the slightest hint of patronising her. The other two were oblivious, probably assuming they were having a cosy chat, which would have delighted Janey. The rest of the evening went well. Before lifting her cutlery, Terri glanced at Dickie, who gave her a subtle nod. The waiter with the stony face poured the wine at the table, so she didn't have to worry about whether it was safe or which glass to use. She had no such reservations about dancing and felt far more at ease on the dance floor than at the dinner table.

\* \* \*

The desert, vast and cool in the early morning, was a welcome contrast to the chaos of Cairo, like drifting in an ocean of sand. The tranquillity was a revelation.

Janey squealed as the huge camel beneath her pitched forwards, then backwards, before rising to its full height and beginning to move. The boys thought it was hilarious. Terri had no intention of offering further entertainment. She swallowed down her apprehension, closed her eyes and let the steady, swaying rhythm of the camel anchor her. The caravan was quiet now, moving slowly and deliberately through the sand. Conversation was difficult from camel to camel, but more than that, the desert, much like the sea, demanded silence and respect. The old man leading Terri's camel told her its name was Jeremiah. It suited him. She spoke softly to the animal as the sun rose higher and the heat deepened.

'It still feels like a dream, Jeremiah…this new world, my new friends, Egypt, Terence. You. None of it feels real. I'm an impostor in my own life. I didn't even know which knife and fork to use at dinner last night. But if this is a dream, I don't want to wake up. I don't want to be back in Beechgrove Street or standing in the rain waiting for the tram to work. I *am* an impostor, but I want this life. Is that so bad? Do you think I want too much, like my mother always says I do?'

Jeremiah grunted his approval and Terri smiled, patting his side.

They plodded on in companionable peace until the guide halted them, pointing towards the shimmering green of an oasis.

'Rest,' he called, raising his arms to signal a stop.

The promise of shade and cool refreshment beckoned through the haze. Another dream.

\* \* \*

The following day, the four travellers drove to Alexandria, once the capital of Egypt, and a city steeped in history. They stayed in a much better hotel near the beautiful Montazah Gardens and spent the rest of the day and the next morning exploring.

They visited the Bibliotheca Alexandrina, built to honour the ancient library, once the largest in the world. Cleopatra was rumoured to have turned to the scholars of the ancient library to shape her formidable education. Afterwards, Terri decided to buy a book as a memento and while the others stopped for coffee, she returned to a little bookshop she had spotted nearby.

The shop was cluttered with books of every shape and size, some on shelves, others piled on the floor. Titles in Arabic mingled with those in a variety of other languages. Terri recognised the sweet, woody smell of old paper and decided the metallic scent in the air was probably ink. She was scanning a dusty shelf when an elderly man approached. He wore a long grey galabeya under a sleeveless scarlet waistcoat. The black tassel of the fez on his head hung over one cheek and small, round spectacles perched precariously at the end of his nose. A leather satchel slung over his shoulder completed the image of a learned and wise scholar. He pointed at the book in her hand and shook his head, then disappeared into a passage between two huge bookcases. Moments later, he returned with a small green volume and a broad smile. He patted the cover and handed it to her.

'This book. You must have this book.'

She looked down at the gold lettering: *The Rubáiyát of Omar Khayyám*. It was beautiful. As she walked away, clutching the carefully wrapped purchase to her chest, Terri knew it was more than a souvenir. She had never heard of Omar Khayyám, but of all the books in his shop, this was the one the bookseller wanted her to have. It felt predestined. This was a book she would treasure. Always.

After coffee, the friends ventured to the Stanley Bridge. The views of the Mediterranean made the long walk worthwhile, though Janey, in her less-than-sensible shoes, was reluctant to agree.

'Terri, why do you have to walk so fast? And do we *really* want to see another historic site? My feet can't take much more. Peter, you'll have to carry me.'

Her moaning continued to the bridge, but even Janey had to admit the view was stunning. The turquoise waters glistened like an endless sparkling carpet, stretching beneath a skyline of elegant buildings. Terri closed her eyes, breathing in the warm sea breeze and listening to the distant hum from the busy promenade. Her reverie was broken by Janey, still focused on her feet.

'I swear I'm not walking one more step,' she warned.

It was agreed that Dickie and Janey would head back to the hotel, while Peter and Terri visited the Roman Amphitheatre and Pompey's

Pillar, which dated back to the 4th century. Afterwards, they stopped at a small restaurant, sitting outside in the shade of a broad palm tree. Peter opened up a little, sharing snippets about his family and army life.

'Like Janey, my father's very senior in the military,' he said. 'So there was no question about my career path.'

'What would you choose, if you had a choice?' Terri asked, sipping her black tea.

Without hesitation, he said, 'I'd be a lawyer. I think it would suit me. But there's no point thinking about it. I'll be a military man, like my father, work my way up and pray there's never another world war.'

Terri couldn't help thinking they were more alike than she had realised. Neither had lived up to their parents' expectations, even if those expectations were poles apart. If she had accepted her destiny as unquestioningly as Peter accepted his, she would still be in Bridgeton, working in a factory and dating a lad from the Locarno dance hall. She shuddered at the thought.

'Are you alright, Terri? You've gone all serious. It's not *that* tragic. I mean, just think of the criminals who'll be better off if I never become a lawyer.'

He laughed, but Terri sensed he didn't often share this much of himself. There was no doubt they had a natural connection. But she also knew Janey was more than interested in Peter, even if he hadn't noticed yet. They made sense together—same background, same confidence. And neither blinked at a formal table setting.

Terri gathered herself and stood. 'Come on. Time to get back to the hotel. Famagusta's waiting.'

'What? That's not fair, Coulter. You know my secrets. Now you have to tell me yours. Besides, I'm enjoying this… just sitting under a palm tree… chatting. Aren't you?'

Terri knew he was flirting and though she enjoyed his company, she had no intention of telling him about her life. What would be the point? She did what girls often do in moments like this—she changed the subject.

'You just don't want to drive back to Cairo, Hastings. I'm determined to stay awake this time. I'm sure I missed loads on the way here. And I can't wait to see what kind of naval vessel Dickie's organised for our trip to Famagusta.'

The spell was broken, precisely as she had intended. Terri decided to avoid being alone with Peter for the rest of the holiday. She didn't want to give him the wrong idea or risk jeopardising her friendship with Janey. Life was complicated enough.

Spending time with Janey, Peter, and Dickie had made her think about Terence. How would she ever manage the differences between them? She hadn't noticed the cutlery on their one and only date, but formal military functions were part of his life.

*Even if I learn everything about etiquette and place settings, would I ever fit in?*

She and Terence knew very little about each other's lives before the army. They had never sat under a palm tree talking about their hopes and dreams. In her letters, she could be whoever she wanted to be. Terri tried to picture Terence meeting Tina, but the idea was so ridiculous it made her wince. She pushed these unsettling thoughts aside. There would be time to worry about all that later. For now, she was determined to enjoy what was left of her stay in Egypt.

'Famagusta, here we come!' exclaimed Peter, leaping out of his chair and linking arms with her, startling the older couple at the next table, who muttered their disapproval.

## 27. Terri. Egypt. Late September 1949
### The Engagement

It was a particularly warm late September night. Janey was out with Peter—the two of them were officially dating now. Through the mosquito netting draped around her bed, faint sounds from the camp filtered in as Terri mulled over her latest letter from Terence. He was now in Southern Rhodesia in his new post as a Mounted Trooper with the British South African Police (BSAP). He told her he spent long days on horseback patrolling the villages in the bush and carrying out escort duties. She knew he loved horses and would be in his element. But his suggestion that it was time to become engaged had taken her by surprise. She hadn't replied or told anyone. Not even Janey. There was a lot to think about. And Terri had done a lot of it in the past few nights. As soon as her head hit the pillow, the battle began.

We've only been on one official date—and that was more than a year ago. *How can we get engaged?*

The connection I felt with Terence was unlike any other.

And It was easy to talk, easy to listen..*That's important, isn't it?*

And every time I looked at him that night, my heart fluttered. *I can't just dismiss that feeling—can I?*

She threw herself onto her back and breathed deeply. A dry breeze carried the tang of dust and smoke through the netted window. Her thoughts darted like fireflies.

But it's one thing to hear about *No Mean City*, quite another to marry a girl from there.

But we're from different worlds. The truth is, Terence is more suited to someone like Janey Dodds, the daughter of an army major.

And so it went on.

Tonight, she was also thinking about Eddie Hughes. They had been engaged when she was just seventeen. He was older and looked handsome in his RAF uniform. After the war, Eddie struggled to find work and joined the men heading for America. He hadn't even discussed it with her. That hurt. She was his fiancée, after all. They had written to each other for about six months, her letters full of questions, his full of nothing much. Then, out of the blue, Eddie wrote and asked her to join him and get married. Her gut told her it would never work. She was happy with her life and happy at Bamber's. Terri had politely turned him down and sent the ring back via his mother. Eddie moved on, met another girl and was unlikely ever to return to Scotland, but she was still friends with his sister.

Terri turned onto her side again. The battle continued to rage.

I never felt my heart flutter or do a cartwheel with Eddie, before or after the engagement.

*That's true.*

And Terence's letters are full of news and affection.

*That's also true.*

Then a bizarre thought: *Will it not be weird for a man called Terence, who signs his letters as Terry, to be engaged to a woman called Terri?*

'Now you're being ridiculous,' she said aloud and laughed.

She knew in her heart and her gut she was going to say yes to Terence. Unlike Eddie, he included her in his life and his decisions. And he would always be Terence to her.

She decided to write to him tomorrow. And then to her parents. The practicalities would sort themselves out later.

She turned one last time. The camp outside was silent, and Terri felt a sense of peace as her eyelids grew heavy. She was engaged to Terence Warr. It was her final thought of the night. The battle was over.

## 28. Terri. Ismailia. October 1949
### A Letter from Home

My dearest Teresa,

   I am sorry it has taken so long to write. I have carried your last two letters in my jacket pocket waiting for the right time to respond. There was so much news and I wanted peace and quiet, which is not easy to find around here. I am in the Gorbals library, one of my favourite places as you know. It feels as if you are sitting here beside me like in the old days. I prefer this library to the one in Bridgeton. It is such a beautiful building and I have so many happy memories of us pouring over books together. I sometimes come just to look at the map of Egypt, to remind myself where you are in this big world. I think of you in the heat of Ismailia, wearing your smart army uniform, working in your hairdressing shop. I hope you are careful, not staying out too long in the sun or working too hard. But then I tell myself you are sensible and you'll be fine.

   I will visit Thistle Street afterwards. Your grandmother always asks after you and I share any news from your letters. Of course, I have already told her the exciting news of your engagement to Terence. She is delighted for you. I must admit it is strange to think of you engaged to a young man we have never met, but he sounds like a dependable chap and very nice too. Your mother had plenty to say about him being English, but she's impressed that he's an army captain. Something to boast about to the neighbours! As I always say, I trust you, Teresa. If you think Terence Warr is the one for you, then he's the one for me, too. Does he have a family? You never mention them in letters. But it makes no difference. After all, he may not be keen on your family either! I must get more familiar with the map of Rhodesia. Another new country for you to explore, Teresa, even if it is a long way from home. I will miss you every day. But as long as you are happy, I am happy. And that's how it will always be.

   I enjoyed your last letter about the holiday with your friends in Egypt and Cyprus. It sounded exciting and exotic. I can't wait to see the photograph of you on the camel. Your mother and I laughed out loud at your description of the ride. Thank you for thinking of me in the library in Alexandria. After reading your letter, I looked up its history. I closed my eyes and imagined the two of us there, surrounded by knowledge and every book a window to another world. We would read bits to each other the way we always do here. It was a perfect picture and I did not want to open my eyes and find myself alone.

It took me a while to work out how you managed to visit Famagusta, but the map helped. I read that it was a favourite destination for military personnel with its beaches and social life. I also read a piece about the internment camps there, from just after the war. It is hard to believe such places existed so close to those beautiful beaches, but at least they have been dismantled now. Oh dear, I am becoming much too serious. Sorry, Teresa. You know what I am like when I get on my soapbox. And I don't have you to tolerate my lectures. Your mother raises her eyes to Heaven if I mention anything more serious than the gossip from the chip shop or the Steamie.

Wasn't it lovely that you met a local girl in Famagusta who teaches piano in a primary school? And what a privilege that she brought you to her home and played for you. As we often say, it is wonderful to meet real people when you travel. Far better than reading a hundred books like me. I found an article about the first secondary school for Turkish Cypriots in Famagusta. It opened in 1944 in a single room with only 60 students. Wouldn't it be a coincidence if that's where your friend now teaches? You said you exchanged addresses, so you can ask her in your next letter. The article said it's now a large school with its own building. Isn't that a lovely story? I know we both believe that education is more valuable than wealth. It is progress when internment camps empty and schools expand. Oh goodness, I am back on my soapbox.

I wish we could sit and discuss these things, the way we always do. The library seats around me seem more empty because you are not here. I like the sound of Janey and your army friends. They seem to look out for you and that is precious. But then, you are a loyal friend yourself. Who wouldn't want to be friends with my lovely Teresa?

There's not much news from here. Your mother is fine. She hasn't lost her job at the chip shop yet. I think it suits her. Young Alec is dating a woman called Margaret. She is a good bit older than him, but he seems happy. And Robert wants to leave school at fourteen, even though I have told him he can stay on. Life is strange indeed.

I am fine too. The job at the shipyard is steady, and it feels good to have a wage. I don't take it for granted after being out of work so long. Sometimes I meet a few of the men for a game of pool, but not too often. The house is quiet without you. Well, until your mother gets a bee in her bonnet about something. They all miss you.

Live your life, my darling girl. Always be true to yourself.

Your loving father,

Alexander.

## 29. Maureen. Perth. November 2020
### *Friends and Friendship*

I have no memory of Mum ever going out on her own when we were growing up. She didn't seem to have female friends living locally. One morning, over coffee, I asked her if I was right.

'I was just busy. If I wasn't looking after all of you, I was down at the shop.' She skims the froth from her latte as if there's no more to say.

I have discussed this subject with my brother, Joe, who took over the business when Dad retired. He worked alongside Mum for fourteen years.

'The business *was* Mum's friend,' he said, as if it were obvious. 'I think she found something she loved and was good at. Family and work were enough for her.'

There was truth in his response. It was hard to picture our mum having 'girly' chats or gossiping, enthusing about a new lipstick, or confiding her secrets. As a couple, Joe and Terri, our mum and dad, had lots of friends. Like her, Dad left school at fourteen. He had a sharp mind, loved to read and could quote Shakespeare, Oscar Wilde, even Chaucer. Terri's role in their couples group was different: she was vivacious, always well-dressed and a great dancer. She could whip up sausage rolls or mince patties in a flash. People loved Terri, but her inner world stayed private. She avoided intellectual debates, assuming Joe knew more about those things than she did.

I think of Mum's stories and the friendships she has talked about with genuine affection: Janey Dodds, Mae Brown and even Mandy Peterson. There had been fun, frivolity and closeness. I start by asking, 'What happened to Janey, Mum? Did you keep in touch after Egypt?'

I expect her face to light up, but my question has the opposite effect. I see sadness in her eyes, and make a clumsy attempt to change the subject. 'I was thinking we might… '

'I've thought about it over the years,' Mum says, 'although not much recently.'

I don't interrupt.

'None of it matters now. Poor Janey is dead. It's true, we were great friends in Egypt. But it wasn't the same back in Civvy Street. She became an officer and married Peter. I went to the wedding, but they were posted overseas and Janey wasn't one for writing. You were all young. We had the shop and no money. Maybe I didn't fit into her life anymore.'

Mum pauses for a few moments. 'But I kept in touch with her parents, especially Mrs Dodds. I often visited her in Bexhill and she wrote to me for years. I still have those letters upstairs. Sadly, Janey always had a strained relationship with her mother.'

Mum sips her latte. It must be cold by now, but I don't want to disturb her train of thought.

'I used to wonder if Janey thought Peter had a notion for me. If that was why she kept her distance after we demobbed.'

Another sip.

'Then I wondered if she resented me being so close to her mother.'

Another sip.

'Then I stopped wondering and got on with my life.'

'Do you think Peter could have been interested in you?' I ask.

'I don't think so,' she says.

I note the lack of a vehement denial.

'The three of us were close. Did a lot together before and after our holiday in Egypt and Cyprus. I never thought about it at the time. I knew Janey was sweet on Peter. It wouldn't have occurred to me.'

I try to take it all in. I have heard the stories about Egypt and her connection with Peter in Alexandria, but I have no doubt Mum's sense of loyalty would have trumped any emotional confusion. Still, it's sad if it cost her a friendship.

'Could Janey have been a little jealous of you in general, Mum? From what I can gather, you always seemed more confident than she was.'

Mum shakes her head. 'I was never outgoing, Maureen. Never the centre of attention. Janey was very beautiful, striking.'

I feel a wave of love for this woman who still doesn't believe she deserves centre stage, though even now, at ninety-one, she exudes something that unobtrusively commands it. Maybe Janey saw it too.

'I think you had, and still have, an inner confidence, Mum. A self-belief. A gritty determination. I never knew Janey, but perhaps there were thoughts in her head she didn't understand, or things in her life she couldn't share. Maybe it was easier to walk away. Or just maybe, life got in the way and nothing was wrong.'

I tread carefully now, pondering the contrast between Mum's closeness to Mrs Dodds and her difficult relationship with Tina, her own mother.

'I suppose we can never fully understand a relationship unless we're part of it. And even then, we can't see inside someone else's head. It's complicated.'

Mum says nothing. I know I should leave it there. But another question slips out before I can stop it.

'Did you ever talk about it? Ask Janey if something was wrong?'

'No. I never did,' she murmurs.

Then her tone brightens. 'But I became friends with her younger sister, Maureen Dodds, who lived near their mother. We've stayed in contact over the years. And it was lovely to see her again when you and Colette came with me to Bexhill recently. We had a great time, didn't we?'

And indeed we did—lots of fun and laughter. I have a vivid memory of accidentally setting fire to my napkin when we were out for dinner with Maureen Dodds and her daughter, Alex. I begin to say, 'Remember the night when I… ' but stop. The melancholy look has returned to Mum's face.

'Both of Janey's children died,' she says, barely above a whisper. 'And she had dementia in her final years. Peter was very kind and cared for her until the end. That was a blessing.'

Mum stares at her hands, neatly folded on her lap. Pain, long tucked away, has stirred like dust in a forgotten drawer.

As if reading my mind, she lifts her head and says, 'You know, Maureen, sometimes friends are given to us for a reason. And only for a season in our lives. We were great friends in Egypt. I loved every minute together. We thought it would never end.' She pauses. 'But it did.'

I leave the room quietly to let Mum rest in the soft, late morning light. I hope she is dreaming of friendship and fun, not rejection and loss. Autumn sunlight spills across the pink carpet, revealing its hidden stains and frayed edges. Too late now to be repaired. Best left alone.

## 30. Terri. Ismailia. November 1949
### *The Story of the Cook*

By early November, the searing desert air, once sharp enough to make your skin feel on fire, had cooled to a more tolerable 80°F, softened by the shift from summer to autumn. Early mornings and late afternoons were even cooler and more pleasant. Families of local people spent evenings outdoors, enjoying the balmy breeze and a reprieve from the sweltering summer heat.

Terri was in the NAAFI canteen, grabbing lunch before a packed afternoon of appointments and an evening of GHQ makeup and wig management.

'Where's Hilda? I haven't seen her for a few days. Have you got her stuck in the kitchen all day?' Terri asked the new girl behind the counter.

Unlike Hilda, the girl had no chat and simply spooned the tagine onto her plate without making eye contact. 'Sick,' she said, adding bread before moving down the line.

Terri resolved to check on Hilda the next day. The salon was closed on Sundays and the theatre company had a rest day. As much as she loved work, Terri looked forward to her weekly day off and the chat with Hilda after Mass at the café in town. If Hilda didn't appear, Terri would pop into her hut with some cake after Mass. But the next morning, to her surprise, Hilda was waiting for the bus with the usual churchgoers.

'Great to see you, Hilda. Are you feeling better?'

The bus arrived before Hilda could reply and they found a quiet spot on one of the wooden seats. Hilda turned her face to the window, pulled a handkerchief from her bag and dabbed her eyes. Terri was startled.

'Hilda, what's the matter? Is it serious? Are you alright? Can I help?'

'Not now,' Hilda said, eyes still not meeting her gaze. 'I'll tell you over a cup of tea at the café. I just have to get through Mass first, Teresa. Do you mind? I'm not trying to be difficult or anything. I just can't go into it right now.'

Hilda was the only person in the camp who refused to call her *Terri*.

'Teresa's the name you were born and baptised with,' she had said, 'and that's what I'll be calling you.'

'Of course, Hilda. We'll catch up properly later. I'm right here beside you,' Terri whispered.

Hilda dabbed her eyes again.

Terri found it hard to concentrate during the service. Poor Hilda. Something must be very wrong. She was usually so calm and practical. That was part of what bonded them. She and Janey were great friends and did everything together, but she shared something different with Hilda. They came from similar backgrounds and religions. Hilda had left school at fourteen and worked as a cook in a local restaurant until she plucked up the courage to join the WRAC and request a posting abroad. She came from a poor estate in Liverpool and sent most of her wages home to her elderly parents.

*Oh God, maybe one of her parents is sick or has died,* Teresa thought during the Offertory. *Maybe she's terminally ill herself and doesn't know how to tell them,* she pondered, as the bell rang for the consecration. Terri usually had a list of people and intentions to pray for, but today her head was scrambled. She struggled to focus. The sooner Mass was over and they were settled with a cup of tea, the better. She was driving herself mad with possible scenarios, one worse than the other.

After Mass, they sat in the little café in silence until the tea and cake arrived. Terri poured.

'Hilda, talk to me. Whatever it is, it can't be worse than I'm imagining. Please. I'm your friend.'

The words had barely left her mouth when Hilda blurted, 'I'm pregnant,' and buried her face in a crumpled handkerchief, muffling deep, heaving sobs.

Of all the possibilities Terri had considered, pregnancy was not one of them. She paused. Took a breath. What she said next mattered.

'Oh, Hilda. I know it's not what you planned. I can see how upset you are. And that's completely understandable. But... is there any positive side to this at all?'

Terri intended to say more, but the words stuck, lodged somewhere between thought and speech. She felt stupid and inadequate. Hilda stopped crying and blew her nose, which seemed to steady her. She looked at Terri with bloodshot, swollen eyes. Her pain was palpable. Terri felt it in her own throat, her own heart.

'I suppose I was flattered, Teresa. The oldest story in the book isn't it? I'm in my late thirties and not exactly an oil painting.'

She tried to smile, but her eyes remained glazed. 'He was so handsome, Teresa. I let myself believe he cared for me. I knew he didn't want to marry me. I'm not that daft. But we talked, we laughed, and… well, one thing led to another. I should have known better. Of course, I should. It's no different from home… Once they get what they want, they're off. And that's exactly what happened.'

Terri saw Hilda's lip tremble.

'Hilda, I am so, so sorry. I truly am. What a…' she stopped, searching for a word she could say in public. '…coward. He's a coward. And this sort of thing… well, it could happen to anyone in…'

'But it wouldn't happen to you, Teresa,' Hilda's voice cut in gently. 'You know it wouldn't. You'd have known how foolish it was. You'd have stopped the bastard in his tracks. Sorry. I never swear on Sundays. But you know I'm right. Girls like me get caught… the ugly ducklings who're easily flattered, easily led. Especially by handsome men in uniform.'

Her head dropped again. Tears slithered silently onto her tightly clasped hands. Hilda was right… The man was a bastard as well as a coward. But certain questions still had to be asked. Terri took another moment, bracing herself.

'What are you going to do, Hilda? How can I help? Do you know when you're due?'

Terri cringed at the last question. She hadn't dared say the word 'baby.' That would make it too real. And Hilda was Catholic, like herself. There would be no options to consider.

'I'm almost six months pregnant, Teresa. Everyone will know soon.'

Her voice was barely audible. Then, after a pause, it steadied. 'The dress I cook in is large, shapeless and white. It's been easy to hide until now. But the other day, one of the kitchen girls commented about me putting on weight. She meant it as a joke. I laughed. But that night, reality hit me like a train. I couldn't face anyone the next morning, so I called in sick. Told them I had a gippy tummy.'

Terri was stunned again. Six months. That meant the baby would be due in about another three. She didn't know much about pregnancy, but that much she could figure out. She wondered if the sullen girl in the canteen had been Hilda's joker. Terri's first impression of her hadn't hinted at humour. Or compassion.

They sat for another hour, ordered more tea and cake, and discussed practicalities. Hilda decided to go to Lieutenant Compton and explain everything. She hoped to stay in the camp and have the baby in Ismailia. She knew of a girl who had not declared her pregnancy in time and had been shipped home after giving birth locally. It was easier to arrive home with a baby than tell your parents you were expecting one. They both agreed this was the best option.

'I don't think my parents will disown me,' Hilda said. 'They'll be disappointed, of course. But mostly… I just don't want to worry them.'

Terri wasn't sure whether it was worry or fear that Hilda was avoiding, but said nothing. It was typical of Hilda to think more of others than herself.

* * *

Terri had been swamped with appointments at the start of the week and *Othello* didn't close until Wednesday evening. It was Thursday before she had an opportunity to follow up on Hilda's meeting with the lieutenant. She assumed it had taken place since Hilda hadn't returned to work. She made her way to the catering staff quarters, but there was no sign of Hilda. As she turned to leave, the sullen girl from the canteen appeared from one of the rooms and spotted her.

'If you're looking for Private Kelly, she left yesterday. Some camp for pregnant girls until they're shipped back to England.'

Terri swallowed the bile that surged in her throat and tried to keep her voice calm. 'Do you know where that camp is?'

'Not a bleedin' clue.' Then, as an afterthought, 'You'd think she'd know better at her age.'

The girl headed off towards the canteen, no doubt to ladle out food in truculent silence for the rest of the day.

Terri was too upset to speak. Probably just as well, as she might have found herself up on a charge. She couldn't make sense of it. How had Hilda disappeared in just a few days? Where was she? Why had no one said anything?

As Terri turned to leave, she wiped away tears she could no longer hold back, vowing to find out where Hilda had been sent. She would write to her—something, anything to remind her she was not alone. Yet, the cruel truth was that Hilda *was* alone. Alone in a strange camp. Pregnant. Frightened. Ashamed.

Meanwhile, an officer was swanning around camp, convinced he had simply had a fling with one of the cooks. No harm done. Terence would be appalled. Hilda refused to name him, only saying he was a handsome officer with blond hair and a moustache. Just as well Terri had no idea who the culprit was. Had he ever set foot in *Chez Elizabeth,* she could think of several razor-related accidents that might have occurred.

## 31. Maureen. Perth. 4th December 2020
### From Coffee on the Go to Let's go for Coffee

This morning, we are at the café attached to the Black Watch Regiment Museum and Castle, once home to the Earls of Kinnoull. It is one of Mum's favourite spots, where she regularly meets her pals. The Soroptimists are having their first tentative gathering since Covid and have invited Mum.

'You look as stylish as ever, Terri,' says Avril, the secretary, her warm smile visible even behind a mask.

Mum's delighted reaction makes the hour and a half it took to prepare for the meeting worthwhile. She chose her outfit with care, coordinating colours and jewellery to match her new green coat from Primark. Avril leads her to a table, where the other ladies greet her with genuine enthusiasm.

I find a sofa at the far end, order a latte and begin jotting notes. I want to record some of these coffee dates I never imagined possible during Covid.

Mary Cockburn is one of Mum's closest Keep Fit friends and a fellow volunteer at the Perth Royal Infirmary hospital café. The two friends often end the day with a catch-up call. We recently met Mary at the Mustard Seed, another of Mum's favourite places and it was wonderful to see so many older people mixing again after months of shielding. At ten o'clock, the café was alive with conversation, like birds celebrating spring after a long, silent winter. Mum and Mary added their own notes to the music, giggling and swapping stories behind Perspex screens, oblivious to social distancing. Life is full of small magical moments.

Although the café was busy, hospitality staff continue to face challenges. They must collect customer details, gently enforce distancing protocols, provide hand gel, and clean tables and chairs between customers. The industry is desperate for normality, but it comes at a price.

I glance over at the Soroptimists, chatting in well-spaced groups. Observing them now, it is clear these women are true friends, not just acquaintances. Mum's involvement in the floristry business first connected her with the Soroptimists, giving her the sense of status she once craved. She has travelled the world with them and believes deeply in their mission to support women and expand access to education. But what I sense today is simply genuine respect and affection. Terri Reilly belongs. She is one of them.

Mum's Keep Fit group includes women in their eighties and nineties. I have joined them at the theatre and for after-show dinners. They may walk with sticks or rollators and wear hearing aids, but when they gather, discussions include politics, art, music, and more. They also know a good bottle of wine and how to enjoy it. What unites them is a zest for life, not a fear of ageing or dying. And Terri Reilly belongs. She is one of them, too.

My thoughts drift to Teresa Coulter of the Gorbals and East End of Glasgow, Terri Coulter in the Middle East, Terri Reilly in the hairdressing and flower trade. Were they the same person? Different people? Or have they merged into who she is now? We know our mothers as mothers and sometimes, if we are fortunate, we come to know them as women too. My mother is ninety-one and I am nearly sixty-five. I am piecing together fragments of her early life and matching them with the woman I love and cherish. I did not set out to know her better, but with each day and every shared story, I learn more.

When I asked why Mum hadn't nurtured friendships while we were growing up, I think I was fishing for a logical answer. I wondered if she had been affected by the Blitz, when some girls never returned to class. But her stories of Mae, Janey and Hilda suggest otherwise. And witnessing her relationships here in Perth makes that highly unlikely. Perhaps there is no mystery. Maybe she simply had no time to maintain friendships during her busy adult life. Still, she is blessed to have formed close connections later in life: people who value her for who she is now, not who she was or where she came from. And I am grateful Covid did not rob her of these precious friendships when time is finite. Mum's own explanation is probably the truest: *sometimes friends are given to us for a reason and only for a season in our lives.*

I notice movement among the Soroptimists. Coffee time is over. I help Mum with her coat and we say goodbye, careful to avoid the usual hugging. She cannot resist a meander through the shop before leaving. We stroll, arm in arm, past scented soaps, candles, hats and scarves, and shelves of military memorabilia. At the jewellery stand, always dangerous, Mum picks up a long necklace with a large silver star on the end.

'It's nearly Christmas,' she says. 'It'll go nicely with your red sweater.'

She places it on the counter. 'I'll take that.'

## 32. Terri. Ismailia. November 1949
## The Meeting

Terri arranged a meeting with Lieutenant Compton, desperate for information about Hilda: What had happened? Where was she now? How could she be contacted? Terri had grown to like and respect the lieutenant, which made her reaction all the more shocking.

'Kelly is in a holding camp and will be sent back to England as soon as possible after the delivery. It is not the first time I have had to deal with this kind of thing. The rules are made clear to all female military personnel. And that includes the catering staff. There are consequences for such behaviour. You should know that, Coulter.'

'But the transfer was so sudden, Ma'am. I had no opportunity to say goodbye to...'

Terri's voice cracked with more emotion than she had intended. Lieutenant Compton was glaring up at her now.

'These things are best handled quickly and quietly. Kelly will be looked after by the appropriate people.'

She scribbled the address of Hilda's holding camp on a page of headed notepaper and threw it across the desk at Terri, as if touching it had somehow made her an accomplice to a crime.

'Now, if there's nothing else, I have work to do... And so do you, I imagine.'

The lieutenant lowered her head. The discussion was over.

Terri stood to attention, turned and left the office. Her heart felt as heavy as her feet as she descended the stairs, hand on the banister to keep her steady. Disappointed. Disillusioned. This was the woman she admired and wanted to emulate. This was the army she had come to see as her home, one she had believed shared her values. This was the life she thought she wanted. Lieutenant Compton clearly saw her sympathy for Hilda as some form of insubordination. She was probably as disappointed in Terri. The words stuck in Terri's head: '...this kind of thing...these things...' Hilda was not a *thing*. Her pregnancy was not a *thing*.

Her father had taught her that every person should be treated with dignity and respect. She had believed this to be the ethos of the army. Discipline was strict and rules were to be obeyed—she knew that. But her father had also said that respect must be earned by those in authority, not simply awarded by virtue of rank or power. There had not been an ounce of compassion in Lieutenant Compton's words. Her quickness to judge echoed the culture of blame Terri had overheard around the camp. No one mentioned how Hilda had a kind word for everyone, how she kept the canteen open for latecomers, how she listened without ever betraying a confidence. How she was funny, generous and thoughtful. How she was a human being. No one wanted to talk about any of that—only about how stupid she was to get herself pregnant. Terri noticed they didn't say she was stupid to have sex, only stupid enough to get caught. It made her blood boil. Her father was not the only one who could stand on a soapbox. She pictured the two of them side by side, spouting about injustice. The image made her smile. A small, wistful, watery smile for the man who never disappointed her.

\* \* \*

It was Sunday, but Terri could not face the prospect of Mass. No doubt she would benefit from some Divine inspiration, but her legs simply would not make the journey. She ordered tea from the sullen girl who was not Hilda and sat nursing it, feeling sorry for herself—not like her at all. Life offered plenty of opportunities for self-pity, but Terri Coulter didn't normally pander to them.

She stared at the letter in front of her. She had written to Hilda as soon as she left the lieutenant's office, trying to be reassuring, promising a visit as soon as she had leave. Now, she looked down at her own handwriting on the envelope marked *Return to Sender*. Inside, a short note stated that WRAC Private Kelly, H had been dispatched to England aboard HMT *Empire Windrush*. The note added: '...*a baby was delivered stillborn prior to her departure.*'

Terri thought about Hilda and how they had travelled to Mass together every week. She thought about that final Sunday and Hilda's life-changing news. She thought about how distressed Hilda had been in the café and how she had tried to give her a little hope.

'It may not be what your parents had planned for you, Hilda, but when they see your beautiful baby, they'll be filled with joy and be happy for you.'

The worst of it was that Hilda had perked up and said, 'Do you know, Teresa, you might be right. My mum and dad were older when they had me. They've probably given up any hope of becoming grandparents at this stage.'

But Terri had no right to say any such thing, no right to suggest that everything would be okay. It had all turned into a disaster for poor Hilda, discharged from the army, with no baby for them to love. No baby for Hilda to love.

Her eyes stung. Tears plopped into the cup of tea in her hand, like raindrops in a puddle. They were not just tears of self-pity. They were tears of empathy for her friend, grief for the baby she had lost. They were also tears of frustration, anger, and a deep sorrow she could not yet verbalise.

## 33. Terri. Ismailia. December 1949
### Choices

As 1949 drew to a close and a new decade hovered on the horizon, the camp hummed with talk of the future.

Terri's extra eighteen months had been completed and she was due to demob in February 1950. Men completing two years of National Service were invited to remain as professional soldiers. Although women had not been conscripted, members of the WRAC could also apply for a permanent army role. This morning, Terri stood at attention in front of Lieutenant Compton's desk for the second time in a month. Her thoughts tumbled over one another and her stomach churned. Why had she been summoned? The answer stunned her.

'I think you would do well in the army, Coulter. I believe you are an officer in the making. You could stay on in your role as a WRAC hairdresser, but you would also be in a prime position to retrain and move quickly through the ranks.'

The lieutenant smiled and added, 'You might be sitting in this very chair one day.'

Terri wished she could sit down now before her legs gave way.

Through the confusion she managed, 'Thank you, Ma'am.'

Seconds later it was back to business.

'Think about it, Coulter, but don't take too long. Let me know as soon as possible, otherwise, I will be forced to organise your demobilisation.'

Terri had been dismissed.

She descended the office stairs and leaned against the building, trying to recover and make sense of the past ten minutes. Lieutenant Compton had asked her to apply for a permanent position in the army. But how? Why? Had she forgotten their previous meeting? What about Hilda—was she forgotten too? Terri smoothed her jacket, straightened her beret, and walked slowly back to her billet, breathing deeply as she repeated her calming mantra to herself:

*One, two, three, four,*
*Jenny at the cottage door*

# Small Shoes

*Five, six, seven, eight,*
*Jenny at the cottage gate...*

A year ago, even a few months ago, she would have been flattered by the lieutenant's encouragement. Delighted. She might even have accepted the offer. After all, it ticked all the boxes: a secure job, good pay, opportunities to travel, status, and the chance to further her education. Terence would have been delighted. *Why am I not jumping at this opportunity?* Gradually, the fog lifted. Of course, Hilda's pregnancy and transfer had been forgotten, and her questioning tone overlooked. She was not going to be disciplined or transferred. This was the army. Lieutenant Compton had done her job and moved on. *Why can't I move on?*

Terri threw her beret and jacket aside and dropped onto the bed, staring at the roof. She had received a letter from Terence this morning, which only added to her turmoil, her dilemma. He had suggested she demobilise in Nairobi, the British military hub in East Africa. He could meet her there, and then travel together to Southern Rhodesia for her to '*have a look at the place.*' He assumed they would live there after they were married. His letter made it all sound possible. Not just possible—exciting.

'*Just think, Darling, we will be living our own lives in a new country. All the other wives on the base will keep you company. It will be such fun. And of course, you won't have to work or worry about safety, as our house will be in an army compound for officers and their families, with a driver to take us wherever we want to go...*'

Talking aloud was easier than wrestling with her thoughts in silence.

'But do you want to go?' she asked the roof.

She remembered her father's letter and his parting words: '*Be true to yourself.*'

'And what does that mean?' she said to the roof.

She thought about Hilda, the lieutenant's attitude, the curt note about her baby.

'How did that make you feel?'

The roof stayed silent.

'There's only one real question, Terri Coulter. What do you want from life?'

She gave a short laugh. 'Oh, is that all?'

The door flew open. Janey flopped onto the other bed, glowing.

'Oh, what a day. Peter and I went... Terri, are you even listening? You don't have someone hiding under there, do you? What were you laughing at when I came in?'

'Nothing. Just life.'

'Oh, is that all?'

Terri laughed again, but this time the sound was blurred by tears.

\* \* \*

As she walked to work on that pleasantly warm morning in early December, with birds singing on a scented breeze, Terri's decision had been made. Her important question was answered—at least for now.

Mohamed was dozing on the veranda as she approached *Chez Elizabeth*. He jumped to his feet, greeting her with his usual broad, toothless, red-stained smile. He drew his shawl tighter around his shoulders.

'Cold,' he said, making an exaggerated shivering gesture. 'Tea?'

Terri had been teaching him some English words and he had taught her a few in Arabic.

'La, daffi,' she replied, which translated as *No, it's warm*. Then she laughed and nodded. 'Yes, let's have some chai.'

Mohamed scurried off. She would miss their morning ritual. She would miss Mohamed. She would miss Egypt.

As Terri sat on the veranda waiting for her chai, Terence's letter came back to her. His vision of military life in Rhodesia did not give her butterflies. She felt no thrill of adventure, of travel, of a new beginning. She just wasn't ready yet.

'I need time,' she said to the cloudless blue sky.

'I need to be at home for a while. I need to take stock.'

This time, the birds sang their approval.

Mohamed looked puzzled when he returned to find her talking to herself. She accepted the proffered clay cup and smiled. There was no point in trying to explain. Terri lounged back in the wicker chair, while her loyal assistant sat cross-legged on the floor beside her. They drank tea in contented silence, just as they did every morning before starting the day's routine.

Terri reassured herself, as she sipped the hot, sweet liquid. She hadn't realised how good it would feel to make a choice—to make *this* choice.

She was going home. Terence would understand. They had their whole lives to be together. Things would work out.

It should have been hard to leave the army. She had loved every minute of it: in Egypt, in Edinburgh, in Guildford. It should have been hard to say no to Terence's plan. She longed to be with him. Terri didn't know what she wanted from the rest of her life, but she knew what she wanted for now. Returning to Glasgow was the right thing to do. In her gut, she knew it was the right choice, the only choice.

She wasn't looking forward to telling Janey. However, becoming the new face of the WRAC recruitment campaign had given her the confidence she thought she lacked, the confidence needed as an officer.

Janey was on her way.

They both were.

Just in opposite directions.

*34. Terri. Perth. 8th December 2020*
*Reflection: The Answers to Hard Questions*

Maureen is in the dining room, wrapping Christmas presents to deliver to the doctors' surgery and a few other places. I like to show my appreciation for all they do. It's nice to be appreciated. I want to help her, but I'm just so wabbit. I can't seem to get out of this chair to do anything today. Honestly, as Mae Brown used to say, *It would sicken your dickie and make your tie squeak.*

We've been out and about in town a lot. It's good to see the shops getting busy again. I can't imagine how the flower business would have survived if I'd still been working when the virus hit. I often fall asleep during the news, and I can't keep up with who's allowed into what bubble these days. But then, what do I know about the price of fish?

It'll be a funny old Christmas. Maureen will be gone, but Colette is coming. She works very hard. I hope I'll have enough energy to look after her. She loves my mince, even at Christmas. I think young Joe will make an appearance on Christmas Day after he leaves his girls. He spends Christmas Eve with them every year. Three of my family are divorced now. It's hard to believe, but there you go. You have to move with the times. Of course, I don't stand for any snash from Paul and young Joe. Paul's wife, Jules, is lovely and very kind to me. I haven't met Joe's new girlfriend yet, but she sounds like a very nice girl. He seems keen and I hope something comes of it this time. I want Joe to be happy. He deserves it. But I also have two daughters-in-law. I can't drop them like a ton of hot bricks just because they're no longer married to my sons. That's not who I am or how I operate.

Maureen asked me a funny question yesterday, or maybe it was the day before—it doesn't matter—but it's been on my mind. She asked me who the love of my life had been. It was a strange question, especially when she thought her dad was the bee's knees. And he was. I didn't answer at first, but when Maureen wants an answer, she keeps probing.

'I suppose it was Terence Warr,' I said eventually, because I suppose it was in a way. But only in that romantic notion of love. Like in the films.

# Small Shoes

We've been talking about him recently. There's a picture of Terence on top of my dressing table upstairs. I've no idea why it's there. I think one of the girls fished it out of my underwear drawer. The family all knew his name and used to laugh at his photograph, in his army uniform and twirling moustache. It never bothered Joe that I kept it. He used to say:

*And on her back, I'd hang a sign,*
*Keep off the grass, this girl is mine.*

Joe knew I loved him, and he loved me. And that was that. I mean, what's true love anyway? Three of my family thought they knew what it was when they walked down the aisle. The fact is, I didn't really know Terence Warr. I met him once for dinner and the rest of our relationship unfolded over a series of letters, even after we were engaged. They'd call it a fling now, and there was certainly no hanky panky. It wouldn't have worked with Terence. I wasn't cut out to be an army wife, doing what I was told and socialising with the other wives. Work was a huge part of my life and that wouldn't have suited Terence. He was handsome and charming, and a Captain in the army. I couldn't believe he was interested in me. He made me swoon. But you have to do more than swoon to survive a marriage. Joe didn't make me swoon—well, not in the same way. But I truly loved him. He knew what made me tick. I don't talk about it much, but I still miss him every day, even though he's been gone for more than twenty years. When my father died, Joe was my rock and that never changed.

I don't want Maureen to get the wrong end of the stick about Terence, so I think it's time to tell her a bit more about how I met her dad. She already knows the C to Z, but I'd like her to know the A to Z, and understand the kind of love we shared. Joe wrote very romantic letters when we were courting, and long after. And when he sang about love, I always knew he was singing to me. Yes, maybe I should get Maureen to ask that question again. And give her a different answer.

I wonder if I'll stop thinking and dreaming about Egypt after Maureen leaves. Sometimes, I can't tell whether I'm in Perth or the Middle East. At my age, that's not a good sign. As if the question about the love of my life wasn't bad enough, Maureen has asked me more than once to talk about why I came home to Glasgow when I was demobbed. I suppose I can see her logic. I told her Terence Warr was the love of my life, albeit in a romantic, unrealistic way. So why did I not agree to demob and meet him in Nairobi?

'I thought all you wanted was to get away from Glasgow?'

That was the truth. I stalled for time.

'Maureen, it was all such a long time ago.'

But she wasn't put off.

'All your stories are of happy times in the army, especially abroad. You had a job you loved. You were respected. You had friends. There was sunshine and holidays, and dances. And there was your handsome captain. What wasn't to like?'

I can't remember exactly how I answered, but I think I said, 'It was the right thing to do.'

Because that was also the truth. I knew it was the right thing to do at the time. I just didn't know how to put it into words. Make Maureen understand. How do you describe *the right thing?* It's a feeling, not a fact. We left it there, but I don't think she was convinced. It upset me, if I'm honest.

I changed the subject and told her about poor Hilda. I had forgotten her name until I started telling the story. It just popped into my head, the way names and words do when you're older. The funny thing is that I wasn't really changing the subject. In my head, Hilda was always associated with my decision to leave Egypt. When I got home, I remembered wanting to learn more about the pregnant Irish girl who came to stay. My father and I were sitting on either side of the fire in the kitchen of Beechgrove Street.

'Something on your mind, Teresa?' He knew me so well.

'Dad, I was thinking about that girl, the pregnant one in Abbotsford Place. I mentioned her in one of my letters."

'You mean Mary?'

I stared into the flames and blurted, 'Would you have thrown me out if I was pregnant?'

My father spilled tea on his lap, clearly shocked by my question.

'Of course not, Teresa. I would never have thrown you out for any reason. We're family and you look after your family. You don't judge them. You should know better than to ask.'

I never forgot his words. Always wise. And he was right—I should never have asked. What happened to Hilda affected me in so many ways. My father wiped the spilled tea with the end of a towel and told me the rest of Mary's story.

'She worked in the dairy. That's how your mum and I knew her. Then she was conscripted to work in the munitions factory on night-shift during the war. Some blighter took advantage of poor Mary. She probably didn't even know what was happening. Thank God, her old man took her back in the end. The baby was due any day and the penny dropped that he was going to be a grandfather.'

There was no difference between Mary and Hilda, except that Mary's story ended happily. I've no idea what happened to Hilda. I hope she eventually found someone to look after her. I worked with The Society of the Innocents in Glasgow after I had my own family. We didn't have all the answers, but we tried to support pregnant girls who had nowhere to turn, or who turned to the wrong people. Girls like Hilda. I may not have remembered her name, but I often thought of her.

I wonder how Maureen is getting on with the wrapping. I hope she remembers to use the red and gold ribbons to decorate the parcels. I might have time for a snooze after all.

## 35. December 1949
### Midnight Mass in Malta

At 0300 hours on December 20th, 1949, HMT *Empire Windrush* sailed into Valletta harbour

Unlike the journey to Egypt, there were no flotillas or noisy klaxons to greet their arrival on that chilly night. As Terri disembarked, she looked back, struggling to distinguish the black sea from the dark sky, except for a few stray stars doing their best to twinkle.

The ship had encountered engine trouble and had to be docked in Valletta for repairs until the 27th of December. This would allow both military personnel and crew to spend Christmas on dry land. The mood among the returning troops was mixed: some were disgruntled at not being home for Christmas, some wished they had stayed in Egypt and some didn't care, as long as there was a celebration. Terri didn't quite fit into any of those groups. It wasn't that she wanted to avoid home. She was just content to have a few days in Malta to gather her thoughts before returning to Glasgow. Christmas was always busy and stressful, no matter where she worked. This year, she was looking forward to walking through the city and attending Midnight Mass on Christmas Eve.

Christmas lunch had been organised by the Major General stationed in Valletta and everyone on board was looking forward to it, even those who would rather be somewhere else. It was not lost on Terri that Hilda had sailed home to England aboard the same ship, with very little to celebrate.

\* \* \*

As she wandered the historic streets of Valletta in the mild winter sunshine, Terri soaked up the festive sights, sounds and traditions. Groups of singers performed Maltese carols on street corners, while shop windows glowed with elaborate nativity cribs. One smiling shopkeeper explained that these cribs, called *Presepju* in Maltese, were part of a tradition dating back to the early 1600s. The sweet aroma of treacle rings from a bakery was too tempting to resist. She ate one while walking along the street, feeling decadent and content.

The Catholic presence in Malta was unmistakable, with churches lining nearly every street. Terri caught her breath at the sight of St Paul's Anglican Pro-Cathedral. She tilted her head to take in its 200-foot spire, soaring like an arrow toward heaven.

\* \* \*

Terri was mortified that her request to attend Midnight Mass had caused such a fuss. She stood at attention before Captain Wishart, the officer responsible for army personnel who had disembarked from the *Windrush*.

'34266 Private Coulter,' she said in response to his first question

'Glasgow, Sir,' in response to his second.

Then, as his eyebrows lifted, *'No Mean City*, Sir'

Officers like Wishart had usually only heard of Glasgow because of the book. The captain flushed. 'Ah. Yes… right. Of course,' he said, eyes dropping to the paper on his desk. 'And you say there's no one else from your ship attending?'

'No, Sir. But I'll be perfectly fine on my own.'

She was tempted to say *No one messes with a girl from 'No Mean City'* but decided against it. The captain looked far too serious for that kind of remark. She wanted permission to attend Mass, not a night in the brig. She stared ahead and waited.

'You'll be assigned two MPs. Officers, gentlemen and Catholics. They will pick you up in the Jeep at 2300 hours and return you safely after the service. Happy Christmas, Coulter.'

\* \* \*

And so it was that Terri attended Midnight Mass in the stunning Valletta Cathedral, flanked by two handsome officers. Hardly the worst company for Christmas Eve.

It had been as difficult to say goodbye to Janey as she had anticipated. They had hugged and promised to keep in touch. Now, as she knelt, she prayed for her family at home, for Janey and Peter, for Dickie, and everyone she had left behind in Egypt. She prayed for Mohamed, whom

Terri knew she would never see again. And a special whispered prayer for Hilda Kelly, wherever she was.

*I'm thinking of you, dear Hilda, on this Christmas Day. I am filled with sadness for your lost baby. I pray life will treat you kindly and that you will be loved and respected, as you deserve to be.*

Lieutenant Compton had seemed disappointed when Terri declined the offer to join the professional army. And Terri, in turn, had been disappointed by the lieutenant's indifference toward Hilda. She had loved every minute of her army life, particularly in Egypt and she would remember it always. It was time to leave, at least for now. Who knew what the future would bring? Sometimes you simply had to play it by ear and choose a direction on instinct. This was one of those times and her instincts had led her to the ATS. They hadn't let her down yet.

Terri had been unable to trace a forwarding address for her friend. The girls in Hilda's hut had no idea and the powers that be would not provide one. She looked up at the ornate altar surrounded by festive flowers and felt at peace for the first time in weeks: at peace with herself, and with the world. It wasn't a perfect world, but that was okay.

\* \* \*

The Jeep stopped in front of her accommodation and the two officers insisted on escorting Terri to the front door.

'Goodnight, Gentlemen. Happy Christmas. And… thank you for a lovely evening,' she told the handsome duo, her voice a little louder than necessary.

It was late, but Christmas revellers were still enjoying themselves. As she made her way slowly through the lobby, Terri couldn't help basking in the looks of admiration from the girls in the bar. She had learned a thing or two from Janey Dodds, after all.

*I wonder if Glasgow is ready for the new Terri Coulter,* she whispered to herself as she climbed the stairs to bed.

## 36. Maureen. Perth. 10th December 2020
### *Bright Day and Dark Night*

**11:15 a.m.**

The fancy Christmas bags, bought in bulk from the card shop, are in the hall, packed and ready for delivery. We stand with our coats on, Mum in red to mark the occasion. She admires the scene.

'I don't think I've ever been more organised for Christmas.'

I believe her. A large drawer at the side of her bed is crammed with a miscellany of potential gifts collected over the year, but they rarely make it into the light of day before January or February. Today is a major achievement and I allow myself a pat on the back. The nuns taught us self-praise was no honour—or something along those lines—but I am useless at wrapping presents and I worked hard to fill those fancy bags. Mum supervised from the safety of her office chair in the next room, instructing and interfering at regular intervals. But it was worth it to see the look of triumph on her face this morning.

'Okay, let's get the sleigh packed and try to drop Santa's goodies down the right chimneys,' I say, lifting the first batch of bags.

Mum may not be the most organised with Christmas presents, but she never forgets anyone. Not just the doctors and nurses at the surgery, but every receptionist. Not just the hospital consultant—his secretary. Not just the pharmacist and assistants—the man who delivers her medication. The same goes for her ileostomy supplies and audiology products. And of course, the neighbours and their families, the window cleaner, the gardener, the refuse collectors, the postman, and probably others I know nothing about. She has little money these days and her gifts are not extravagant, but the giving is what matters to her. My brothers occasionally get frustrated:

'What am I supposed to do with another gadget from the pound shop?'

'I don't need anything. I wish Mum would spend the money on herself.'

Having heard so many stories from her childhood, I wonder if the ability to give is, in itself, a kind of gift. Not in any sanctimonious way, but as a practical expression shaped by her history.

'Looking at this lot won't get it shifted,' says Mum.

The boss is back.

\* \* \*

**6 p.m. that evening**

Lemon sole for dinner, which I hope Mum will eat. We are in our usual places in the living room, me with red wine, Mum with a glass of Lindisfarne mead. We munch on crisps and mull over the day.

Mum raises her glass. 'Here's to you, Maureen. I could never have done it without you. A good job well done. And it's only the 10th of December. I still can't believe it.'

She laughs, takes a sip. 'Lovely. Stocks are running low. I hope Paul sends a bottle for my Christmas.'

I know two bottles are already en route, but say nothing. I am thinking about tomorrow. About leaving.

These weeks have been special, filled with shared laughter and animated discussion. Of course, some days were hard. Days when Mum would not or could not eat. Days when she looked frail, unable to talk. Days when I did not know what to say, how to help. Days when my back ached from bending, or my heart ached for no reason, or lots of reasons. But there have been so many unexpected treasures: gallivanting around town, stopping for lattes, chatting in vibrant coffee shops. Just ordinary days, filled with fun and love. Those are the memories I want to bottle and keep. Mum is quiet now. I suspect she is thinking about tomorrow, too.

I feel the usual swirl of emotions: the thought of being home with Martin and the boys for Christmas lifts me, yet the thought of leaving Mum, especially at Christmas, fills me with dread. I try to lighten the mood for us both.

'Colette will be here in a few days. Make sure you've got your hair and makeup done. Otherwise, I'll get the blame for letting standards slip.'

Mum plays along. 'Yes, I'll do my best or there'll be wigs on the green! She'll come in like a whirlwind and notice everything. She can wrap the presents for the neighbours and the family. That'll keep her busy. Pity she doesn't drive. My shopping days are over until you get back.'

'I think we've done enough shopping damage for now, don't you, Mum? It's alright for you. I'll be in quarantine for two weeks and I haven't bought a single Christmas present. No point. I can't fit another thing into my rucksack anyway. Right then, this fish won't cook itself.'

\* \* \*

**About 11.30 p.m.**

I am in bed, cosy under the duvet, the electric blanket working its magic. A long soak eased my back, still throbbing from all the bag-carrying. I am packed and ready for the morning. I don't want to keep Lorna waiting. Barney is working tomorrow. I said goodbye to him last night when he and Gus arrived on their walk. He took the wee car back home, where I have no doubt it was warmly welcomed by his daughters. Without it, we could not have done the shopping or the Santa bag deliveries. Or stopped for all those lattes. Or relished that precious freedom: out in the world on our small adventures, making unexpected memories together. I turn off the blanket and pull the duvet up to my chin.

Mum was not fit enough to climb out of the car and greet the recipients of her gift bags, but every single one instructed me to pass on their kind regards and wish Mrs Reilly a Happy Christmas. Her smile broadened with every message. We also paused mid-delivery for a latte and carrot cake at the Mustard Seed with Mum's Keep Fit pals, Mary and Una. Yes, it was a good day and I am delighted this visit concluded on such a positive note.

As I switch off the lamp, I hear Dad's words in my head, the ones he always said on days like this: *God is in His Heaven, all's right with the world.* I think they were written by Robert Browning.

I turn on my side, ready for sleep. And WHAM!

A sudden, crashing, red-hot, paralysing pain explodes in my back and down my right leg.

I can't breathe. I can't move. All's not right with the world after all, Dad!

Impossible to Fill

## *Glasgow Tram*
## *University via Charing Cross*

# PART 3
## *GROWING WISER*

## 1. *Maureen. Perth. 16th December 2020*
### *I am the Patient*

Today is December 16th. It is the first day I have lifted a pen or even thought about writing a single word since the lightning strike. Since the vice-like back pain that struck with sudden, breath-stealing viciousness the night before my return to Sligo for Christmas. My brain remains fuddled, my thoughts like scraps of paper dancing in the breeze. I cannot grasp them. Sometimes, I can't even see them. I have been consumed by my pain: trying to avoid it, control it, manage it and accept it. Most of all, I am exhausted by it. But today I am writing, and it feels good. It feels normal.

My memory of that night is vague and disjointed. Out of sequence. Like the trailer for a bad film. I must have shouted when the initial spasm hit because Mum was standing beside my bed. I don't remember what she said, but I have a clear vision of me pleading, barely above a whisper, afraid to use even my vocal muscles. Mum is not wearing her hearing aids. She cannot hear me.

I just repeat the words 'My back. My back. Help me. Help me.'

She understands, but she can't help. Poor Mum. What a fright to give her in the middle of the night. I reach for her. A savage fist digs deep into my spine and twists it in a vice-like clamp. I scream. I upset Mum. She is crying.

God, now that I am documenting it, my behaviour was pathetic. In my defence, even the slightest movement caused another wave of pain, another white-hot spasm. Another strike by the vice.

Nothing makes sense. I think of that other incident—accident. When my Nissan Micra was hit by a Land Rover. The shock. Thinking, this isn't happening. Can I please go back? Just five minutes? Just one minute? Just ten seconds? Please. I was going home from work. I am going home tomorrow. I am going nowhere.

I cannot see Mum properly, locked in an awkward position, partially facing the other way. The brutal fist hovers, poised to clench with the slightest provocation. I concentrate on being still. I concentrate on slowing my breathing. I hear her voice soothing me. I absorb its comfort, its reassuring tone. I am a child again. I am hurt, but my mum is here. I will be ok. Everything will be ok.

She holds my hand. Her grasp is light, but it feels strong. It feels safe.

I concentrate on being still. I concentrate on slowing my breathing.

I hear the word: 'Ambulance.'

I say, 'No, No fuss. No ambulance. No hospital.'

But the vice feels the movement. Hears the voice. WHAM! It reaches inside my body. Twisting, turning, tightening, cramping. I TOLD YOU NOT TO MOVE.

Mum is crying again. My poor wee mum. This is so unfair.

I concentrate on being still. I concentrate on slowing my breathing.

'You don't get to keep me in Perth by shipping me off to hospital.' I say, loud enough for her to hear, but not loud enough to annoy the vice. *An attempt at humour. I must be ok.*

The rest of the night is foggy. After a few hours, I begin to analyse the pain. It starts in my lower back, travels down over my backside and thigh, across my knee and down the front of my right leg into my foot. I can stave off most of the spasms if I stay completely still. It is harder than it sounds.

I am calm now. I am not dying. I close my eyes.

As I add a script to the bad film clips of my memory of that night, I am ashamed that I cannot remember if Mum goes back to bed, sits down, or stands beside the bed all night. I just know her presence is my anchor.

I become aware of another sensation. An insidious approach this time. Not sudden or dramatic. Quiet and persistent. Oh no.

*I am going to have to get out of this bed or wet it. Which is it to be?*

The bathroom is adjacent to my bedroom. Only a few steps. It might as well be another country. I procrastinate for as long as possible.

'I can't do it, Mum,' I wail like a baby. 'I can't do it.'

'Yes, you can, Maureen. We'll do it together.'

She is still here beside me.

Where has my frail, terminally ill mother gone? First, she was the reassurance and comfort from my childhood. Now, she is calm and authoritative. This is *my* voice, my nursing voice, the one I sometimes use when caring for Mum. The world has turned upside down in the space of a few seconds. *I am the patient. I don't like it.*

I choose pain over humiliation. I imagine my brother Barney arriving in the morning, finding me in a pool of urine. It spurs me on. Somehow, we reach that other country, shuffling like a pair of conjoined turtles. I am not paralysed. My back is in spasm. It is not earth-shattering, just bloody sore. But there is no way I will be home for Christmas. And that is a different kind of pain.

## 2. Maureen. Perth. 18th December 2020
### *Adjustment*

There was my brother Barney early the next morning. There was a follow-up visit from his GP colleague, Johnny, who had agreed to look after me. There was a phone call to tell Martin the news. There was the realisation that I was not going home for Christmas. There were tears of self-pity. Eventually, there was some relief from the pain.

Sleep deprivation is debilitating. As the cocktail of prescribed medication kicked in, I would close my eyes and begin sinking into peaceful nothingness. But the vice was vigilant. Devious. Clever. Waiting until I was fully asleep, then WHAM! It would dive into every muscle and sinew from my back to the toes on my right foot, wrenching me awake. Laughing. Gloating.

My brother Paul, a retired consultant rheumatologist, advises the best way to manage nerve pain is to use distraction tactics. Thus begins a macabre game between me and the cruel vice. It strikes without warning, squeezing and contorting. I act quickly, applying either Deep Heat or Deep Freeze. Those red and blue tubes become my weapons.

*'Right, you bastard, you want heat, well, this is cold, so fuck off.'*
Or
*'Right, you bastard, you anticipate cold, well, this is heat, so suck it up.'*
And then I became even more cunning.
*'Right, you bastard, you are getting used to the creams, well, this is a tap with gushing, freezing water. Let's see you deal with that!'*

On reflection, I think I was half out of my mind. Medication, pain and lack of sleep are a powerful combination, and not in a good way. Sometimes, it felt as though I was in a claustrophobic tunnel with no light at the end. But of course, there was a light, even if it was blurred. And that light was kindness and love. I realise, even as I write these words, that they sound trite and schmaltzy, like a phrase from a self-help book. But I have to document the truth as I remember it. And that is what I remember amid the awfulness of those days.

\* \* \*

It had been planned that Colette would arrive on 13th December to look after Mum while I was at home in Ireland for Christmas. Instead, on her arrival, she found me in bed in a distressed state, and Mum, who was consumed with worry about my distressed state. Two patients for the price of one. Not exactly a bargain. It is fair to say my sister is not the *nursing type*. However, she appeared like an angel to me that day, which may or may not have been drug induced. Every morning, Colette gave Mum her breakfast in bed and then produced a tray for me. We ate and chatted before she left to help Mum and attend to the daily domestic chores. I continued my nighttime routine: getting up and down to apply hot and cold cream or thrust my leg under the tap. But the vice gradually loosened its grip, the fog began to clear, and the light at the end of the tunnel became closer each day.

As I write, it is one week until Christmas Day. I can mobilise with my dad's walking stick, which he hated and never used. I cannot share a bed with Colette in my current state, so she has moved into the wee room that was my writing space. My brain is too fuzzy to write anything sensible, but I miss listening to Mum's stories. They make me feel as if we are stepping into Doctor Who's TARDIS and travelling together to a world long gone but not lost. In those moments, there is no cancer, no looming farewell, only the reality we create in images and words. It strengthens my connection with my mother in a way I could never have anticipated. I miss that feeling. I am not ready to let it go. Not yet.

Colette has been cleaning the house, polishing the silver and putting up the Christmas tree. She works with frenetic energy, but the atmosphere can be tense at times. Mum and I agree she needs a break before she blows a gasket, with us in the firing line. Tomorrow, if Colette takes a well-earned rest and a trip into town, I will focus my fuddled brain and jump back into the TARDIS with Mum. It will know where to take us, even if I cannot recall our previous destination. I have a vague memory of us discussing Terri adjusting to life in Glasgow after de-mobbing in 1950. I toss my stick onto the sofa and manoeuvre myself down beside it. The idea of Mum adjusting to life after Egypt and me adjusting to life after the lightning strike makes me smile. Very different scenarios, and yet, not so different. Isn't life just one long series of adjustments? Or maybe the drugs are turning me into a philosopher. Who cares?

There's an old proverb that says *It's an ill wind that blows nobody any good.* In my case, it felt more like a hurricane. My back injury means I will spend Christmas with my sister and my mum. It will be her last. I want to treasure this unexpected gift of time, rather than dwell on the disappointment of not being in Sligo as planned. I will take a leaf out of Mum's book and simply *play it by ear!*

## 3. Terri. Bridgeton. March 1950
### *Back to Reality*

The basin of water reached just over Terri's ankles as she stood in the scullery. The water was warm, but she shivered as she ran the cloth up and down her arms, around her abdomen, then down her tanned legs. She towel-dried quickly, wary of interruption. It was the daily routine she had followed before joining the army, yet now she felt awkward, self-conscious and freezing. It wasn't that she had grown used to plush surroundings or private bathrooms. Far from it. But standing in a basin in a tiny room next to the kitchen felt undignified in a way she had never noticed before.

She hated the toilet on the landing: the stench of urine, the newspaper squares in place of toilet paper, the lack of cleanliness. Although she had shared toilets with a lot more people than in Beechgrove Street or the Gorbals, army latrines were pristine. It was always someone's job to keep them clean or face the consequences. She heard the family stirring. As she rushed to dress, Terri prayed she would settle soon and stop thinking about the life she had left behind.

After a week in Brighton filling in forms and undergoing medicals, w/342468 Private Coulter T.J. No. 2 Squadron, Scottish Command Signals, Royal Corps of Signals, was officially demobbed and rejoined civilian life on 6 February 1950. When she saw her father waiting at Central Station, her heart almost burst with happiness. He wore his good grey suit and a hat that looked new and stylish. At first, he seemed older, but when he smiled, the years and miles between them vanished. She ran to him, flinging her suitcase onto the platform and her arms around her favourite man in all the world.

'Oh Dad, I can't believe you're here. I've missed you so much! But how did you know which train I'd be on? I didn't tell you. I didn't want a fuss. Yet here you are and I couldn't be more pleased. Did I mention that I've missed you?'

Alec's face creased into another beaming smile. He bent to pick up her suitcase, watched closely by Terri, who knew the move was to hide his moist eyes.

'A state secret, Teresa,' he said, lifting his head, and the case. 'I'll have to kill you if I divulge my source.'

They laughed together and linked arms, pushing through the busy station crowds. What a different atmosphere from the day she boarded the train for Guildford. This time, the tears he tried to hide were happy ones. It felt good to be home.

Tina had clearly been to the hairdresser, her short, wavy hair with a hint of colour and neatly styled. She wore a green gingham dress and a fitted yellow cardigan and looked younger than Terri remembered. Though touched in a way she couldn't quite explain, Terri said nothing. Her mother was not one for compliments and would only have deflected one with a sharp remark. Terri noticed and appreciated her mother's effort in silence.

'Hello, Teresa. You look good,' Tina said, holding out her arms. 'Army life must have suited you. Young Alec is doing his National Service now, too, you know. But I suppose your father's told you all about it in one of those long letters of his.'

Terri thought she caught a note of irritation, but ignored it.

'Mind you, Alec's only in Stirling, so he gets to come home on holiday. Of course, it's not as exotic as Egypt, so it wouldn't have suited you.'

Yes. Definitely more than a hint of irritation. Her mother couldn't help herself. She walked towards the scullery, satisfied she had made her point, whatever it was. Then she turned and added, 'I've got the fritters in batter, ready for the pan. Nice and crisp. Just the way you like them. Sit yourself down. It's good to have you back.'

It was hard to fathom Tina Coulter, so Terri didn't try. She probably regretted her comments, but if they were in her head, they were bound to come out of her mouth. That was just how she was.

'Thanks, Mum. Oh... and by the way... I like to be called Terri now... Terri with an i,' she called from the kitchen table. Her timing was not ideal, but there was never going to be a good time. Better to get it out there. Then came the panic. *Oh God, I'm turning into my mother. Am I going to be just like her?*

From the corner of her eye, she saw her father's forehead wrinkle and his eyebrows draw together, a sign he was worried Tina might flare up. Terri rushed to clarify.

'But I don't expect you and Dad to call me Terri. Obviously. Teresa's fine. It's the name I was born with and there's nothing wrong with it. I just fancied a change. Thought I should let you know in case you hear someone use it.'

Her father's smile, usually open and sincere, turned into his other one: the half-hearted version he reserved for sidestepping conflict with Tina.

'That's lovely, Dear. Your mother and I will call you Teresa. But Terri is also a lovely name.'

Of course, her mother had the last word, shouting from the scullery over the sound of the crackling chip pan. 'Terri's a boy's name. With or without an i.'

That was the end of that conversation.

*　*　*

The day after she arrived in Glasgow, Terri went to Bamber's to ask about her job. At her debriefing in Brighton, they had been told employers were obliged to reinstate them because they had completed military service. Still, she knew Ava, the girl who had taken her place. After all, Terri had trained her. But she needn't have worried. Ava was cooperative and understanding, saying she had been expecting the change. Mr. Thompson's face lit up when Terri entered the shop.

'Miss Coulter, what a joy to see you back where you belong. When can you start?'

They agreed on a few days of crossover with Ava working for a further week. Mr. Thompson confided that they had been looking for a reason to let the girl go because she was a member of a union.

'…and as you know, Miss Coulter, we are not a unionised shop.'

His tone shifted from conspiratorial to flamboyant. 'I should add that I love the name change. Terri suits you, Darling. Much more panache than Teresa. A rose by any other name, as the Bard would say. But of course, you will continue to be Miss Coulter at work.'

He bounded off to take Mrs. Lambert from under the large hairdryer. Terri noticed more dryers than before and that the shop had been painted and modernised. Mrs. Skinner's glass cabinet was gone, replaced by a small table for the cash register and appointment book, with shelves of cosmetics and perfumes behind it.

Small Shoes

Terri didn't spend the week before returning to work twiddling her thumbs. She visited the Glasgow and West of Scotland Commercial College, opened while she had been away. She was interested in the City and Guilds Diploma in Hairdressing and arranged a meeting with Mr. Templeton, who had recently returned from two years' conscription in the Royal Navy.

'You sound like you've plenty of practical experience, Miss Coulter,' he said. 'This diploma is a three-year course, with written and practical exams each year. Judging by what you've told me, I believe you could join the third year directly. Classes start the week after Easter... let's see...'

He consulted a large wall calendar. 'Tuesday the 18th of April. Classes are every Tuesday and Thursday at 7 p.m. How does that sound?'

Before she could take it all in, he stood to shake her hand. His smile was warm and genuine. Terri's 'Thank you, Mr. Templeton' felt inadequate. She shook his hand enthusiastically, barely able to stop herself from hugging him or dancing around the room.

When she found her voice again, Terri straightened her shoulders, the posture of attention still ingrained. 'I'm ready, willing and able to start any time, Mr. Templeton. I feel confident I'll pass the final exams this year. I won't let you down.'

Thankfully, the tears didn't come until she closed the office door and stood in the bustling corridor. She thought of her two old teachers, Mrs Dixon and Mr Douglas.

*I won't let you down either,* she thought.

Mr. Thompson was delighted when Terri shared the news on her first day back at work. She had worried he might think she was getting above herself, but he clapped his hands with glee.

'I'd have expected no less from you, Miss Terri Coulter. But you'll have to wait until I retire if you're hoping to take over my job. Now... are you too high and mighty to make the coffee?'

\* \* \*

## Teresa. Commercial College, Glasgow. 18th April 1950

The classroom was large and well-lit, but under-heated. Terri looked at the four rows of desks, neatly spaced, unlike Sacred Heart School, where they were crammed together. She was early, but a few students already sat with notepads open. She chose a desk in the middle and hoped she wasn't encroaching on someone's territory.

'I haven't seen you here before. My name is Sheila. Sheila Thompson.'

The girl with neatly-styled auburn hair and slightly protruding front teeth smiled and reached across from her desk. Terri shook her hand, trying to channel the confidence the army had taught: firm handshake, eye contact. But her sweaty palms betrayed her nerves.

'Terri Coulter. First evening class. I'm joining the final year. I hope I'm up to it. Is this someone's seat?'

Sheila didn't seem to notice her anxiety. She was friendly and engaging.

'Wow, that's impressive. You must be really good. They wouldn't let you in otherwise. This seat's normally free. It's been waiting for you, Terri Coulter. Maybe I'll finally pass my exams this year!'

Sheila laughed, a distinctive laugh that made her teeth more prominent and her eyes crinkle. Terri began to relax, though her senses remained alert. It reminded her of school days, waiting for the teacher to arrive, body tingling with the anticipation of learning something new.

She took her brand new notebook and brand new pen from her brand new briefcase. She was ready to begin.

## 4. Terri. Perth. 19th December 2020
### *Reflection: Give and Take*

Colette has gone into town. I'm pleased she's having a break. She's been working like ten men and a wee fella since she arrived. Colette's a shopper, like me. When I travel to Monaco, she takes me down to the luxurious Metropole in Monte Carlo. We wander around but don't buy much. It's too expensive. And when you look through the shop windows, it's hard to work out what they're selling. I like going to the markets in Italy or Menton, where I always buy towels or scarves for the Keep Fit ladies. Then we have lunch looking out at the sea. It's odd to think I won't be back in Monaco. I've attended lots of the ISM School graduation ceremonies when Colette is in charge of the choir. I get to dress up and Colette's friends make a big fuss of me. It's very different from the way I left school at fourteen, without so much as a handshake or by-your-leave. But I've done the best I could. Maureen asked me recently if I had any regrets. It came out of the blue, as her questions sometimes do. She doesn't miss and hit the wall!

'No,' I said without hesitating. I saw the look of shock on her face and thought I'd better explain.

'I suppose I've always lived every day as it comes… played it by ear. Still do. But I also made the most of every opportunity. That's why I've no regrets.'

Maureen seemed happy with that, but I wasn't finished.

'I believe in mind over matter. I also think we need a bit of luck. And I've been lucky all my life. Still am.'

Maureen has gone to make us a latte while Colette is out. Poor Maureen. I feel guilty. If she wasn't here looking after me, her back wouldn't have gone. I felt useless at the time. I couldn't do anything for her. She's out of bed now and can walk with Joe's old stick, but she won't be at home for Christmas. I get upset when I think about that. It isn't fair. She says her back was already bad from years of nursing, but I don't believe her. And the worst of it is, I'm thrilled she'll be here for Christmas. That makes me feel even more guilty. I told her it was my fault, but she got mad.

'Mum, you were always there for me, and for all of us. You were there every time I had one of the kids or moved house. And God knows how many times you helped Colette move from one apartment to another in Geneva or France. You ferried Paul and Barney up and down to Aberdeen University when they were medical students. And you worked side by side with young Joe in the shop for 14 years. You are allowed to be looked after for a change. It is not a chore, it's what we want to do. It's what I want to do. I'm here because I want to be here, back pain or not.'

It was a lovely speech and I suppose those things might be true. But they happened a long time ago. I know Maureen means what she says, but she forgets she's not as young as she used to be and much older than I was when I helped the family in the ways she described. I've tried to stay independent because I like making my own decisions and doing things my way, as Frank Sinatra would say. And of course, I'd rather look after them than the other way round. I still worry about them all.

Maureen comes in with the coffee and custard tarts. I think she's glad of the chance to talk about the old days without Colette here to add her twopence worth. I watch her struggling to walk and sit down, yet she looks more like her old self. I'm trying to remember where we left off. I want to make it easy for her, but I don't know how or where to start. Were we talking about the Middle East, or maybe Terence Warr? No, I remember now—I was back in Glasgow and about to tell her how I met her dad. He liked to quote Rabbie Burns and was particularly fond of this one:

*Gather ye rosebuds while ye may,*
*Old Time is still a-flying,*
*And this same flower that smiles today*
*Tomorrow will be dying.*

You were so right, Joe!

## 5. Terri. Maryhill, Glasgow. August 1950
### Terri meets Joe

Terri stood close to the wall of the large Parochial Hall attached to the Church of the Immaculate Conception in Maryhill. She was trying to keep a low profile and wondering how her friend, Sheila, had persuaded her to come tonight. It was an 80th birthday celebration for a man called Tom Boyle, the musical director of the church choir.

'Oh, please, Terri. My aunt was supposed to go with her friend, who sings in the choir. Her friend can't go now and my aunt won't go without her because they'll all be Catholic. She gave the invitations to me. I said I would go, but I don't know a soul there. You can't let me attend an elderly man's birthday party on my own. Pleeeeeease!'

They were having lunch together in Bamber's. Sheila Thompson from her evening class now worked there, thanks to Terri's recommendation.

'You should be on the stage. Or you could always join the choir and then you'll know everyone at Mr. Boyle's birthday bash. Imagine...all those lovely Catholics. Your aunt would be thrilled. Anyway, why would either of us want to be seen at an 80th birthday party?'

'Well, we know his daughter, Mrs. Reilly, who comes in to have her hair done. She's the nice lady in the wheelchair. Mind you, I think she's a bit wary of you. Maybe it's because you've been in the army. You know what they say about army girls, especially the ones who travelled abroad.'

Terri was scanning the newspaper and had noticed a hair colouring course in London with Wella Rapid. Ignoring Sheila, she said, 'This looks quite...'

The bullet of rolled up bread from Sheila's sandwich hit her on the forehead and landed in her lap.

'Careful, Miss Thompson. Just because you share your name with our senior stylist—who only gave you a job here on my say-so—doesn't mean he'll tolerate sandwich throwing. And incidentally, I heard your snidey comment.'

And with that, Terri tore the crust from her sandwich and was about to throw it in Sheila's direction, when Mr. Thompson came into the back shop.

'God, I'm as parched as the Sahara. Are you two nearly finished?'

Terri stuffed the crust into her mouth and said 'Mmm' as discreetly as she could, then washed her cup and plate without daring to look at her friend. She was helping Mrs. Delaney take off her coat in the salon when Sheila passed behind her and said, 'I'll take that as a yes, then.'

\* \* \*

So here she was, in Maryhill Church Hall, trying to melt into the wallpaper while Sheila, who had gone off to find them a drink, was deep in conversation with an auburn-haired young man. She watched as they smiled at each other. Then she saw Sheila, pointing a finger in her direction and heading towards Terri with the young man in tow. No sign of a drink.

'Terri, this is Joe Reilly. He's in the choir, but he's also Mr. Boyle's grandson. And he has a beautiful baritone voice.'

The young man was obviously embarrassed at the gushing compliment and Terri wondered how Sheila knew about his voice, beautiful or not? He stood between them with nothing to say after shaking Terri's hand and mumbling, 'Pleased to meet you.'

After a few minutes of awkward silence, Joe spotted an elderly lady standing on her own and quickly excused himself.

'She's my Aunt Nellie. She's quite deaf and finds large crowds difficult,' he said by way of explanation before walking away.

'Looks like she's not the only one,' Terri said, more to herself than Sheila. Then she noticed his limp. Joe Reilly wore a large black boot on his left foot, which made him tilt to one side when he walked. She instantly wanted to grab back her comment. Thankfully, Sheila's attention had been distracted by yet another young man across the room.

'I'll just go and get us a drink.'

'That's what you said last…' but Sheila had disappeared into the crowd.

By ten o'clock, Terri was more than ready to abandon the party and decided to leave her friend to her own devices. Unlike her aunt, Sheila seemed to have no difficulty mingling with Catholics. She spotted Mr. Boyle's daughter sitting in the middle of a small group.

'I have to go now, Mrs. Reilly, but I had a lovely evening. Please convey my thanks to the family for inviting me.'

Mrs Reilly looked up from her wheelchair and smiled. She was wearing a fur piece with the head of a small animal dangling at the end, probably a mink. Terri wasn't sure if she was imagining it, but Mrs. Reilly's smile did not seem to reach her eyes, making her look formidable, especially with a dead animal around her neck. *Maybe she's just tired or in pain,* Terri thought. After all, Mrs. Reilly had multiple sclerosis. She was about to turn and go when a tall, distinguished-looking man wearing a dinner suit, white shirt and black bow tie, came striding over. Unlike his wife, Mr Reilly's smile held genuine warmth as he firmly shook Terri's hand.

'Did I hear you say you were leaving, Miss Coulter? We can't let you wander the streets on your own at this time of night now, can we? Joe will drive you home.'

Terri tried to tell him there was no need and that she was used to travelling alone at night. She had no intention of spending a whole car journey in silence with Joe Reilly. But her efforts were to no avail. Bernard Reilly had already summoned his son and the young man with the limp was coming towards her. This time, she noticed the striking auburn colour of his curly hair. She had to admit he had a kind face.

They sat in his father's comfortable Rover, each struggling for conversation.

'Bridgeton. Oh. I've never been there,' he said when Terri told him the address.

She could see the side of his face as he stared through the windscreen, noting the look of disapproval.

'No, I don't suppose you have,' she said.

'Have you lived there long?' he asked.

'Since we moved from The Gorbals.'

She scrutinised his face for a reaction. If he thought Bridgeton was bad, he would surely raise an eyebrow at The Gorbals. None. She knew it was cheeky, but added, 'Just as well you don't have to drop me there. Gangs on every corner, you know.'

Terri suspected Joe Reilly was well aware of her sarcasm when he replied, deadpan, 'I always carry a switchblade in my dinner jacket pocket. Just in case of such eventualities.'

It was Terri's turn to look shocked. Then they both burst out laughing. The barrier of tension between them dissolved and Terri Coulter felt an unexpected flutter.

After their initial slow start, they found plenty to talk about on the journey to Beechgrove Street. It turned out they shared a love of theatre. Terri told him about her involvement with GHQ productions in Ismailia, and how her work in Bamber's gave her access to some performances in Glasgow venues. Joe was duly impressed and reciprocated by telling her he was a member of The Savoy Club, an amateur musical theatre company. Terri was quick to inform Joe that this was where they differed.

'Don't get the wrong end of the stick, Joe Reilly. I have no voice and no acting ability whatsoever.'

'From the very little I know of you, Teresa Coulter, I very much doubt that. I think you are a natural performer and have all the attributes required of a leading lady.'

Terri knew he was flirting, but it was innocent. There was no harm in enjoying some banter. She would probably never see him again anyway.

'And just to be clear,' she said, with more than a hint of mischief, 'I have no intention of joining your grandfather's choir…even if you are renowned for your beautiful baritone voice.'

Without missing a beat, her chauffeur said, 'Pity. The sopranos are all over sixty and most of the altos have moustaches.'

'That is such a pathetically male comment, not to mention very unkind, Mr Reilly. I'm surprised at you.'

The car turned off London Road. 'It's the next turn on the right,' she said.

'Right it is then,' he said. She noticed his voice had lost its playful edge.

The evening had ended. The car stopped outside her tenement. A puddle underneath the towering gas lamp beside the car shimmered like a tiny lake. They sat, unsure what to do next, each waiting for the other to speak, neither wanting to be the first to say goodnight. A different kind of silence from earlier in the evening.

'What happened to your leg?' Terri blurted, instantly regretting it.

She wasn't sure whether Joe was happy to talk about it or just keen to keep the conversation going a little longer. But he explained how he had contracted tuberculosis as a boy and spent two years in the hospital.

'They removed my left hip, which, in turn, shortened my leg,' he said. 'I'm 5ft 10 ½ on the right side and… well… the other side depends on whether or not I'm wearing my big boot.'

Terri knew he was trying to make light of it, but even in the dim light, she noticed sadness in his hazel eyes. Terri guessed it was not a subject he often discussed and she was grateful he had shared the story. She was about to say something when he added, 'I was only seven. At first, I used to wonder what I had done wrong to be taken away from home.'

There was no way to respond. She squeezed his hand.

That night in bed, Terri asked herself why she had felt grateful. Why should she be grateful that a man she had never met before had told her something so intimate about himself? Joe had walked her to the top of the outside stairs. He hadn't asked her for a date. He simply smiled and said,

'I'll see you anon, Teresa Coulter.'

She did not ask how he planned to see her. Yet, as she closed her eyes that night, Terri knew Joe Reilly would make it happen. And that was fine with her.

## 6. Maureen. Perth. 31st December 2020
## The Festive Season?

Covid has made this a very different Festive Season for everyone, not just me. I am content to be with Mum and my family in Scotland, but miss Martin and my family in Ireland. Christmas Day was spent with my cousin, Lorna, and her husband and son, known to all as the 3Gs. Mum made sure she looked her best—*tickety boo* as she would say. She wore a beautiful black and white outfit, accompanied by a red scarf and matching red, snazzy ankle boots. I wilted with pain as the day progressed. On the plus side, it was a tonic to see Mum playing Giant Snakes and Ladders after our sumptuous dinner. As I watched her throw the enormous dice, I thought of all the years she had worked in the flower shop until late on Christmas Eve.

Flowers are pretty to look at, but working with them is messy and tough. Every Christmas, Mum came home with soil under her nails and scratches from thorns, not to mention muscles screaming from lack of rest. Even after a long day, she would sit at home making bows for the bouquets, her hands moving so fast it was like watching a magic trick. By the end of the evening, she often disappeared into a cloud of colourful ribbon. Christmas meant business and business was a tyrant. But what I remember most about our mum on Christmas Day itself was her transformation. She looked as excited as we felt, fully engaged with the day, hair and makeup immaculate, and dressed in something festive and elegant. It was hard to reconcile this radiant vision with the drudgery of the preceding weeks and frantic final days. I remember her beautiful smile on Christmas morning, as if she had slept all night instead of not at all. Thankfully, there is no business now, but nothing else has changed—especially the smile.

A new year will dawn tomorrow: 2021. I cannot let the day pass without an entry in my journal. I am sitting at my tiny bedside desk. The setup is unsuitable and even more uncomfortable than the suitcase and tray. God, I miss my beautiful desk at home. I miss Martin and the family.

I stare at the page in front of me. It is blank and intimidating. I try to write something meaningful, write anything at all. But the page returns my stare, belligerently blank. On 1st January 2020, I couldn't wait to open this journal, holding it in my hands, smelling its pages. There was something exhilarating about the idea of 2020. It felt positive and clear, like 20:20 vision. I turn back to that first page of the year and read aloud:

*1st January 2020, the New Year, a new decade. It is a beautiful, calm morning in the Glencar Valley, bright with optimism and promise. I have my blank page of hope, of all that is to come. And, as I sit at my desk with the sun streaming onto the paper, I am a very content woman.*

And indeed, I was a very content woman. Mum and my closest friend, Clare, both had cancer, but they were stable at the time. Sarah, our beautiful daughter, was coming home from Dubai in mid-April to be married and I planned to retire at the end of March to prioritise the wedding. I was determined to relish every moment without the stress of work. It was to be a whole new chapter in my life. I would write, and Martin and I would celebrate our 40th wedding anniversary in September 2020, with a holiday somewhere warm and romantic. We might even stay for a whole month. Why not? Of course, that was before Martin's cancer diagnosis. Before Covid. Before Mum was deemed to be *terminally ill*. Before plans became obsolete. Robert Burns, the famous Scottish poet, wrote:

*The best-laid plans o' mice and men*
*Gang aft agley.*

I think it is fair to say that 2020 went more than a little 'agley' for me, and for the whole world!

Sarah turned thirty yesterday. She and Niall will marry next year, no matter how many guests are permitted to attend. Currently, the limit is twenty-five, a far cry from the 200 invitations sent out for the original date. However, in the context of Covid-related devastation, a postponed wedding is a disappointment, not a travesty.

I recall one news report about a grieving widow at her husband's funeral. She sat alone on a church pew. Aware of his mother's distress, her son moved from his assigned seat to comfort her. The funeral director intervened. Covid regulations. The deep sorrow and palpable grief of that family felt symbolic of our lost humanity as well as lost lives. I cried for the mother and son. I cried for all those whose lives have been damaged and irrevocably changed by a virus none of us had even heard of when I opened my journal for 2020. Perhaps it is fitting that its last page should remain blank. Perhaps it is better to end the year with a comma rather than a full stop. Perhaps it leaves space for hope.

### 7. Terri. Perth. January 7th 2020.
### Reflection: The Winds of Change

Maureen leaves tomorrow. Back to Martin and her real home. I am delighted for her. But since this bladder cancer, I don't feel quite the same when she's gone. I know that's selfish. I don't tell anyone how I feel. She is upstairs packing. Maureen carries everything in a rucksack. She says it's easier to have both hands free, now that she walks with a stick. Colette is like me—we always have a decent-sized suitcase with plenty of outfit choices. I don't know how Maureen manages. Last year, she and my grandson, Mark, went to Wimbledon and slept for two nights in a tent. Colette and I thought she was mad. I think my travelling days are over. It would be too exhausting deciding what to pack and then fit it all into a case. I've been all over the world, so I don't mind. I always wanted to travel. And I did. I loved my time in the Middle East, but I also have lots of happy memories of family holidays abroad and trips with the Soroptimists. I spent ten years gallivanting all over the place in my sixties. Sometimes, you have to wait a few years to achieve the things you dream about when you're young.

I was happy when I came back to Glasgow after demobbing—happier than I anticipated. I learned a lot at Night School and that knowledge reinforced my hairdressing skills and ambition. I was working in Bamber's with Sheila, and getting closer and closer to Joe Reilly—flirting, to be honest. As I said to Maureen, I was just having fun. But in my heart, I knew it couldn't go on like that. I was engaged to Terence Warr. Decisions had to be made.

## 8. Terri. Charing Cross. March 1951
### Work, Play and an Ultimatum

Terri and Sheila had managed to manipulate the lunch rota in Bamber's so they could chat—or 'gossip' as Mr Thompson preferred to call it.

'Miss Coulter was not as frivolous before you joined our staff, Miss Thompson,' he had said one lunchtime.

'Perhaps that's more to do with her joining the army than me joining Bamber's, Mr Thompson,' Sheila replied.

'Perhaps,' said Mr Thompson. But as he walked away, he added, 'Still, I imagine army life is based on discipline, not chatter. It may have done you some good.'

Mr Thompson always had the last word.

They closed the back shop door to the salon and giggled, hands clasped over their mouths to stifle the sound. Terri was mortified by Sheila's cheek, and Mr Thompson was right—she was not as giddy before Sheila arrived. But there was a grain of truth in what Sheila said. Terri did not blush as easily these days or feel intimidated. Army life was about discipline, but personnel were also encouraged to speak up, take initiative and act when needed. Terri had absorbed it all.

Sheila settled herself into the most comfortable of the mismatched chairs, feet curled under her, both hands wrapped around a mug of tea.

'Well, tell me all about it. What's happening with you and Joe Reilly? On or off? You've been seeing him for seven months and talking about ending it for... let's see... seven months. And you're still seeing him. What are you doing, Terri? Is it Joe or Terence today? I can't keep up!'

Terri had no idea how to answer. She wasn't sure she even *had* an answer.

'Who knows,' Terri said, biting into her sandwich to stop herself from saying more. She and Sheila had become close since meeting at Commercial College, but it didn't take much for rumours to spread. That was not going to happen, no matter how hard her friend pressed.

Sheila pulled back her lips, large teeth protruding and threw back her head in a hearty laugh.

'Well, if *you* don't know, then things are not good, Terri Coulter. I'd go as far as to call this *frivolous behaviour.*'

There was no doubt Joe was keen—too keen at times. And there was no doubt Terri liked him. She appreciated his sense of humour, his thoughtfulness and his honesty. She liked that he was clever, yet didn't realise how clever he was, which only made her like him more. One Saturday, she had organised to bring Sheila on a double date with Joe and his friend, Charlie Hunter. The two of them had organised a second date, and Sheila had given Joe her seal of approval.

'He collects you from work or Bridgeton,' she said. 'And he puts up with your mother's direct manner. God, remember when she asked him how long he'd been a cripple?'

It was true, especially his patience with her mother, who must drive him mad. More importantly, Joe and her father got on well, chatting about books, history and even politics. Terence, though, hadn't had the chance to know Alec. There was nothing to say they wouldn't find lots to talk about.

Still, despite all his good points, Joe could be gauche and impetuous. Terence, on the other hand, oozed confidence and always thought before he acted. Terri admired those qualities. And that was the problem. She was in an impossible situation, one that could not go on much longer.

*　*　*

It was Saturday evening and Terri was putting on her coat, ready for her date with Joe. Tina was still at work in the chip shop and Alec sat beside the kitchen fire reading the paper. He lowered it onto his lap and looked at her.

'I'm not interfering, Teresa, but maybe it's time you decided what you want. You can't keep the poor bloke on tenterhooks, wondering if you're going to disappear off to South Africa.'

'I know, Dad. I promise I'll decide properly soon. I've never hidden the fact I'm engaged to Terence, but Joe just says, 'I'm here and Terence is there.' And that's it. But it's not that simple.'

Alec raised the paper again. 'Oh, but I think you'll find it is.'

'I'm meeting Joe downstairs. See you later, Dad.'

Of course, she'd heard him, but what was there to say? She ran down the three flights of stone stairs as if speed could scatter her thoughts.

Joe stood waiting at the open passenger door of his father's Rover, like a chauffeur from a Hollywood film.

'*Mademoiselle*,' he said with an exaggerated French accent, bowing his head as she slid into the soft seat. He closed the door gently, walked around, and got in.

Her mood instantly lifted.

'You are impossible, Joe Reilly. Let's get out of here.'

Later that night, outside her building, the light-heartedness had faded. They sat in the parked car, a heavy silence full of all that was unsaid, until Terri broke it.

'You're pushing me, Joe. You said you wouldn't.'

'I know. And I'm normally a man of my word. But I can't sleep, I can't eat, I can't think straight. I just need to know if I stand a chance. I'm not asking for undying love…although that would be nice. I'm starting to see that Terence chap's smug face everywhere. His moustache, that cheesy smile. He's haunting me.'

Terri was tired. She wanted to go upstairs before her mother came down, or worse, shouted from the kitchen window. She opened the door without waiting for Joe and stepped onto the pavement.

'I knew I should never have shown you that photograph,' she said, then slammed the door and marched towards the Close.

'Wait, Terri. Wait. Please. I know. I'm sorry. I won't mention it again. I promise. Just let me walk you to the landing.'

It had become routine for them to part on the landing between the middle and top floors. Nobody lived there because it housed the shared toilet. Her mother always asked a million questions if Joe walked her to their door and usually managed to embarrass her. Besides, Joe had to be up early for work.

'I don't know what's worse,' he had said the first time they stood at the big window overlooking the back court, 'the smell when the door opens, or the sight of people going in and out.'

He wasn't wrong, but she couldn't let it pass.

'Don't be such a snob, Joe. Just be glad you don't have to use it. I do.'

The stairs on the landing had been washed, and the smell of disinfectant still hung in the air. She waited for Joe to comment, but instead he straightened his shoulders, standing as tall as his boot would allow. A full five foot ten and a half.

'Terri. Or Teresa. I don't care what you call yourself. Your father says Teresa, so technically, that's who I'd be marrying. But I think Terri Reilly sounds better than Teresa Reilly.'

'Joe, stop. Please. You promised five minutes ago you wouldn't do this again. It's not fair.'

'You're right. It's not fair. On either of us. You've reduced me to a blithering idiot and I don't like it. Not one little bit. You have to choose, Terri. Is it the moustache-lipped lothario with the mealy-mouthed smile? Or me?

And just so you know, if you choose him and run off to some God-forsaken corner of the Earth, I'll be waiting at the other end. I'll stalk you for the rest of your life.'

Without waiting for a reply, he stormed down the stairs, his uneven footsteps ringing through the Close. As he went, Terri noticed a strip of white escaping from under his trouser leg. It unravelled further with each step, like a narrow wedding-train of elastic bandage. She knew he sometimes wore it when his leg was sore. If the moment hadn't been so serious, it would have been funny.

She turned to the window. Mrs O'Hara's sheets flapped under the dark sky. She always put them out at night to get a head start on the other women in the Close. It drove her mother mad.

*Yes, Joe Reilly, you are gauche and impetuous,* she thought. *But you've just been solemn and dignified, passionate and dramatic.*

She peered over the banister. Once he had safely reached the bottom of the stairs, she called out: 'Joe Reilly, I repeat… You are impossible!'

And although she couldn't see his face, Terri Coulter knew he was smiling.

## 9. Maureen. Glencar, Ireland. January/February 2021
*Home sweet home*

**8th January 2021**

I'm sitting in a wheelchair, parked beside an empty row of seats in Edinburgh Airport.

'We're short-staffed,' says the kind man from Special Assistance.

'Most people have been let go for now. God only knows how long they'll be off. The whole thing's a shit show. I'll be back as soon as I can. Don't worry, you won't miss your flight.'

He rushes off.

The airport is deserted and freezing. My legs feel numb and I have to choose between frostbite and doing a 'Lazarus'. I worry that someone will see me walking and think I'm a fraud, undeserving of the precious Special Assistance resources. Looking both ways, I limp across the floor and back to the chair, repeating the ritual whenever my legs threaten hypothermia. It is enough to keep the circulation going so that I can manage the aircraft stairs when the kind man returns.

I sit on the flight to Belfast City with a scattering of other travellers, each of us braving the elements. And Covid. I am on my way home. At last.

\* \* \*

**Sligo. January 2021**

Bloody Covid. Bloody quarantine. Bloody regulations. No Christmas hugs. No bedroom cuddles. Just tears of love and words of welcome from behind masks. Then banished to the bedroom. Again.

This is my third time in quarantine. On this occasion, I also have sole access to the lounge and don't have to wait seven days to escape the confines of the bedroom's four walls. It is filled with flowers and Christmas presents, making me feel grateful and tearful. The gift of human contact will have to wait.

I continue my nerve confusion therapy, alternating heat and cold as required, but I am happy to say I no longer swear or address my leg like the enemy in a sci-fi film. Still, focus is a struggle. The continuing clouded thinking and restlessness from the nerve pain medication have taken me by surprise. I cannot settle at my desk to write. I cannot settle anywhere. My thoughts are erratic. Irrational. Something has to go. I begin tapering the medication, following the advice of Johnny, my wonderful Scottish GP.

Little by little, the clouds lift, like morning mist over the Glencar Valley. Then one day, the world looks brighter. My thoughts, sluggish for so long, start to sharpen. My brain feels normal. Not perfect—but *me*. I am myself again. And it feels glorious.

The first day I write a complete sentence without moving from my desk is magical. I feel a rush of joy and spontaneous tears. Martin gets such a fright when he walks in and sees me crying that he nearly drops the tray of tea and lemon cake. It is a perfect celebration. I have a lot of writing to catch up on, but one sentence will lead to another and another, until I have documented the wonderful stories Mum told me before I left Perth.

*  *  *

**1st February 2021**

It's a wet welcome to the first day of spring, I have been home for three weeks now. Ireland remains in level five lockdown, so while I am free to hug Martin and go for walks, life is far from normal.

I have had plenty of time to reflect on my recent conversations with Mum and now that my elusive writing mojo has returned, the words are pouring onto the page and onto the screen. Mum must have faced difficulties trying to fit into life in Glasgow after the army, especially after her time in the Middle East, but she tends to gloss over them. She told me:

'My accent was different, although I didn't realise it until my mother begged me not to talk to the neighbours. She said I would embarrass her. That was hard to imagine."

Mum imitated Tina's Glasgow accent putting on a posh voice. The performance was hilarious.

'You'd think you were brought up in bloody England, Teresa. All la-de-da. This is how you sound: 'Hell-e-oo, Mrs O'Hara. Hoaw are yoou today?'

We were in a café at the time, both instantly lost in shared, happy memories and uninhibited laughter.

Yes, Mum is good at playing down challenges. I have tried to understand why Terri returned to Glasgow at all. I have asked in different ways, but as yet have not received a clear answer. It was surely a pivotal decision. Mum has said it was 'the right thing to do', but doesn't explain what she means. Still, it makes sense in the context of our mum, Terri Reilly. Duty, and doing what is right, have always mattered to her. The more I listen and get to know her as a young woman, the more I understand. Not just her past, but the mother I grew up with and the woman she is now at 91.

Mum wanted to escape and better herself, to travel and meet new people. She did not look back. She chose to leave the Middle East and return to Glasgow. She did not look back. And the Terri Coulter who decided to marry Joe Reilly, not Terence Warr, did look back. After hearing the story of their romance and then how she met my dad, I was more than a little curious to hear her account of breaking off the engagement with Terence. I was not disappointed and look forward to bringing that story to life in a vignette before returning to Perth.

I have wondered: Does Mum know she is dying? Does she know and not want to talk about it? Will she ever tell me how she feels about the end? When I reflect on the way she has spoken about past choices, I now believe Mum accepts the facts as they are. She does not pontificate or speculate. There is a quiet dignity in her choice not to discuss what is coming.

The family may laugh about our mum's tendency to *cry over spilt milk:*

'I should've taken that blouse. It was a good price.'

'I shouldn't have bought the mince in Tesco's. Morrison's is better.'

'I meant to send a card, but I didn't have time to go to the post office.'

There are many more examples. But when it comes to the big decisions, there is no such hesitation. Her expression would be: *taking the bull by the horns.* The only direction Terri Reilly knows is forward. Forward means living. And living is what she will do every day; Until she stops.

## 10. Terri. Perth. 5th February 2021.
### Reflection: Memories and Feelings

It's hard to get used to the stage in life where you are a *responsibility*. Don't get me wrong, I am blessed that my family wants to look after me. It just takes a bit of getting used to. But nothing stays the same, not even me! Maureen will be back in Perth soon, but in the meantime, there are rotas and schedules for family visits to make sure I'm okay. It doesn't sit well with me.

I sleep a lot these days, but I don't get mad at myself the way I used to. I just go with it. When I'm not asleep, I'm remembering. When I'm remembering, I fall asleep. And when I'm asleep, I'm dreaming about remembering. It's like living in two places at once. In the real world, I'm ninety-one, wondering how much time I have left. In my other world, life is ahead of me. The remembering feels so real. Maybe it's because I'm not busy anymore. Not out and about the way I used to be. Or maybe it's talking to Maureen about stories for her book. I always say it's important to *stimulate the phagocytes*. Discussing the past has got me thinking and my phagocytes are working overtime! I could always recall the places I'd lived and worked: the Gorbals, Bridgeton, Bamber's and all my army postings. But now, I can visualise the people I had completely forgotten. I can remember how I felt all those years ago. And that's unsettling at times. I've always kept the bright side out. Still do. I wasn't one for feelings back then. I suppose they were a luxury. Maureen says I am one of the *Silent Generation*. Apparently, we are hardworking, resilient, loyal, conformist and uncomplaining. I'm not so sure about the 'uncomplaining' bit, but she has a point. When life was tough, we just got on with it. She also said,

'Before you pat yourself on the back, Mum, your generation was also referred to as *The Lucky Few* because you were well positioned to take advantage of economic opportunities after the war.'

She added that both expressions were American, which didn't surprise me. But having said that, it describes me to a tee. I knew what I wanted and went for it. But the war gave me the opportunity to work in Bambers, and to join the ATS and travel abroad.

'You are so right,' I told Maureen. 'And I can sum up what I wanted in one word: more.'

'M-O-R-E!' she said, doing her best *Oliver Twist* impression.

I laughed and tried to do the same. 'Yes. M-o-r-e than a life as a factory girl...' But I didn't have the voice or the energy for the full dramatic effect, so I added in plain English: 'More than a life without education. More than a life in the Gorbals or Bridgeton. Just more.'

When I think about it—really think about it—what I wanted was to be anything other than my mother. I didn't know that at the time. I just knew that *more* meant getting away from my life as it was. It's only now, when I tell my stories out loud and relive the memories, that I remember how I felt. Maybe my decisions weren't based solely on facts, the way I always thought they were. That's a revelation to me. I'm finding that hard to digest. When I go back in time, I feel the humiliation, the anger, the sadness, the joy, the shame, the disappointment, the excitement all over again. And it's like experiencing these emotions for the first time. Not easy to talk about. Most people my age have learned to keep their emotions in check. Not like the young ones. They like to tell everyone everything.

The more I talked to Maureen about what happened to Hilda, the more I remembered. I thought about how she was treated. Not just by the man who took advantage of her, but by the army. I had forgotten that I was so angry and disappointed. I believed the army was where there was a right way and a wrong way. Everything was clear. Not like at home, where my mother wavered between the two, depending on her moods. But looking back, it wasn't fair of me to judge the army or the lieutenant so harshly. They had procedures and the lieutenant was just following hers. The army was there when I needed it most. Maybe it was my time for me to ask questions and decide what was right and wrong for myself. I used to think I came home because of what happened to Hilda. In truth, it just made me think differently about things. I couldn't explain it properly then. And I certainly can't explain it now after more than seventy years!

I must have dozed off because it's dark now. I hate the dark nights. But we've passed the shortest day and spring is on its way.

I venture up to the toilet, hanging onto the rail on the staircase. But it takes a long time to get up there these days. It's exhausting. Maureen's husband, Martin, says, 'Terri, if you fall and break your hip, that's it. Game over.'

So, I try not to fall. My Guardian Angel watches over me. Like the time I fell on the bus. And when I lost my footing on the stairs, trying to swipe at a bluebottle. I didn't break anything. That was my Guardian Angel.

I'm safely back in my chair. Young Joe, my Joselico, will be here soon. He's bringing dinner. We'll have some crisps and a drink first, and maybe Barney will pop in after work. Life is good. I keep the television on the BBC. The news brings me back to reality. The virus is still around. There's a lot of talk about the vaccine. I'll be getting it soon. Even the news can't keep me awake. It all sounds...

## 11. Maureen. Perth. 17th February 2021
### *Shedding Secrets*

In what feels like a heartbeat, I am back with Mum. Colette is also in Perth as it is mid-term at ISM, where she teaches in Monaco. Once again, it is a delight to witness the brightness she brings with her, and I look forward to the easy chat and laughter we share when she is here.

I am loath to call Mum a hoarder, not only because I dislike attaching glib labels to people, especially my mother, but also because there are so many other facets to her colourful personality. However, it cannot be denied that two garden sheds full of paraphernalia, most of which has been hidden from view for fourteen years, is excessive. How can one wee old lady need a three-bedroom house and two sheds, one might ask. Have you met Terri Reilly? one would answer. Under Mum's supervision, Colette and I cleared and cleaned the smaller of the two sheds during the summer. However, she is physically unable to oversee the same process with the large shed. As a result, the project has become a secret operation. We do not have Mum's permission and it doesn't sit well with me.

'Better now than after,' we agreed last night, neither of us articulating what 'after' meant.

\* \* \*

It is barely light on this chilly early February morning as we stand outside the shed at the top of the garden wearing sweaters, coats and woolly hats over our pyjamas. Neighbours peeking through bedroom curtains will assume we are completely mad. And who could argue?

'Right, open up and let's have a look,' I say.

Colette unbolts the padlock, more decorative than functional. She creaks open the door and we stare into Aladdin's Cave, though in truth, it smells more like a flooded basement. The giggling starts.

'Oh, my God. What if there's a mouse in there?' says Colette. 'Or worse.'

I ignore her. 'Where and how will we start? We've only got about an hour before I take Mum her breakfast. We need to get a move on.'

We continue staring, waiting for inspiration. More giggling. No inspiration.

'Well, it won't empty itself,' Colette says and steps inside.

I join her, even though there is barely room to stand. The largest item is Gran's gateleg table, so called for the hinged swinging legs supporting its leaves. I remember being mesmerised as a child when Gran wheeled it into the room and transformed it into a regal-looking table. Covered in dust and cobwebs now, and riddled with woodworm, it looks far from regal.

'Dump,' says Colette.

In the corner: a bag of retired golf clubs, a rolled-up windbreaker from 1960s holidays in Rothesay and an antique lawn mower.

'Dump. Dump.'

Dotted along the shelves: several fancy cushions, probably lifted directly from chairs in Skelmorlie and thrown unceremoniously from the removal truck into the shed. Temporary storage became permanent.

'Dump. Dump. Dump,' Colette chants as the shed empties and the garden fills.

The rest of the floor space is dominated by soggy, sad cardboard boxes. At least three are stuffed with receipts and invoices from the flower shop, dating back to the 1970s. Mum insisted on keeping them.

'In case the Inland Revenue come calling,' she would say when challenged.

There are also boxes of newspapers, comics, magazines and Annuals. We briefly consider trawling through them in search of a gem, but years of dampness have taken their toll. I hold up a frazzled copy of *The Victor Annual*.

'What about this?'

Colette lifts her head from a plastic box. 'Nope. Dump,' she says, holding up a *Blue Peter Annual*.

'Do you think kids still read Annuals?' I ask. 'We were always given one for Christmas. It was obligatory.'

'Haven't a scoobie, Maur. Unlikely. Too many video games and stuff online. Look at this…'

Without warning, betrayal stabs me in the gut. Mum would never have approved of us going through her shed, let alone dumping things without her knowledge. It feels like rummaging through her life.

Colette senses my change in mood and pulls a brand-new shower cap from a polythene wrapper. She puts the flowery pink hat on her head.

'I like this,' she says, hands on hips. 'I think I'll take it home with me. It was probably meant for my Christmas fourteen years ago anyway.'

Her antics have the desired effect and we laugh loudly, no longer trying to stifle our girlish giggles. Sometimes, humour is the best medicine.

We close the shed door and replace the pretend padlock, ready for tomorrow's trawl. The remaining boxes are filled with an eclectic mix of bits and pieces needing further investigation. We carry as many as we can through the patio doors into the house, hidden from Mum's view. I am grateful for my back support, and for Colette's strength. It's time for breakfast and the beginning of a normal day.

\* \* \*

When Mum is safely back in bed upstairs and chatting to Colette, I begin sifting through our recovered stash.

The first box holds two small brown suitcases, each crammed with sheet music. The musty smell of old paper makes me sneeze. Some of the titles bring back memories of songs my father, uncle and grandfather used to sing. I feel sad, knowing they will probably end up in the dump.

The next box is a mix of coloured folders filled with recipes, beauty tips and articles about health, all cut from newspapers and magazines. Mum has carefully placed each one in its own plastic pocket before filing it away in its designated folder. I smile as I turn the pages. They have lived in the shed for fourteen years and I know they now belong in the recycling bin, but I also know each article was gathered with love, in preparation for sharing with Colette or me.

*Oh God, this is hard. How much harder will it be... after?*

I push the contents—and the thought—under the table, dabbing away stray tears before opening the third box. Inside, I find black-and-white photographs of my father's family in one brown envelope, and pictures of us as children in another. But I am flabbergasted to see several photos of our parents' wedding tucked into a large, unlabelled envelope. In the name of God, what are they doing in a damp cardboard box, in a shed with a wet floor and a leaking roof? These precious photographs could easily have been destroyed by water, mice, or over-enthusiastic family members intent on a thorough clear-out.

Under a stack of *Interflora* floristry magazines, which I'll give to Joe, I find a rusty tartan tin with an old-fashioned image of Edinburgh Castle on the lid. I hope it doesn't contain ancient shortbread. I am just about to open it when Colette arrives with two glasses of Baileys.

'Did you find anything exciting in the boxes?' she asks.

I tell her about the music, the folders and the photographs. We begin oohing and aahing at the old pictures, laughing at ourselves as children. But I am still curious about the tin. Colette leaves down her glass and wrestles with it until the lid opens with a metallic snap.

'Letters,' she says, emptying the contents onto the table and selecting one at random. Carefully, she unfolds the first few pages. We immediately recognise Dad's handwriting.

'June 1951… before Mum and Dad were married.'

She picks up another. 'Here's one from Mum… also June 1951. The address is New Malden in Surrey. She must have been staying with Mrs Dodds, Janey's mum.'

I spot another of Dad's letters, this time dated August 1951. My eyesight is not up to reading the words. I shine my phone torch on the page and make out the address. Dún Laoghaire, Ireland.

'This time, Dad must have been away, Maur. Let's try to put them in order.'

We devise a system: I search for dates and addresses and Colette reads the letters aloud. We group them into two bundles, June and August 1951, and clip together Joe's letters and Terri's for each month. We laugh and cry. These are love letters from our parents, written when they were apart for two weeks at a time. Terri was away in June, Joe in August. It feels as though we are voyeurs, invading their privacy. We are, and yet we can't help ourselves. That Joe Reilly pursued Terri Coulter relentlessly is clear, but so is his love, his wit and his wonderful writing talent.

Terri's letters are more practical and newsy, as we'd expect of our mum. Yet her growing love for Joe—Joey, as she sometimes calls him—is just as obvious. Who knew our dad was ever called Joey!

'Listen to this, Maur,' Colette says, holding up one of Joe's letters.

*Terri Darling,*
*I miss you terribly. As often as I breathe, I think of you. There's not one moment of the day when you stray from my mind, and I damn the convention which places you and I at opposite ends of the country, even though I know you need a holiday, even though I know you are with friends who care for you as I do, and even though I know that in two weeks, you will be back to sooty old Glasgow you loathe, and to me.*

'Damn, that's good,' I say, and repeat the phrase aloud. 'As often as I breathe, I think of you.' Now that's what I call A-Level romance, Dad!'

Colette is only half-listening. She is reading from another June letter.

*Darling Girl,*
*I have been missing you something shocking and the days have been dragging past, elongating themselves into eternities.*

'I wish someone would say something like that to me.'

We are physically exhausted from the morning's effort, and emotionally exhausted from our intimate glimpse into the relationship between Joe and Terri, our mum and dad.

'Re-read the beginning of the letter Terri sent to Joe on 27th June,' I say. 'It's so, Mum.'

*Darling,*
*Two letters! A book will no doubt be looked for by all and sundry within the next few days. Joe Reilly is taking to literature. How do you do it? Of course, receiving two letters, one Monday and one Tuesday, is spoiling me. I naturally looked for one this morning, but woe is me, I was sadly disappointed.*
*I did intend to do the odd spat of writing yesterday, but it was wet and miserable and depressing, putting me off. In any case, I was out in the afternoon and then washing hair, etc, later.*

'You're right, Maur. It's crazy to think Mum wrote that letter at the age of twenty-two and yet she's recognisable as Terri Reilly at ninety-one.'

'I know. She is playful and probably flirting with Joe, but has no problem admitting she put off writing to him because she was too busy. So like Mum.'

'Washing her hair.' Colette adds, 'Just like the kind of excuse I'd make. And mean it! Ok. There's only one more envelope to open. It seems to have two letters inside.'

Colette unfolds the two letters as I stand up, ready to leave the room. I can see, even from a distance, that one of the letters is from Dad. The other is a small square letter. Colette has no intention of hurrying, so I sit down again.

'This is a very different letter from Joe to Terri,' Colette says. 'It's not a bit lovey-dovey. He's angry because she's dating him and still engaged to Terence Warr.'

'What's the date at the top?'

'Sunday 15th April. I presume it's 1951. Wow! Dad doesn't mince his words.'

Colette sets aside the April correspondence and tentatively opens its companion, a fragile, blue airmail letter. It reminds me of letters received from relatives abroad in the days before WhatsApp took over. Every corner and inch of space on the tissue-thin paper is filled. The writing is unfamiliar. Colette lifts her head and stares at me across the table.

'My God, Maur. This letter was written on May 21st 1951 and you'll never guess who it's from.'

I stare at the envelope. I don't have to read the words to know they were written by Terence Warr.

Mum was upset recounting the story of the difficult decision she had to make in May 1951. She spoke of two letters: one from Joe, the other from Terence. She did not mention the contents of either. Just said, 'It was a very long time ago.' I still can't believe we found them, or that she kept them together, as if they were inexorably bound for life.

\* \* \*

We tidy away the letters, and I flop onto the bed, eyes closed. Sleep is impossible. My back throbs, my lower leg tingles, but the deepest pain is in my heart, a physical ache from the effort of stifling the sobs rising in my chest.

*Oh Mum, we've shared so much during these past few months. I hate not telling you about the letters in the shed. I would love to know how those words from Dad made you feel. We could have laughed about how romantic and determined young Joe Reilly was. But I can't tell you about the letters without telling you about the shed. And how we rummaged through it behind your back. My silence is the silence of a traitor. I'm so sorry, Mum. I've let you down when it mattered most.*

The thought causes another surge of pain. I bury my face in the pillow when I can no longer hold back the dam of tears.

\* \* \*

## Morning of 18th February

I must have fallen asleep, because after what feels like minutes rather than hours, I am roused by Mum's bed creaking and her familiar shuffle as she gets up.

My eyes are puffy, and I have an overwhelming urge to turn over and go back to sleep. Colette is still deep in slumber when I stagger to the floor and make my way to Mum's room. She is on her way to the toilet and pauses to smile at me.

'Good morning, darling. I hope I didn't waken you.'

Her radiant smile feels like a warm, comforting embrace. My chest tightens again, but this time with tenderness and love, not guilt and grief. My emotions these days are drawn from a shuffled deck of cards. I never know which one will slide from the pile and am constantly surprised. When I expect sorrow, I feel joy. Instead of feeling ashamed this morning, I feel blessed and grateful. Grateful for today, for this moment, for my mum, my family, my memories. And with the benefit of a few hours' sleep, I am thankful that we found the letters and that I could share them with Colette. I didn't just need her sight. I needed her company. Her empathy. Her love.

Later, in my journal, I write:

*Thank you for keeping those precious letters, Mum. I will treat them with dignity and respect. I will write your story with the insight you have gifted me and with the honesty you would expect of me.*

## 12. Terri. Beechgrove Street. 28th May 1951
### The Moving Finger

The key turned in the lock and Terri clutched the letter tightly in her closed fist. Her father came into the scullery and sat down to remove his boots. He was particular about this ritual: his jacket hung up, his boots off, his hands washed under the big tap, then into the kitchen for a cup of tea. He always found time to clean and polish his boots for the following day.

'From your sweetheart at home or abroad?'

Alec was laughing, but Terri felt her cheeks flushing

'Dad, it's not like that. It's…'

'I'm only teasing, Teresa. It's none of my business. I know you'll work it out when the time's right. It's just… I can see you're not quite yourself these days. Can't be easy trying to keep two men happy… even if one is far away. Maybe *especially* if one is far away. But I think you know, my Darling Girl, that comparing letters won't give you an answer either. Now… I'm gasping for a cuppa. Have time to join me?'

'I'd love to, Dad, but I'll be late for work if I dilly-dally any longer.'

She hesitated, then added, 'It's from Terence. He's thinking about applying for a new job. I won't be late. Catch up with you later.'

She planted a kiss on his cheek and was out the front door before he could say more.

She knew her father wasn't fooled. He was alluding to the fact that Joe Reilly sent as many letters as her fiancé. And he lived in the same city. She had to write to Terence. But what was she supposed to say?

\* \* \*

Work was hectic and Terri was grateful to find the house quiet when she staggered through the door of Beechgrove Street that evening. She kicked off her shoes, sat on the scullery chair and rubbed her aching feet.

Silence. Good.

She peeled off her stockings and wiggled her red toes. They needed a good steep in warm water and Coleman's mustard powder before bed if she had any hope of fitting into those shoes tomorrow. Too tired to eat, she headed straight for the kitchen recess and sat on the edge of her bed. Peace. There was never any peace these days. She closed her eyes and in an instant, was back on the veranda of *Chez Elizabeth*, sinking into the wicker chair as she waited for Mohamed to bring her a cup of chai. Enjoying the peace.

She straightened up, annoyed with herself.

'You're in the real world now, Terri. And in the real world, you have issues to deal with.'

She took Terence's letter from her handbag, unfolded it and placed it carefully on the bed. The thin airmail paper felt brittle. He had fractured his hand some months ago and said it affected his handwriting. It looked unfamiliar, felt distant.

You're looking for excuses, Terri Coulter, and it just won't do. It's not Terence who's changed, it's you.

She read aloud from his letter, dated 21st May. He was planning their future, and she was dating Joe Reilly. It was wrong on every level.

*Darling, would you mind if we stayed in the B.S.A.P and did not go to Northern Rhodesia? There is a possibility I might get a staff job, that of Assistant Dogmaster. If I do it will mean that I'll be attached to the CID in Salisbury and will be stationed in that fair city. I need a change from bush life and it will be a lot better for you too.*

Terence went on to talk about the pay and how he loved life with the British South African Police, but that it was time for promotion. There was no talk of a job for Terri. Terence loved working with animals, and she knew he would thrive as a dog handler within the Criminal Investigation Department. But was it the life for her?

Would I be in Rhodesia if I hadn't met Joe? That's the real question. She smiled, thinking of the big question she had asked herself in Ismailia. What did she want from life? She had known what she wanted then. Did she know what she wanted now?

She skipped to the end of the letter.

*Darling, that Saturday night seems a long way away at times, but at others, the memory of it comes back and you are very near, but at the same time so very far away, like the Evening Star in the bush sky. Terri my sweet, I must be in love.*
*God bless Pet.*
*Love Terry.*

Terence was right about that night. It had been thrilling, but it was so long ago. Joe was persistent. Persuasive. No tingles, but he made her feel special. Happy. They chatted easily together. He listened, and cared about her plans for her own salon. He was kind. Funny—*except when he was writing nasty letters.*

Both men were polite and well-mannered. That mattered to her. Terence was well-educated, but Joe was naturally clever. Always reading. Curious. Just like her father. And he could work magic with flowers. She liked that too. But he could also be infuriating. She had never hidden her engagement, but it hadn't put Joe off. At first, she thought the chase appealed to him. But over time, she had seen the truth. His feelings were genuine. Reluctantly, she had to admit hers were too. But Joe's latest letter had not helped his cause. Terri laid it next to Terence's. So different—the letters and the men.

Joe's letter stared up at her. It was hostile. Not like him. Not like him at all. She had driven him to anger. Lifting it from the bed, she read it again. Torturing herself one more time.

*28, Cumlodden Drive, Glasgow NW,
Sunday, April 5th 1951.*

Being of a pensive frame of mind this evening, I take pen and paper, and start writing. What will be written, I do not know. It's not easy to transfer to paper the kind of thoughts running through my head. Truth to tell, I'm just plain lonely. I'm lonely for the love which from you is not forthcoming. I see you practically every day, it's true, but the girl I'm seeing is not my girl. The girl I'm kissing is not my girl. So far down, where nobody sees, is a great emptiness. You ask me not to feel bitter. What a stupid thing to say, and what a dreadful lack of understanding it suddenly reveals.

You tell me you are being nice to me. Nice! What a milk-and-water word that is. If your idea of 'niceness' consists of imitating and pretty well too, the conduct of a girl in love, at the same time feeling only mildly interested, then you can keep it! I have waited too long for my ideal to come along to be put off by second best, in the form of half-hearted love. Truly, I feel insulted that such could even be offered to me. If you can see me as often as you do and still be firm in your resolve to marry any other, then you fall into one of two categories. Either you are an extraordinarily nice girl who has fallen in love in the usual way, or you are a thoroughly worthless type of girl who, safe in the knowledge that her fiancé will never know, is conducting a love affair with a harmless young man, with all the effrontery of a Jezebel. Now then, I think I am a better judge of character than to allow such a creature to lead me so far up the garden path. If I am proved wrong, then I shall never again trust a girl. You must realise yourself that I can never believe such a thing of you. Yet you tell me you don't love me and force me to believe it.

At first, you thought you could let me take you out once you had told me all about it. You were pretty sure it would fritter out. How wrong you were.

It did not occur to you that someone would fall in love with you and you with him. Yes, I know what I'm saying, though Heaven knows it feels like sacrilege to say so. You can fall in love, you know. It's a custom still in practice in this modern world of shallow feelings. You have been telling yourself for so long that you can never fall in love again that you believe it. Baloney! If you're not in love with me at this moment, then I wouldn't have you in a gift and the worry of how ultimately to dispose of me is a worry you will never have to face. I shan't play the role of sordid lover to a girl looking only for an outlet for her emotions. Find yourself another safety valve and *next time make sure you light on someone with as leathery a heart as yourself. Darling, for goodness' sake, make me stop thinking along these horrible lines. Tell me, at least, the truth and let me either love you wholeheartedly, or not at all, because this suspicion is eating away the roots of what otherwise might be a truly beautiful romance. And that's all I have to say!*

It was unlike any letter she had ever received or ever wanted to receive again. Joe had not even signed it. His angry words still stung, though not as badly as the first time. Then, it felt like someone had stabbed her in the chest and sucked the air from her lungs. Hurt had quickly turned to rage. *How dare he speak to me like that!*

But later, once she had calmed down, Terri re-read the letter. Joe had a point, even if he had gone about things the wrong way. She needed to make a decision. Not because he was pressuring her, which he was, but because it was time. He had tried to call later that day and every day for a week, but she refused to answer. She did not acknowledge the flowers either. Joe eventually contacted Sheila, telling her he had stood at the post box wishing he could pull the letter out. But that was the problem with words. Once written, they could not be unwritten, especially when they were sealed in an envelope and dropped through a slot.

Terri reached for her little green book, the one she had bought in Alexandria. No need to check the page. She knew it by heart.

*The moving finger writes and having writ, moves on: nor all the piety nor wit shall lure it back to cancel half a line.*

The words rang true. Never truer. She knew that when the letter to Terence had been written, her words could not be retracted. How had she managed to fall for two men, two very different men? Yet both had qualities she admired. She was being unfair to both of them.

Terri took her letters and precious book and placed them all carefully back in her bedside drawer. Fully aware of what she had to do, Terri decided to procrastinate a little longer.

This was hard. So hard.

## 13. Terri. Glasgow. 11ᵗʰ May 1951
### The Big Decision

After an appalling night's sleep, Terri sat on the number 3 tram the next morning, trying to make sense of the chaos in her head. She hated chaos. Prided herself on being ordered, disciplined. Life had been pandemonium growing up, but the army had suited her. It made sense.

The tram was always packed at this time of day and Terri usually chatted to a neighbouring passenger or listened to their troubles. This morning, she let the rhythmic clunk of tram wheels on the tracks and the murmur of voices wash over her. She thought of Terence and imagined life as his wife: organised, comfortable, predictable. She thought of Joe and his impetuous charm, grand gestures, unpredictable behaviour. She pictured Rhodesia in the sunshine and Glasgow in the rain. She only realised she was smiling when the conductor, hovering beside her with one hand on the ticket machine and the other gripping the overhead strap, said in a loud, cheery voice:

'Och, it's grand to see a lassie wi' a smile on her face! Keep that grin goin'. I like happy folk on my tram. No them ones wi' a face like a dreich weekend!'

Laughter rippled through the tram and Terri had no choice but to join in.

*  *  *

Terri had the keys to open the shop that morning and was grateful for the silence as she pulled on her overalls and began the preparations for the day. The routine required no thought, which meant her mind could return once again to the dilemma of her love life.

'A penny for them.'

She spun round, cloth in hand, to see Mr. Thompson standing beside her.

'You were lost in thought, my dear. Just as well it was me and not a band of robbers or ne'er do wells sneaking into the shop undetected,' he said, walking towards the back to hang up his coat.

'I'm so sorry, Mr. Thompson. I'm just a bit distracted this morning.'

She returned to scrubbing the sink, a little too vigorously, until Mr. Thompson gently placed a hand on her elbow.

'Miss Coulter. Teresa. Terri. Whatever you're calling yourself these days. That poor sink has been cleaned within an inch of its life. I think you should leave it in peace and come in for a cup of tea. I've taken the liberty of putting the kettle on. First customer isn't due until 9:30 and Miss Thompson will no doubt arrive at 9:29 precisely.'

'I don't drink tea anymore,' she said. But she put the cloth down and followed him into the back.

'No, I don't suppose you do,' he replied. 'Which is probably why we now have a jar of coffee in the cupboard.'

They sat on two old salon chairs, cups in hand. Mr. Thompson broke the silence. Terri knew he wouldn't press her. He would simply wait, allowing her the space to speak. That was his way. It was now or never.

'How did you know Mrs. Thompson was the one?' she asked.

He took a long sip of coffee, then placed his cup on the table between them. 'Well, you never cease to surprise me, Miss Coulter.'

He sat back in his chair, fingertips pressed together—his thinking pose. 'I suspect this is one of those loaded questions with quite a bit hanging on my reply. If I tell you it was love at first sight, you'll think me impetuous. If I say she was a suitable match, you'll think me cold and calculating. And the truth is... neither is correct.'

'You once told me to love every... bugger... and marry none,' Terri said, hesitating slightly over the swear word.

She needn't have worried. His laughter was spontaneous and sincere.

'Touché indeed,' he said, though his expression quickly sobered. 'Love isn't linear, dear girl. It's full of lumps and bumps, ups and downs. As Shakespeare himself declared in *A Midsummer Night's Dream:* "the course of true love never did run smooth."'

Mr Thompson paused, either for effect or emphasis, before continuing.

So... how did I know she was the one? I didn't. I have fallen in and out of love with Mrs Thompson more times than I can count. Some days, I adore her. Others, I want to walk out the door and never come back. But of course I don't.'

He stood, rinsing his cup at the sink, as he always did. Terri assumed the conversation was over, but he turned back.

'I apologise for the "love every…person" remark. I must have said it during one of my less loving periods. I have known you for several years now. And in all that time, I have never known you to be indecisive. Even when your choices were not easy or popular. Matters of the heart are complicated. But I believe you will make the right decision, whatever that is.'

He paused again.

'I'll leave you with another of Mr. Shakespeare's pearls of wisdom:
*Our doubts are traitors,*
*And make us lose the good we oft might win,*
*By fearing to attempt.*'

As he left the room, Terri swallowed the lump rising in her throat. Mr. Thompson had known her since she was a cocky fifteen-year-old, boldly asking for a job in a posh salon.

The familiar jingle of the front door interrupted the moment, announcing Sheila's arrival. Terri glanced up at the wall clock and smiled. 09:29. She felt so much better than when she had walked through the door. It was funny how you could talk for hours and remain confused, yet a single conversation could shine a light so brightly, it changed the course of your life.

Her choice held no fear now. When it's the right thing to do, it's the right choice. And she was certain about this one.

'Oh, my God, Terri,' Sheila said, as she breezed past into the back shop. 'Daydreaming will not get Mrs McGoldrick's hair colour mixed in time for her grand entrance in ten minutes.'

No point arguing, or telling her a life-changing decision had just been made. For Sheila, it was just another day in the salon.

## 14. Terri. Perth. 3rd March 2021
### Reflection: Romance

Maureen is upstairs writing. We've been talking a lot about her dad. They were very close. Kindred spirits. I enjoy our discussions about Joe. It makes him feel close. We lived together and worked together. We spent a lot of time worrying about the family and the business. Just life. It has been good to remember how we met and the happy times when we were young and courting. Joe was romantic and I was the practical one. Maybe I was too practical at times. But Joe understood. I may not have been as romantic as Joe, but I cried telling Maureen about the night he proposed. He had a great way with words and a lovely singing voice. And he used both to win me over. It was September 1951, before my dad was sick. He really liked Joe and was very happy for us. Talking about Joe and my father in the same breath is not easy. Tears are never far away. I think I'll snooze while the memory of that night is still fresh in my mind. I remember it was a Tuesday because we both had a half day on Tuesdays. We had been for a drive to Loch Lomond and Joe dropped me off in Beechgrove Street. I'll be dreaming about that night while Maureen writes about it upstairs.

*  *  *

**Terri. Beechgrove Street. 8th September 1951**

Joe walked her to the half landing as was their custom after a night out. They stood at the big window and Terri waited for her goodnight kiss. Joe made no move towards her, which was unlike him. Then he carefully retrieved a little red velvet box from his trouser pocket and opened it in front of her.

'You can forget it if you expect me to get down on one knee, Teresa Coulter. Unlike the Phoenix, I might never rise again.'

It was almost a full moon that night and when Joe placed the diamond ring on the fourth finger of her left hand, it gleamed like a single star in the night sky. Terri opened her mouth, but all she could manage was a breath. She tried to speak, but nothing came. She stared at the ring on her finger, feeling like a Hollywood film star. When she finally found her voice, she whispered,

'I'll make you happy, Joe.' She could hear the tremor.

'We'll make each other happy,' he said. 'And I'll take that as a 'Yes!''

'I don't recall you asking a question,' she said in a steadier tone.

Joe Reilly kissed her newly ringed finger and without any sign of a tremor, sang:

*'Down in yonder meadow where the green grass grows,*
*There, Terri Coulter was hanging out her clothes,*
*She sang, she sang, she sang so sweet,*
*That she sang Joseph Reilly across the street.*
*He bought her a ring and he asked her to wed,*
*The heart on his sleeve missed a beat when she said,*
*I'll sing, I'll sing, I'll sing so sweet,*
*I'll become Terri Reilly and live on your street.'*

There was no chance of another word being uttered now, so she just hugged the man she was going to marry. With her arms wrapped around her fiancé, she thought of the night he had declared his love and stomped off down these very stairs with his bandage unravelling. She had feared her own life was unravelling at the time. The O'Hara twins came racing up the stairs, chasing each other as they passed the cuddling couple, and shouting, 'Yuck' as they ran past. Joe and Terri paid no heed.

'Let's go and tell your mum and dad the news,' said her future husband.

Her brothers were understatedly pleased about Terri's engagement. Young Alec and Robert were at the stage where events were measured by how they affected themselves. But they were happy for her. Tina was thrilled and poor Joe had to tolerate her splattering multiple kisses on him when she saw the ring. But it was good to see her mother genuinely enthusiastic for a change.

Her father hugged them both after the announcement and winked at Joe. He did not appear surprised. Joe told Terri later that he had visited Alec one evening the previous week when she was working late. He had asked for her father's permission to propose. Terri knew there had never been any doubt in Alec's mind that Joe was serious about his daughter. In fairness, Joe had never kept it a secret, even when she was engaged to Terence.

'I wondered if you might wait until Christmas to pop the question,' Terri said when they met the next day.

'I think I made it clear in one of my letters from Dún Laoghaire that it is… and I quote… *both pretentious and predictable to propose to a girl during the festive season.* And I am neither,' he said, taking both her hands in his.

No matter how much in love, Terri couldn't resist a comeback to his confident statement.

'Well, I agree you're not predictable, Joe Reilly… but I'm not so sure about the pretentious bit.'

## 15. Terri. University Cafe, Glasgow. 22nd September 1951
### Lornevale Beauty Salon

Terri had toyed with the idea of changing the name of the new shop. Joe made lots of humorous suggestions and although they made her laugh, she didn't think Maryhill was ready for Joe Reilly's wit.

'What about Hair Today, Gone Tomorrow? or Hair To Stay? or A Cut Above The Rest? or Head and Shoulders Above The Rest. Or even plain old Terri and Sheila's Gaff?'

They were sitting in the University Café on Byres Road in Glasgow's West End, one of their favourite places to meet after work. The café had been established in 1918 by Alfred Verrecchia, a former ship's carpenter who designed the interior to resemble a luxury cruiser. It had been handed down through the family ever since. With its polished wood panels, well-worn booths, and soft lighting, the place felt intimate and welcoming. The cafe was nestled between Glasgow University and the Western Infirmary, which also added a cosmopolitan feel. Joe and Terri faced each other on long, padded bench seats. They were never made to feel they had spent too long nursing cups of coffee and a shared toasted cheese sandwich. This evening's chat focused on her move from Bamber's to her new shop and Joe was on a roll.

'Perms and Potions? Locks and lotions?'

'Stop, Joe. Please stop! The hair on my head is standing on end just listening to you. We've decided to keep the original name—Lornevale Beauty Salon. It's well-established and on Lornevale Road. I also like that it has *Beauty Salon* in the title. If the shop was fully mine and not leased between the two of us, I would probably have opted for something simple like Terri's Hair and Beauty Salon. But if we included both our names, S comes before T and I'm ashamed to admit I wouldn't like to play second fiddle to Sheila.'

Joe sprang to her defence as he always did.

'How could you play second fiddle to Sheila… or anyone else for that matter?

'Not that you're biased, Joe Reilly.'

She smiled at him. They had been engaged for two whole weeks now. Terri felt happy. Truly happy. She had set her sights on the salon months ago, but its location on Maryhill Road, close to Joe's shop, was ideal. It hadn't taken long for Joe to suggest living in the area after they were married. She lifted her left hand and admired her solitaire engagement ring. It still felt new and the diamond sparkled under the low-hanging chandelier light of the cafe. Terri stopped to look at it several times every day, which made Mr. Thompson and Sheila raise their eyes to Heaven and the customers to *ooh* and *aah* with delight.

Letting go of Terence had not been easy. He would always hold a special place in her heart, but it would never have worked. And she knew she would be on the verge of opening her own hairdressing salon as an army wife in Rhodesia. Terence had been as gracious as she knew he would be, and more understanding than if she had written the same letter to Joe. The sadness was there, of course, but mingled with it was an unexpected sense of relief. She wondered if Terence had felt it too. Yet she also secretly hoped there was still a tiny space in his heart for the girl from *No Mean City*. She looked up and realised Joe was talking to her.

'Anyway, you're a much better hairdresser than Sheila. Lovely girl and I'm glad she's stepping out with my good pal Charlie, but she's not in the same league as my Terri when it comes to coiffuring. Even my mother says so... and that's saying something.'

'Yes, your mother,' she said, trying to keep the edge from her voice.

Joe's mother was not overjoyed about her precious son being engaged to an ex-army girl. She didn't mind having a hairdresser on hand, but drew the line at one marrying into the family. Even his older brother, Bernard, had been sceptical about this girl from the Gorbals and Bridgeton. Apparently, after their first date, Joe had sent a letter to Canada, informing his only brother he had met the girl he was going to marry.

*Not impetuous at all, Joe,* she thought, helping herself to another quarter of toasted cheese.

Terri could understand Bernard's initial reaction, and everything had since been smoothed over and repaired. But Joe's mother, Mary, whom everyone called *Mama*, was not so easily persuaded. She was always polite, but never warm. Joe claimed her overprotectiveness stemmed from his two years in hospital as a boy. That made sense. Still, Mama

Reilly had already pictured Joe marrying Everina, a nice girl from Maryhill. Terri's sympathy didn't stretch that far.

'You should have married her and given me some peace,' she teased Joe when he told her. 'But that would have ruined my devious plan to annoy you for the rest of my life,' he replied, throwing his arms around her.

Joe polished off the last of the toasted cheese and ordered two more coffees and a slice of homemade apple tart to share.

'What are you grinning at, soon-to-be Mrs Reilly?'

'Oh God! *Mrs Reilly* makes me sound like your mother.'

'Exactly. So… you were saying… my mother… What about her?'

'I don't think she likes me much.'

Joe leaned in. 'My mother will come to love you as much as I do. And if she doesn't, that's her loss. Look at the progress I've made with Tina. She gave me the biggest plate of fritters last week. Even tousled my hair when she passed behind me.'

'You hated that,' Terri reminded him.

'Of course I did. But it still counts as progress. Mind you, if she does it again, I may have to kill her.'

They erupted into the kind of laughter that makes other customers glance over. Terri slapped Joe's hand, then noticed the owner, a senior man, clearly one of the family, whispering to a woman at the next table. They were both smiling, watching the young and in-love couple in the booth.

Terri wasn't so sure about winning over Joe's mother. Mama had a way of glancing at her skirt length that left no doubt about her disapproval. Terri would do her best to build a relationship with Mrs Reilly, but she had no intention of changing her hair, makeup, or style for anyone.

She steered the conversation back to the new shop. Just two more weeks until she could hold the keys in her hand. Most of the equipment and supplies were already ordered.

'I'm so excited, Joe. But I'm also terrified. What if the business falls flat? What if I give up my job, convince Sheila to do the same and it all goes wrong?'

Joe took both her hands in his, rough from working in the flower shop, but strong and steady.

'Teresa Coulter, as I live and breathe, I've never heard you express doubt about anything. Well, except about marrying me, and even then you were pretending. Lornevale Beauty Salon is going to be a huge success. The only real problem you'll have—and I'll have it too—is turning customers away when it's time to close up.'

She kissed his hand. This was what love felt like.

## 16. Terri. Beechgrove Street, Glasgow. November 1951
### The Worst of Times and the Best of Times

Terri's father had refused to see a doctor when he became constipated in late September. She had heard him talking to Tina—well, listening—as she begged him to go. When Tina was worried, she was vocal. Alec had been suffering for weeks and had lost a lot of weight. He was a calm man, but also stubborn. He'd listen to Tina, then ignore her or say something like,

'It's under control, Tina. I got some good laxatives and they're bound to do the trick soon. I'd better book the lavatory for the day when they start working.'

Then, much to her mother's annoyance, he would wink at Terri and walk away. Terri had been distracted by the new salon and wedding talk, and she had accepted his excuses. Tina was probably overreacting, blustering about nothing.

The laxatives didn't do their job, and one evening in mid-October, Alec was in so much pain and looked so ill, they thought he might die in front of them. Her brother Robert ran to the phone box to call 999, and within minutes their father was in an ambulance. He hadn't wanted to be taken to hospital. The Royal Infirmary always signified death. As a boy, he had waited in the corridor outside the surgical ward, after his father, Alec Coulter Senior, had already died. As a man, he stood there again, learning that his sister Isa, aged forty-four, had died of the same bowel cancer. And now, the cancer that had ravaged and killed them both was rampaging through his own body. No wonder he didn't want to go.

Alec had surgery and was discharged three weeks later with an ileostomy. It wasn't a word any of them had heard before. They never saw it. Their father insisted on managing it himself. Then one evening, he gathered them all together.

'I don't want you to be curious or worried,' he said. 'So I'll tell you about it. Then I'd like it if we didn't discuss it again.'

Alec sat in the chair beside the fire. The rest of the family gathered around the kitchen table. Tina looked shell-shocked, stripped of her usual bravado. Terri's brothers stared at the floor in silence. Terri, though, held her father's gaze, willing herself to stay engaged. Later, she noticed marks on her hands, and realised she had been digging her nails into her palms the whole time.

'My bowel was obstructed because of a large tumour,' he said. 'They had to remove it. I've got a bag now on the outside of my tummy. It collects the waste that used to go to the toilet. I'll get used to it and so will you. I'll handle the cleaning, the emptying... all of it. Now Tina, I could murder a cup of tea.'

Terri wanted to throw her arms around him and promise it would all be fine, but she knew he wouldn't want that. Her father was doing everything he could to normalise things for himself, and for them. So she played her part, and rose quickly from the table.

'I think we've got a handle on that, Dad. Graphic, but clear as mud. Now, who's for tea?'

Their laughter was uneasy, but it helped. And as she passed him on the way to the scullery, Terri caught the discreet smile of gratitude on his pale face. He winked. She didn't dare breathe, afraid a single breath might release her sorrow.

\* \* \*

Two weeks later, Alec sat between Tina and Terri in Professor White's office for his follow-up appointment.

'You lot... the Coulters... seem to have a tendency towards this kind of cancer,' the professor said, scanning the notes in front of him.

His tone was matter-of-fact, but carried an undertone of accusation, as if the Coulter family had somehow brought the cancer on themselves. They sat upright in uncomfortable chairs, like three frightened pupils in the headmaster's office. The professor lounged back in a large leather seat behind his polished oak desk. Terri struggled to absorb what he was telling them.

'...probably make it until Christmas... no guarantees after that... time to put your affairs in order... sorry it's not better news, old chap...'

*Old chap*, she thought, resisting the urge to scream. *My father is forty-six years of age. He's far from an old chap, you insensitive...*

Alec sat in the centre, quiet and stoic, just as expected. Tina sobbed inconsolably, also as expected. And Terri was numb. A wave of nausea hit her like a punch, the one reaction she had not expected. Her world had crumbled, slipping silently from beneath her feet. She was tumbling into an abyss. The medical profession could do no more for Alec Coulter, the man who was her inspiration, her strength. He was the man who had looked after his family through countless medical dramas when there was no money for doctors or medicine. And now, there was nothing for him, no one to help the anchor who had steadied them all.

Terri had no memory of how they got home, nor of any conversation on the tram. What stayed with her were her father's words as they walked together along the green-tiled, antiseptic-smelling corridor to the Royal's front door:

'I will die at home, Teresa, with some dignity. No condescending, efficient matron is going to inform my family that I am dead.'

Tina walked behind them, weeping noisily into her handkerchief. Terri grasped Alec's trembling hand and managed to whisper, from the pit of her heaving stomach:

'Absolutely, Dad. Absolutely. You have my word.'

She hadn't cried in the hospital when they were given the worst possible news. She hadn't cried when he told her he wanted to die at home. But later, when Joe wrapped his arms around her, she wailed raw, deep, primal, undignified tears. Joe held her until the torrent eased into sporadic sobs. He did not offer platitudes. He knew there were none. All that remained was the reality of making the most of every day.

Tina threatened to give up her job in the chip shop after they visited the Royal Infirmary, but Alec insisted he would tell her when the time was right. Always thoughtful. Always diplomatic. Tina would suffocate at home. She genuinely wanted to care for him, but her life revolved around company and gossip. She was better off at work. Everyone knew it. Everyone except Tina.

\* \* \*

Christmas came and went and, thank God, her father was still with them. Terri should have known Alec Coulter would defy the odds and prove the doctors wrong. They could cut out the bad bits, but he understood more about health and healing than any of them. He no longer slept in a bed, believing the cancer would spread faster if he lay down. Terri doubted there was medical evidence to back it up, but she believed him. Or at least wanted to.

She and Joe had set a spring wedding date and Terri prayed her precious father would be there to see it. She knew he wouldn't be able to walk her down the aisle, but could not bear the thought of marrying without him, even if he was only watching from the side. She wanted to bring the wedding forward to Christmas, but it wasn't simple. The Reillys were paying for the reception because her parents couldn't afford to. April was the earliest they could organise a function. Joe would have happily eloped to Gretna Green, but Terri knew that was no way to start married life. Her father would never have approved, especially if he was the reason for the elopement. The wedding was only six weeks away. She believed he would make it.

That night, as Terri lay in bed, turning from side to side and trying to warm her feet, her thoughts drifted to Mrs. Dixon in the Advanced Division. On the day school resumed after the Clydebank Blitz, she had opened their English lesson with the first lines of *A Tale of Two Cities*. Most of the girls had switched off at the mention of Charles Dickens, but Terri had been mesmerised. Mrs. Dixon told them it was important to remember kindness and community spirit, not just destruction and devastation.

Terri had found the book in the library after class and learned the passage by heart. Now, the words came tumbling back:

*It was the best of times, it was the worst of times,*
*It was the age of wisdom, it was the age of foolishness,*
*It was the epoch of belief; it was the epoch of incredulity*
*It was the season of Light, it was the season of Darkness,*
*It was the spring of hope, it was the winter of despair.*

Her father was going to die. She was running her own hairdressing salon. She was about to start a new life with Joe Reilly. Truly, the worst of times coexisted with the best of times. Grief and happiness. Loss and love.

That was life. That was hope.

## 17. Terri. Maryhill Road, Glasgow. March 1952
### The Visitor in Black

Mrs Dixon's words still echoed in her head as Terri sat on the tram the next morning. She was determined to focus on the best of times now and make the most of the lead-up to her wedding. Joe and Charlie had organised an Easter weekend break for the four of them. It was to be a final outing before serious preparations began in a few weeks.

At Maryhill Junction, the tram whined and screeched to a halt. Lost in her plans for the day, Terri did not notice Mr Henry until he shouted from across the road.

'Morning, Miss Coulter.'

He stood outside his grocery shop in a long white apron, hands on his hips. It was half past eight on a chilly March morning, but Mr Henry never seemed to feel the cold. Always nipping in and out: arranging the fruit, blethering to customers, then back behind the counter to serve them. Mr Henry had owned the grocer's for over thirty years and had an opinion on everything. Terri did not have time for chit-chat, but keeping local shopkeepers on side was wise.

'Good morning, Mr Henry. It's a cold one, but spring's on its way. Have a lovely day,' she called, and unlocked the door of Lornevale Beauty Salon without waiting for a response. The shop opened at nine, though no customers were booked before half past. Terri had her own daily pre-opening rituals while Sheila often arrived just in time—something that would have amused Mr Thompson. She missed him. Missed his support, his dry humour, his Shakespeare quotes.

'It was only a matter of time, Miss Coulter,' he had said when she told him. Then, with his usual need for the last word: 'Good luck with Miss Thompson and her interesting attitude to timekeeping.'

Once inside, Terri turned on the lights, heated the water, cleaned the sinks, checked the equipment, and replenished the trolleys. She thrived on routine, and had a habit of double-checking Sheila's station. In the back shop, clean towels were drying on the pulley. Terri folded them, singing Joe's proposal song under her breath.

The bell jingled.

'Sing up, Terri. That's one way to scare the customers off!'

Sheila rarely entered without a comment. Terri poked her head out from the back shop and lobbed a towel. Sheila caught it and fired it back. The day was underway.

Thursdays were always hectic. During a welcome lull in the middle of the day, Terri was in the back, checking shampoo stocks when Sheila entered, arms folded, grinning.

'You've got a visitor. Says his name is Father O'Flynn. You didn't tell me you were expecting a visit from a priest? Too bald for a haircut, if you ask me.'

Terri peeked out. A man in black shifted from foot to foot, staring at the floor, clearly feeling uncomfortable in a beauty salon.

'I wasn't,' she said. 'That's the parish priest from the Immaculate Conception. I wonder what he wants. God, I hope nothing's wrong. Maybe Mrs Reilly had a fall.'

'If it's the priest and not the doctor,' Sheila whispered. 'I'd say that's a bad sign.'

Terri stifled a laugh.

'You're awful, Sheila Thompson. I won't be long.'

She dried her hands, removed her overall and went out to greet her visitor. He was a small man of about fifty, though his serious face and round glasses made him look older. He removed his hat and gave her a tight smile. Terri guessed Donegal from the lilt, like many of the Maryhill parishioners.

'Miss Coulter, 'tis lovely to see you again. We met after Mass, when you accompanied young Joseph and his wonderful parents... two of our finest parishioners.'

His simpering tone grated.

'Yes, Father. That's right. How can I help you today?'

'I thought I'd take you for a cup of tea... if that's a suitable request for a priest to make to a lovely young girl.'

Something in his manner unsettled her. The invitation wasn't straightforward. He had a reason, and she was curious to find out what it was.

'Hold the fort,' she shouted to Sheila, bolting for the front door before her partner could respond.

At the café, he ordered tea for two. No offer of coffee. No biscuit. No chat.

# Impossible to Fill

'Teresa... may I call you Teresa?' He didn't wait for permission. 'I come on behalf of dear Mrs Reilly...that remarkable and holy woman. Despite her disability, she still finds time for the Missions. And of course, her daughter, Sister Mary Christine, is a Servite nun.'

He paused, then got to the point. 'Mrs Reilly is worried, Teresa.'

Now he had her attention.

'She's concerned about the effect your worldly ways may have on her daughters. I mean no disrespect. But take this fashion item, for instance...'

He waved vaguely at her new knee-length, swing coat. Terri was too shocked to speak. He mistook her silence for acknowledgement.

'Mrs Reilly understands that army ways are not always Catholic ways. She holds you blameless, of course. It is the subtle influence that troubles her.'

*I can't listen to any more of your vile nonsense*, Terri thought.

She wanted to leave, yet felt rooted to the spot.

'I notice you have blond hair,' he continued. 'Forgive me if I presume it's not natural. But you'll understand... it can be seen as... suggestive.'

The waitress arrived with tea. Neither of them spoke.. She sensed the tension and hurried away.

*Please stop talking, Father, or I may be forced to behave like the kind of woman you think I am.*

But he carried on.

'Mrs Reilly means no offence. She asked me to speak with you only out of concern. Fashion is fleeting, Teresa. Temptation is everywhere. You seem like a respectable girl. I know you'll consider how your appearance could affect Joseph's innocent sisters.'

Terri held the corner of the table and slowly rose to her full five feet, three and a half inches. She did not trust herself to speak.

*You're lucky it's me sitting here and not Joe Reilly. He'd have you on the floor for half of what you've said.*

The thought lifted her spirits. She took a deep breath and smiled sweetly. 'My customers are waiting, Father. Enjoy your tea.'

She closed the cafe door behind her, resisting the temptation to slam it. Mind over matter. She was just glad the wedding was in her parish and not Joe's.

\* \* \*

Terri and Sheila worked well together as equal partners. Sheila was more laid-back, but Terri liked to take the lead and they always discussed business decisions. Joe's situation could not have been more different. Though the sign said *Bernard Reilly & Son*, his father called all the shots and Joe earned a pitiful wage. Terri liked Bernard, but his quick temper and controlling nature were not easy to ignore, especially when they affected the man she loved. Joe took pride in his work. He had started with three carnations, three roses and a few chrysanthemums. Now, his display window burst with colour and creativity. He ran the shop. He *was* the shop, even if the profits went to his father.

That evening in the University Café, Terri played down the priest's visit when she and Joe exchanged the day's news. She was still shaken, but more than anything, she was angry. And determined. The future was theirs and they had to grab it with both hands.

Joe would thrive in the flower business. All he needed was the right support. And now he had it. Her name was Terri Coulter.

## 18. Terri. Perth. 14th March 2021
### Reflection: Mother's Day

Maureen was irate when I told her about Father O'Flynn lecturing me on morality. I tried to explain it was a different era and no harm was intended, but she just said,

"That's no excuse, Mum. He had no business interfering. He was a priest, for God's sake!"

And of course she was right. But he was only the messenger. And things got worse afterwards. I decided to keep that story for another day, once Maureen had calmed down. What I did tell her was how his visit made me feel. Yes, I was angry, but the emotion I remember most and had forgotten until I relived that day was determination.

'It was a turning point, Maureen. I knew Mrs Reilly disapproved of me. But Joe loved me. And I knew we'd make it work, no matter what anyone said or whatever happened next. Do you know what I mean by that?'

I could tell by the look on her face that she wasn't entirely convinced. But she said, 'So what you're saying is the lovely priest did you a favour!'

Her sense of humour reminds me of Joe. We laugh together as we often do. Like I used to with her dad.

Paul and Jules are here for the week, so there won't be much time for storytelling. They always do a pile of bits and pieces when they're here. This time they brought pre-cooked meals they know I like and even a wee fridge for all their Tupperware boxes. Not to mention two bottles of Lindisfarne Mead. I don't know how they managed to fit it all into the car.

It's Mother's Day today. I've had two glasses of mead, so I'm in bed early. It's only nine o' clock. Maureen doesn't like me having more than one glass, but Paul refilled it. And of course I drank it. I still feel at odds with not working on Mother's Day. Even after all these years. Maureen's family sent a big hamper full of treats for the two of us. A lovely surprise.

When my own family was growing up, they couldn't ask me over or come to us. It was a busy working day and the run-up to it was worse.

Mother's Day came right after Valentine's and Valentine's was just after Christmas. There was no let-up. The days when other people were celebrating meant work for us. I didn't mind. I liked being busy. But it was hard to keep up with everything else in life. The family were all young and looking back, I missed a lot of time with them. I worked with my husband, Joe, then our son, Joe, then on my own. Those three days never got any easier. Then it all stopped when I retired. Now, I get to celebrate like everyone else. It feels wonderful. But it also feels strange.

Paul came in this morning with a bunch of alstroemeria from Morrisons. Different shades of orange and russet. I'd forgotten how much I love them. I miss the flowers in the shop. I was always the business end of things, but I knew which flowers should and shouldn't go into a bouquet. Sometimes my opinion didn't go down well, even if I was usually right.

The vase of alstroemeria is on the table beside me in the living room, I can't see much unless it's close. They're so beautiful. I've decided I'm never going to be without alstroemeria again.

*19. Maureen. Perth. 3rd April 2021*
*The Rubaiyat of Omar Khayyam*

I cannot believe it's April 2021. It doesn't feel like a year since our 2-kilometre restricted walks beside Glencar Lake. Paul and Jules have returned to Somerset and my brother Joe arrived from Inverness this evening. We are chatting and reminiscing, wondering how much time we have left with Mum. I have had similar conversations with each of my siblings, sharing memories, aware that every day is precious. Sometimes, I talk to Mum about the past, then discuss them with Colette or one of my brothers, linking Mum's stories with our childhood memories. Terri is the daughter in one scenario and the mother in the other. I had no idea how deeply this process of weaving together stories, both facts and emotions, would affect both Mum and me.

Terri, the daughter, faced this same reality when her own father, Alec, was diagnosed as terminally ill. And like us, she feared death's nearness but still hoped for more time. She also had to deal with the Reillys and their attempt to sabotage her wedding plans. That story made me even more mad than the one about Father O'Flynn. No wonder Terri, the mother, is resilient.

My brother has gone to bed, and I am sitting in Mum's office chair, musing. A huge oval-framed photograph of my mother hangs on the adjacent wall.. It dominates the room. We're used to it, but it still elicits a gasp or a double-take from visitors. Terri Reilly decided to have a series of professional photographs taken to mark her 70th birthday. I remember thinking she was nuts. It was hideously expensive and unnecessary. But now, looking up at it, I see a confident, beautiful woman whose elegance needs no embellishment. In the photograph, age is irrelevant. Her wistful smile is the same as in earlier portraits. I remember one in her army uniform and peaked cap, and another in a summer dress, pearls, and a wide-brimmed hat. A sash of black lace flows from two carnations on one side of the hat, giving her a sophisticated, mysterious air.

Each portrait feels like a statement of Mum's style and personality at different stages of life. I now think the extravagant photograph was her way of reclaiming her sense of self after Dad died the year before. Joe and Terri were like a verse and chorus of the same song—different, but meant to be together. I didn't understand her need for a portrait at the time, but I do now. Identity mattered to the girl from the Gorbals, especially after losing the other half of her song.

My mind flits around a lot these days. I slip from past to present to future, wondering how I will live without this force of nature, my mum. Sometimes it feels as though I am already grieving, which makes me angry with myself because Mum is still very much alive.

I gaze at the graceful image in the oval frame.

'I don't think a portrait of myself will help me get over losing you, Mum,' I say out loud. I extend my arm and add, 'What am I going to do with you? With this?'

Then I reply to the voice in my head. 'I can't, Mum. I just can't. I don't have a wall big enough for you. I don't have a room big enough for you. I don't even have a house big enough for you.'

I laugh at the idea of transporting this enormous picture to Sligo. Martin is long-suffering, but I doubt even his tolerance would stretch to having a giant photograph of his mother-in-law on our living room wall!

\* \* \*

The following morning, I leave Joe and Mum chatting while I make the mandatory coffee. I return with the tray as the two of them are mid-conversation.

'Be careful, Joe. Roisin might not appreciate your comment. Remember that the moving finger writes and having writ, moves on.'

'Mum, what are you talking about? It's just a text. She'll reply or she won't. Are you losing your marbles or quoting Shakespeare?'

I set the tray down, always wary of my back when I stoop, but curious to find out what I've missed.

'Did I hear you accuse our mother of losing her marbles, Joe? Dangerous territory, don't you agree, Mum?'

Joe and Mum worked closely together in the flower shop and still engage in lively, often cheeky exchanges.

'It's not Shakespeare. It's from *The Rubaiyat of Omar Khayyam,*' she says, as if it's common knowledge, something we should know.

'It's a warning. Once you've written something, it can't be erased. Take heed, Joselico. That's why you should be careful with those text messages. Omar Khayyam was a Persian poet from hundreds of years ago, but his words are still true. In my day, we wrote letters. We had time to re-read them before posting. Nowadays, messages fly around everywhere. No one stops to reflect. And anyway, you're always on that thing.' She points at Joe's phone.

True to form, my brother is glued to his screen.

'Right then. The what... of whom? Let's look it up. I'll reserve judgment 'til then. You see, Mum... mobiles can be useful after all.'

He lifts his head,clears his throat theatrically and reads aloud:

*The moving finger writes, and having writ,*
*Moves on: nor all the piety nor wit*
*Shall lure it back to cancel half a line,*
*Nor all thy tears wash out a word of i*t.

'Wow, that's powerful stuff. I take it back, Mrs R. Your marbles are intact. But I never had you down as a poet.'

I sip my latte and add my tuppence-worth.

'And I know where and when Mum bought the book in question.'

I pause for effect and another sip.

'But you'll have to wait for *my* book to be published before you find out. Isn't that right, Mum? Though I will say... she bought it in Egypt.'

'I'm intrigued,' Joe says. 'You, buying books you don't read? Is this where the obsession started? In some Egyptian bookshop? Tell me more.'

Mum is not fazed by his sarcasm.

'I read that book from cover to cover when I first bought it. And several times since. Just not recently. I think you'll find the verse you read out is number 71 of 101.'

'Wow! Now I'm impressed. How can you possibly remember that? You never cease to amaze me, Mrs R.'

Mum is delighted. She's smiling, not just with her face or her eyes, but with something deeper. Then, out of nowhere, she says:

'Aye... aye... dirty way he done it. Lifted his hat and walked oot!'

Joe and I dissolve into helpless laughter.

Between gasps, Joe says, 'I was right the first time… you're as mad as a bag of cats.'

Neither of us has any idea what she's talking about. Probably an old Glasgow saying, meaning God knows what. It doesn't matter. We're giggling, laughing, sharing, loving.

I have come to realise how often joy and sorrow are intertwined in therapeutic laughter. I know this scene will replay in my head in the weeks and years ahead.

Oh God, I'm doing it again. Stop it, Maureen. Stop thinking about the future. Stay in the present. Mum is sitting in front of you, laughing. Stop projecting. Just enjoy the moment.

But the most precious moment has not yet revealed itself.

'Joe, give me my handbag, will you?' Mum says.

She puts her mug down and forages through the bag on her lap. Then Mum hands Joe a small green book. His jaw drops. He passes it to me without a word. The book is old, its gold title almost worn away. But there is no doubt what it says.

I am holding *The Rubaiyat of Omar Khayyam*, the book Terri Coulter bought in Alexandria, Egypt, in September 1949.

'I keep it with me,' says Mum, like it's nothing out of the ordinary.

This is my mother, who has umpteen handbags, swapped at random depending on her outfit or mood.

My mother, who has sheds, wardrobes, cupboards and boxes of memorabilia.

My mother, who searches for needles in haystacks.

My extraordinary mother, who kept this book for more than seventy years and knew exactly where to find it. In her handbag, beside her, close to her heart, with the rest of her memories.

## 20. Terri. Largs, Scotland. April 1952
### The Final Straw

**13th April 1952**

'Come on, Terri, we don't want to be late. Charlie and Sheila are meeting us at Cumlodden Drive so we can all travel together in the one car.'

Terri could sense from his tone that Joe's patience was wearing thin. She had left him in the kitchen with Alec and Tina while she put the final few bits into her suitcase. From the bedroom, she could hear her mother ranting about how last night's bingo had been rigged and could imagine the look on Joe's face.

'I suppose you've packed enough for a month,' her father teased from his seat beside the fire, when Terri appeared carrying a large suitcase. She was wearing her green swing coat—the one Father O'Flynn disapproved of—with a new hat and gloves.

'My Easter bonnet,' she said, twirling. 'I wore it to Mass.'

'There was no requirement for a bonnet in the choir loft this morning. Nevertheless, we sang a magnificent Easter Mass,' said Joe, standing up from the table and taking the case from Terri. He heaved it into the air, pretending it was far heavier than it was, but he was laughing. 'You didn't tell me we were eloping.'

They giggled their way down the stairs and out onto Beechgrove Street, like teenagers playing truant from school.

'Happy Easter, Teresa Coulter.' Joe said, his hazel eyes shining with undisguised love. 'May I say you look particularly ravishing today. Are you doing anything on 28th April? If not, I thought we might get married. But, of course, only if you have nothing better to do.'

He planted a gentle kiss on her cheek before opening the car door.

'I will give the matter my full attention,' she replied, carefully bending her head to sit into the car without damaging her new hat.

'I dread to think how much luggage you'll need for the honeymoon if this is for a weekend,' he muttered, hefting the suitcase into the car boot.

'I heard that.'

'You were meant to, Darling. Now let's go before your mother comes out to regale me with part two of the bingo crisis.'

* * *

Terri stood with Sheila and Charlie at the foot of the stairs outside Joe's house in Cumlodden Drive. He said he had to pop in for a few minutes, but that was ages ago and they were fed up now. Terri was just about to find out what was going on when the front door opened and Joe almost catapulted down the stairs. If Charlie hadn't been standing at the bottom, Joe would have landed on the pavement. Mr Reilly stood at the top of the stone stairs, red-faced, fists clenched at his side, his brows pulled together in a scowl. His stance made him look even taller than his six feet. Had he really just pushed his son? A suitcase came thundering down the stairs and the door slammed shut. He had. The four friends stood frozen, too shocked to react. Charlie was the first to speak.

'Eh, what just happened Joe? Are you alright?'

Terri felt as if she'd been slapped across the face. Stunned. Winded. Unable to take it in. She threw her arms around Joe, but all she could mutter into his neck was, 'Are you ok, Joe? Are you ok? Oh my God, Joe. Are you ok?'

They clung to each other, unsure what to do next. Joe's face was ghostly. Sheila and Charlie took over. They ushered Joe and Terri into the car.

'I'll drive. You two sit in the back,' Charlie said. 'Then when you find your voice, Joe, for God's sake, tell us what's going on.'

* * *

They stopped at the Sea View café in Wemyss Bay. None of the anticipated holiday banter had accompanied them on the journey. Joe stared out the side window. Terri held onto his hand. She noticed Charlie and Sheila exchanging glances. Everything felt unreal.

Having settled at a table with a view of the dignified old railway station and the dreary-looking Firth of Clyde, Joe finally spoke.

'They wanted us to put the wedding off until September.'

'What?' The chorus made everyone in the café turn round. Terri was beyond shocked at this stage. She grabbed Joe's hand under the table and squeezed it because she had no idea what to say to this man, whom she loved and who was hurting so badly.

'Go on,' Charlie said, throwing his elbows onto the table and propping his chin on his folded hands.

'You can't leave it there. I'm dying of curiosity here, Joe. After all, I'm the one who caught you when you exited your house like a sprinter off the blocks.'

Charlie was a good friend to Joe, and probably the only person who could get away with a comment like that. It worked. While they waited for their soup to arrive, Joe filled them in on the events that led up to his eviction.

'....some tosh about making sure we were doing the right thing. More tosh about Mama not being up to a wedding at the moment. Bloody hell, the wedding is in just over a fortnight. The banns were read in both parishes two weeks ago, for pity's sake. How can they do this to us?'

Charlie intervened again.

'The banns of marriage are read out in church to give people time to object before the wedding. But that's not supposed to include the groom's bloody parents!'

But Joe wasn't laughing. He turned to Terri. His eyes were wide, as if a new horror had just occurred to him.

'The wedding invitations! They were sitting on the table in the middle of the living room, Terri. My parents had no intention of sending them. Remember, we wondered why they hadn't gone out at the same time as the bans were read? We thought there'd been a delay at the printers. It seemed reasonable... until now... how can they do this to us?'

Joe's devastation was palpable, like a heavy shadow sitting with them at the table. Terri felt helpless. They were so happy this morning. She was furious with Joe's parents, and he was right– how could they do this to them? He was suffering now, but she knew Joe would get to the angry stage soon enough. She feared the relationship with his family would never recover.

'Let it go for now, Joe,' she said, with what she hoped was a calm, upbeat voice. 'Let's use these few days in Largs to take stock and blow away the cobwebs. We'll eat fish and chips on benches looking out at the sea. And lick ice cream cones with raspberry sauce from Nardini's as we walk the Prom. We'll talk. We'll get some perspective. We'll work it out together, Joe. I promise.'

Charlie also tried his best to help.

'Yes and we might even indulge in a glass or two of sherry. Or maybe we should have cider. Wasn't that your tipple of choice when we were in Dun Laoghaire?'

Terri could see Joe's features relaxing. They were on a roll and she wanted to keep it going.

'You're right, Charlie. I remember a letter from Dun Laoghaire describing a particular night when too much cider was had. In fact, now I come to think of it, most of your love letters from Ireland mentioned a glass of cool cider. Maybe that's what gave you the inspiration for all those romantic words!'

Joe's expression finally softened into a faint smile. The startled look had gone from his eyes, but the hurt remained. Not something humour or old stories could wipe away. Nothing changed the fact that Bernard Reilly had pushed his youngest son out the door and told him not to come back until he 'saw sense'. But there was no point sulking in Largs for two days.

Four bowls of lentil soup landed in front of them. Terri buttered her bread and stirred the soup, unsure if she would manage to swallow a spoonful. She had been so focused on Joe, she hadn't even started to process her own feelings. First, the interfering priest, and now this. An outright attempt to ruin their wedding. But the Reillys were playing with fire. If Terri gave the word, Joe would walk away from them all without a backwards glance. Of course, she would never do that. Family was family, no matter what. She had learned that from her father. She hated what they had done to Joe. Hated seeing him so wounded. Yet she was also proud. Proud of him for standing up to them. Terri knew this was the beginning of the next phase of his life.

The group sat quietly, focussed on finishing their soup before travelling on to Largs. This time, it was Sheila who broke the silence.

'You know what this is really about, don't you?'

'What?' The trio replied in unison again, this time in a more orderly fashion. Sheila took her time, not quite relishing the attention, but aware of it. She drained the last of her soup from the spoon and said,

'They think Terri's pregnant.'

## 21. Maureen. Perth. April 2021
### *Easter Weekend of Celebrations and Sadness*

**Easter Sunday 4th April 2021**

Mum's visit to Alexandria was more than seventy years ago. The traumatic Easter weekend in Largs took place less than two years later. Very different worlds, and having heard both stories, what strikes me most is how Terri had developed her sense of self during that time.

I open the wardrobe door, looking for something suitable to wear to Barney and Lorna's for lunch. My mobile buzzes. It's my husband, Martin.

'Happy Easter!' I chirp.

'Mum died this morning, Love,' Martin says.

I try to speak, but my jaw won't move. I clutch the phone to my ear with one hand and stretch the other out in front of me, as if it might somehow reach my grieving husband.

"Oh, Martin. I'm so sorry. I'm so very sorry.'

I sit on the bed when I feel my legs wobbling. I tell him, 'I'm so sorry,' over and over. 'I should be there.' Martin knows me, understands my pain, makes it easier for me.

'It's ok, love. I'm sad... but I'm fine... honestly. She lived a long life... I think Mam would be pleased to join her Maker on Easter Sunday.'

It's not easy to keep talking, but we stumble on, finding some comfort in each other's words.

Martin's mother, Philomena, known as Phil, was ninety-five and had been living with dementia for the past few years. She was kind and loving all her life. A devout Catholic, she had deep faith, and Martin was right. There was dignity and grace in her leaving us on Easter Sunday.

Lunch with family is the perfect antidote to the morning's sad news. After coffee and scones in their bright, sunlit conservatory, we sit around Barney and Lorna's big oak kitchen table and put the world to rights. Mum is the epitome of style, wearing a black-and-white themed outfit: a sequinned white blouse, black sparkly headband and a bright green coat to mark Easter Sunday. I take note of every detail, and think about the green swing coat she wore on Easter Sunday 1952.

\* \* \*

## 6th April 2021

Today is my sixty-fifth birthday. A tangle of emotions. At half past ten, the doorbell rings and I open it to find two takeaway cups and a box of croissants, with no clue as to how they had landed. I take the goodies upstairs to Mum in bed.

'Do you believe in fairies?' I ask, peeling off the protective foil and handing her a cup of Costa coffee. I read the message on the receipt and can't speak.

'Maureen, what's wrong? Have you found out who the fairy is?'

'Yes, Mum. It's Paul, my son, your grandson. How in the name of the wee man did he manage to organise lattes from Costa to a house in Perth?'

'It's the idea of the thing, Maureen. It's as good as the coffee itself,' says Mum, taking a bite of her croissant. And she is right. We sit with lattes in our hands and smiles on our faces, Mum in bed and me at the window beside her. It is a perfect start to the day.

In Ireland, funerals take place two days after a death unless circumstances dictate otherwise. I am reassured, knowing the boys are with their dad, and will take care of him. It makes the pain of my absence less acute. Our daughter, Sarah, attends the funeral Mass online from Dubai and Mum and I tune in from Perth. The number of mourners permitted is limited to ten. Ten! Martin is one of eight children, which means spouses and grandchildren must stand outside the church.

I watch as Martin turns in the church aisle and lays a hand on his mother's coffin. I almost don't recognise him. His hair is long and unkempt. His suit, bought before the cancer, hangs loosely on his diminished frame. Such a simple and unimportant consequence of the pandemic: not being able to buy a suit or get a haircut for your mother's funeral. I want to reach into the screen, pull him out, hug him, be with him. Instead, I feel helpless, tears dripping unchecked.

In the evening, Barney, Lorna and their daughters, Stella and Phoebe, come into the house like a whirlwind of catering competence. They unpack boxes full of goodies. Everything you could need or want for a birthday celebration. I am surprised, delighted and grateful. The kitchen and dining room are transformed into a gourmet restaurant with a party atmosphere. It is such a thoughtful gesture on a day when I might have lapsed into grief and self-pity.

The six of us sit around the table again, this time in Mum's house. As various courses are served and cleared by the girls, we chat and laugh, me wearing a ridiculous birthday garland, and Mum in a bright red sweater with matching lipstick and a perfectly coordinated scarf. She holds court at the head of the table, her vibrant smile etched forever in my memory as the most special gift of all.

\* \* \*

## Later that night

The excitement of the day and the sadness of the funeral take their toll on Mum. The family have gone, whisking away dishes and debris with the same efficiency as their arrival. The house is spotless and quiet as I help Mum upstairs. She cannot make it as far as the bed, stopping to rest on the chair outside her ensuite bathroom.

'It's the Blackness, Maureen. I just need a minute.'

'I know, Mum. There's no rush. Take your time.'

I kneel beside the chair as she lays her head in my cupped hands. We have grown accustomed to this ritual, aware that the dizziness she calls 'the Blackness' will ease with rest. Her kidneys are barely functioning now, and we have adapted our routine to include frequent resting places.

'It was a great day, wasn't it, Maureen?'

'It was, Mum. It really was.'

Without warning, my tiny, frail mother lifts her head and sings a melody well known to us both, often sung by my dad and his father before him.

*When you come to the end of a perfect day...*

Her voice is steady and in tune. I am startled and undone by the beauty of the moment. She only manages the first line, but I know the rest of *A Perfect Day*, written by Carrie Jacobs-Bond in 1909. I fix my gaze on a spot on the wall, the only way to keep from breaking down.

*Well, this is the end of a perfect day,*

*Near the end of a journey too,*
*But it leaves a thought that is big and strong,*
*With a wish that is kind and true,*
*For memory has painted this perfect day,*
*With colours that never fade*
*And we find at the end of a perfect day,*
*The soul of a friend we've made.*

When Mum feels able to move, we hold hands and shuffle toward the bed. Me walking backwards, Mum forwards, like a slow-moving engine and carriage. It's the system we've devised to help her walk safely without hurting my back.

I bring the cleansers and cotton wool to Mum in bed, but the skincare is brief tonight. She is barely awake. I gently remove her glasses and hearing aids.

In the sanctuary of my bedroom, I can't hold back the day's mix of emotions any longer. I lie on the bed, staring at the ceiling, and sing the first line of Lou Reed's *Perfect Day*, my voice far less steady than Mum's.

*Oh, it's such a perfect day, I'm glad I spent it with you.*

Then I fall apart.

\* \* \*

## 7th April 2021

I am packing my rucksack for the flight to Sligo. Again. It no longer requires thought: hand gel, toothbrush, medication, a few clothes, my laptop and charger. This trip was unplanned. I never thought I would leave Mum again, but life shifts without warning. I have tried to live one day at a time, not worrying about Martin when I'm with Mum, and not worrying about Mum when I'm with Martin. But this Easter weekend has shown how hard that can be in practice.

I have to go. I have to see Martin. I have to tell him, 'I'm here. Everything will be alright.'

And I have to believe that, eventually, those words will be true.

Barney arrives to drive me to Edinburgh Airport. Again. Phoebe will stay with Mum for a few hours. She has brought Costa coffee, a Cherry Bakewell tart and her lovely personality. I lean over Mum's chair and kiss her cheek.

*Don't make a scene, Maureen.*

'I'll see you soon, Mum. Joe will be down tomorrow night. No doubt he'll bring pizza and a few beers.'

I don't know why I mention pizza and beer.

I don't want to say goodbye. Mum blows me a kiss. She doesn't want to say goodbye either.

*Don't make a scene, Maureen.*

'Bye, Mum.'

## 22. Terri. *University Café, Glasgow. 15th April 1952*
### *The Aftermath*

On the Tuesday after their strange Easter weekend in Largs, Joe and Terri went back to work.

It had not been the relaxing, carefree break they had anticipated, but it was good to spend time together. In addition to their stressful start, the boarding house had double-booked and the boys had no bedroom. The couple who owned the place were apologetic and keen to facilitate them. They suggested Joe and Charlie sleep on the two settees in the sitting room. It was hardly ideal, but accommodation was in short supply. Anyway, hearing about their sleeping arrangements had been a welcome distraction. Over breakfast, Joe regaled them with some of their overnight antics. His storytelling style and sense of humour lifted both their spirits and some of the weight of the previous day.

'The enormous grandfather clock in the corner of the room announced the passing of every sleepless hour by chiming loudly, then thundering out the requisite number of hours. As if that wasn't bad enough, it took great pleasure in dividing each hour into fifteen-minute segments.'

Charlie added his bit.

'At precisely four o'clock, Joe leapt up from his settee. By this time, I was on the floor because he played the *bad leg* card and got the decent one. I heard him fiddling with the clock and getting back onto his *comfortable* settee.'

Charlie emphasised the word comfortable to drive his point home, but the girls were more interested in the clock. Joe took over again.

'Suffice to say, after that, we slept like babies until seven, when Mrs. Daly informed us breakfast was being served in the dining room.'

It was good to see Joe smile. Properly smile. Terri's heart was smiling too.

'A service to humanity, I would say,' said Charlie.

Then Joe started singing the last verse of *My Grandfather's Clock*, which sparked a fit of infectious giggling.

*'Ninety years without slumbering*
*His life seconds numbering*
*It stopped short, never to go again.*
*when the old man died.'*

That afternoon, the four friends strolled arm in arm along the prom, eating chips as Joe sang his song again. They all joined in the last two lines, their choir lost beneath the squalling sea breeze and the cries of the seagulls…

\* \* \*

The shop was quiet that Tuesday. Sheila had taken the day off and Terri was relieved not to have to talk about the Reillys or their weekend. Joe collected her after closing his shop for the half day, and they went to the University Café. In the privacy of a familiar booth, they ordered their usual two coffees and a toasted cheese sandwich. But the mood was subdued.

Terri slid the salt and pepper out of the way and reached across the table for Joe's hand. He looked exhausted. A night of broken sleep in Largs followed by another in Beechgrove Street hadn't helped. He wasn't used to tenement life, even if he was in the bedroom and not the kitchen recess! They both started to speak at once, then smiled, which eased the tension a little.

'No. You first,' he said. 'I was just going to say sorry again for all this. I don't think I'll ever forgive my mother. I know it's her doing.'

'You realise you just went first, don't you?' said Terri, squeezing his hand.

They were still smiling at each other when the coffee and sandwich arrived.

'Ah, what it is to be young and in love,' said the waiter, kissing the fingertips of his right hand and blowing the kiss at them in true Italian fashion.

How could they tell him their hearts were broken?

Joe took a large gulp of coffee. 'I know what we're going to do.'

'You do?' said Terri. 'By the way, it was my turn to speak.'

Joe ignored her. It was as if the romantic gesture had infused him with renewed bravado.

'We're going to get married anyway. The banns have been read. We don't need my parents' approval. To hell with them. If they choose not to come, that's up to them. I'll go to the house tomorrow after closing and tell them. If they want to play silly buggers, then so can we.'

He seemed pleased with his decision and tucked into the toasted cheese with enthusiasm. He hadn't asked Terri what she thought, which annoyed her, but she let it go. Joe was planning to stay at Charlie's until he could find somewhere more permanent. Terri wasn't surprised. If he stayed another night with her parents, they might never make it to the altar. She also wanted a proper chat with her father before agreeing to anything.

'Now, Terri. It's your turn,' Joe said, finishing the last bite of sandwich without offering her any.

*It's just as well I'm not in the mood for an argument, Joe Reilly,* she thought.

## 23. Terri. Glasgow. 15th April 1952
### Wise Words from a Wise Man

Joe dropped Terri at the entrance to the Close at 35 Beechgrove Street. They were both too tired for any more discussion. Terri had told him she wanted to sleep on his suggestion about the wedding. He had been deflated, but perked up when she assured him, she did not care when or where she married him.

'We can always elope to Gretna Green,' she had said after kissing Joe goodnight. Somehow, this ludicrous suggestion had appeased him. But that's all it was, a ludicrous suggestion. Every bit as ludicrous as them getting married without his family. Joe would regret it for the rest of his life and she could not let that happen. It made sense that he was angry at the Reillys. She was too. But someone had to think about the practicalities and that someone was not Joe. He had no idea about the cost of a wedding. She climbed the stairs with feet that felt like blocks of cement.

Alec was dozing in his chair beside the fire. He rarely moved far away from it now. Terri stood for a moment and looked at her wonderful father. How was he going to take her news? Terri didn't care about Tina's response, no doubt loud and opinionated, but she cared deeply about Alec's reaction. She had worked so hard to build a life for herself, a career, a loving relationship, a future. How could it all be crumbling? Her father's eyes fluttered open and when he saw her, his thin, pale face lit up with a smile. A smile so full of love it overwhelmed her. She bit her lip to stop it trembling. He was still with her, but she knew it wouldn't be for long. Maybe not today or tomorrow, but far too soon. She planted a loud kiss on his forehead.

'Where's Mum? My turn to make the tea, I suppose?'

'Yes, that would be about right, Teresa. I think you still owe me 4,380 cups after this one, but who's counting? Your mother's in the bedroom, getting ready for the bingo. And what was the smackeroo of a kiss in aid of? Did I do something to earn it?'

'You've earned so many smackeroos that I still owe you 4,380 after that one, but who's counting.'

She disappeared into the scullery to kick off her shoes, fill the kettle and steady herself.

'That you, Teresa?' Tina Coulter shouted.

She came in, buttoning up her good red coat and adjusting her hat in front of the small mirror.

'I'm off. Mamie O'Hara and I are heading to the bingo in the church hall. I might win a fortune. Young Alec's out for the night with his floozie and I've no idea where Robert is. He bunked off school again today. Won't be late.'

The front door banged and she was gone. Terri stood with a cup in each hand. No time to say anything. She went back into the kitchen, looked at Alec, and the two of them burst out laughing. Father and daughter knew Tina too well. A tirade of talk then out the door before anyone could ask a question.

She was about to sit in the chair opposite her father when he said,

'Why not sit here on the floor in front of my chair, the way you used to when you were a girl? Well, when you were a younger girl. That was one of my favourite times, you know, when it was late and you'd creep out of bed and sit in front of the fire with me.'

It was one of Terri's favourite times too. She wasn't quite as agile as she had been as a girl, but she set her cup on the floor and eased herself down, legs stretched in front of her. She was back in her safe place.

'Now, Teresa. Tell me what's wrong.'

She could never fool her father. Lifting her cup, Terri took a sip and told him the whole sordid story of their wedding fiasco. He stroked her hair as she spoke, saying nothing until she had finished. They sat in silence for a few minutes, both staring into the fire. Her father rarely told her what to do, not like Mr Reilly with Joe. The only direct advice he ever gave was:

'Always listen to your gut and your heart, Teresa.'

That used to frustrate her when she was young and desperate for answers. But he had been right. And over time, she had learned how to listen to her gut and her heart, even if it sometimes took a while to hear them. He was the wisest man she had ever known.

'I don't think Mr and Mrs Reilly set out to ruin your life by cancelling the wedding, Teresa," he said at last. 'But I agree… it was a drastic decision based on a very shaky foundation.'

She had omitted to tell him the part about the pregnancy.

'They believe they're protecting their son, even if they're going about it all the wrong way. Maybe they haven't noticed how much Joe's changed. He's not a vulnerable young man with a disability anymore. He's an intelligent, confident man who knows exactly what he wants and how to get it. Would you not agree, Teresa?'

Terri turned in time to see her father grinning.

'Dad!' she said, slapping his knee, well aware he meant Joe's pursuit of her. But she was not about to be distracted. She hadn't forgotten Father O'Flynn's visit.

'Maybe they like him being vulnerable, disabled and close to them.'

But her father must have read her mind, which wasn't unusual.

'That idiot priest may well have been bending their ear. He might have influenced them more than the other way round. They're probably as upset about all this as you and Joe.'

Terri doubted that, but said nothing.

Terri smiled as he continued. Alec Coulter, always the peacemaker.

'And you'll find they're as keen to find a solution as you and Joe too. I wouldn't say Mr Reilly's a man who likes being backed into a corner, but I don't have him down as totally unreasonable either. And Mrs Reilly will never think any girl is good enough for her son.'

She had to speak now. 'She thinks Everina McGarry's good enough. Joe told me himself.'

Alec laughed and patted the top of her head. 'That's only until he puts a ring on her finger. Then Mrs Reilly might tell a different story. Anyway, Joe knows full well he's found the girl of his dreams. And her name's certainly not Everina.'

Although Alec was still laughing, Terri heard the weariness in his voice. She stood up, with more difficulty than sitting down, and lifted their cups.

'You should rest, Dad. And I'd better get organised for the morning. It'll be another busy day. Sheila was off today and Joe collected me before I had a chance to clean up properly.'

'Teresa, the most important thing is that you and Joe love each other. What difference will a few months make?'

Her father leaned his head against the back of the chair and closed his eyes. Terri was heading towards the scullery when he added quietly, 'Compromise is not defeat, Teresa. On the contrary, it can be a victory.

I've a feeling Mr Reilly will agree to just about anything if you put a deal on the table. One that lets him save face in the parish.'

The next sound she heard was muffled snoring.

## 24. Terri. Perth. 8th April 2021
### Reflection: Family and Compromise

Maureen has gone home to be with Martin. His mother was a lovely woman. We didn't have a lot in common, but we got on well. In the days before she left, Maureen and I talked about the change of date for our wedding. She was shocked. I suppose the subject had never come up in conversation.

'Have a look upstairs in the brown leather pouch in the small box at the bottom of my wardrobe,' I said. 'I saved the invitations for April 28th 1952. They're all there.'

If I thought she'd been furious about the visit from the priest, she was twice as mad when she heard this story.

'I was annoyed at the time,' I told her. 'But it was so long ago and it all worked out in the end. After all, I was married to your father for forty-five years.'

'But how could they delay the wedding, knowing your dad was so ill?' she asked, and before I could answer, added:

'It doesn't make sense, especially when the doctors thought he would be lucky to make Christmas. That was so selfish of the Reillys.'

I had to tell Maureen the story of how we settled the issue. I didn't want her to stay annoyed at the Reillys. They were her grandparents and she loved them. I was never as outraged as Joe about the wedding being postponed. I'm not sure why. I just knew I couldn't be responsible for adding fuel to the fire. My father was wise. So wise. I talked to him and afterwards, I knew what to do. Joe took a bit more persuading.

We visited Cumlodden Drive a few days after our weekend in Largs. Joe rang the doorbell and his youngest sister, Pearl, answered.

'I'll just go and find out what to do,' she said.

Joe was indignant and wanted to walk away. I linked my arm into his and held on tight, more to keep him there than anything else. We were granted entry and led to the front room, the one kept for visitors. That made Joe even madder. Then Mr Reilly wheeled Mama in. Their faces were bleak, as if someone had died. Joe and I sat on one side of the room, the Reillys on the other. It felt more like a standoff than a family discussion.

Maureen laughed when I said, 'I still can't believe I did all the talking.'

She didn't know me back then. It wasn't like me to speak for Joe, especially with his parents. But that day, I said what had to be said and I was delighted with myself. I can't recall every word. It's nearly seventy years ago. But I remember the gist of it.

I told Mr Reilly we were shocked and hurt and that we had seriously considered going ahead with the wedding in April. Without them. That got a reaction. I remember saying, 'We don't need your permission. The banns have been read.'

Mr Reilly went puce. Mama just sat with her hands folded in her lap.

The bits in the middle are woolly, but I finished by saying,

'Joe and I are sensible and considerate adults.'

I think I added that Joe loved them. I didn't dare look at him in case he was scowling. But it was true. Then I told them we'd agreed on a wedding date: Tuesday, 2nd September. I let that sink in and added that I was grateful they were paying for the reception, as my parents couldn't afford it.

But the best part came as we stood to leave. I looked straight at Mama Reilly.

'By the way, I won't be changing the way I dress or the colour of my hair.' I paused. 'And I am not pregnant.'

Mama's face turned scarlet and Mr Reilly's went white. Maureen and I laughed just thinking of it.

When we got to the bottom of the stairs, relieved not to have been thrown down them, Joe held me tight and said, 'I've never been prouder of anyone in my life.' After the bear hug, he looked at me and said, 'O, Teresa Coulter, I love you.'

Now, Maureen and I were both crying. I'm crying now just thinking about it. Joe said those words for the rest of his life. Later, it became *O Terri Reilly, I love you*. He liked saying that. Maureen and the family have seen them written in umpteen cards over the years.

The Reillys weren't bad people. Just too concerned with what others thought. After my father died and my mother moved to New York, they became the only grandparents our children knew for a long time.

In 1957, we decided to emigrate and join Joe's brother Barney and his wife Molly in Toronto. I'd already given up the shop when Maureen was a baby. The tickets were bought, the forms filled in. I was pregnant with Paul, and Joe, being Joe, wrote that we had one and a half children. The Reillys were upset about us leaving. And again, I had to be the one to take a stand.

'I can't do it, Joe,' I said. 'I can't take their only grandchildren to the other side of the world.'

He was stunned, but when we talked it through, he agreed. Neither of us ever regretted staying. We built our own life. Our own family. As I said to Maureen, family is important. Very important. At the end of the day, that's what it's all about.

## 25. Terri. Beechgrove Street, Glasgow. August 1952
### *Precious Moments and Revelations*

'I'm home!'

Terri sloughed off her shoes and hung up her coat in the scullery. Her father's voice was the only response. She was delighted.

'Would that be the lovely Teresa Coulter by any chance?'

Alec was in his chair by the fire. As if reading her mind, he added, 'I'm home alone. Everyone else has scarpered. Come, sit down and tell me about your day. Were you busy? Silly question... you're always busy.'

Terri sat opposite, stretching her hands toward the fire. It was August, but there was already a chill in the evening air.

'Yes, a very busy day, Dad. But a good complaint. Business is booming.' She looked closely at him. 'More importantly, how are you? How's the pain today?'

It was the question she asked every day. Alec usually replied with a vague 'up and down', then changed the subject. Tonight was no different.

He was even thinner. His trousers looked like they had been made for someone twice Alec's size. He said *baggy breeks* made the ileostomy easier to manage, but never explained any further, just got on with it. Meticulous. Private. Using his own basin, burning the soiled rags Tina cut for him. The peppery smell lingered, no matter how wide the windows were opened.

'You've got that concerned look again,' he said. 'I'm fine. And I'd rather talk about you. Now, what does a man have to do to get a cup of tea around here?'

Terri made the tea and placed his cup on the little table beside his armchair. He wouldn't drink much, but he liked the ritual. She threw a few lumps of coal on the fire and sat down again with her coffee.

'That's a cosy fire, Dad.'

'Your mother had a job getting it going this morning. She had to use the newspaper to draw it up the chimney. I didn't have the heart to tell her I hadn't read it yet.'

They chuckled. It was typical Tina, battling with the fire like it was a person.

'What about the shovel trick against the hearth?'

'Didn't work. I thought we'd have a chimney fire before she was done.'

Then the lightness in his voice dimmed. 'I hate that it's become her job now that I'm not so well. And Robert's never here when there's work to be done.'

Terri changed the subject, telling tales of Sheila's antics, her fussy customers, and the cash register with a mind of its own. It worked.

'It's so good to see you happy, Teresa,' he said after a while. 'You had a hard time last year, battling with difficult decisions. But now, you seem like you're back on track.'

Terri nodded. 'I do feel more like myself. But it wasn't just indecision I struggled with, Dad. It was guilt. I told Joe the truth about Terence, but never mentioned Joe to Terence. I did love him, you know, but I think he was more of a dream than a reality.'

Alec leaned back. 'Love's a funny business. You were brave, Teresa. You listened to your gut. I should have done the same. I carry guilt too.'

'You?'

He raised a hand at her objection. He wanted to speak.

'I knew your mother and I weren't suited. She was a good-looking girl, you know. And she was confident and cocky. I admired that in her... at first. Anyway, I fell for her in a big way. My mother, your grandma, warned me, but I paid no heed. I thought love would fix everything. But love and marriage don't change who you are. Our personalities never matched. It was as simple as that. But I wasn't fair to her.'

Terri sat upright. 'But Dad, I've never heard you raise your voice to Mum. You're always so tolerant. How was that unfair?'

There was a shift in his voice, not louder, but heavier.

'Because I gave up, Teresa. I stopped trying. Tina didn't have a mother like mine. She had one who drank and looked out for herself. Tina had to figure it all out on her own. She's a survivor. And when she feels threatened, she lashes out. Not always in anger... sometimes just to protect herself. I never helped her understand the difference.'

Terri hadn't thought of it that way. She simply accepted her mother the way she was. Alec looked so weary, but seemed determined to keep talking.

'I retreated from life. Stopped going to the billiards hall. Stopped taking her to the pictures or dances. I was afraid she'd embarrass me. But I never explained what was wrong. Never gave her a chance to meet me halfway. So no... I wasn't fair. And I wasn't a saint, Teresa. I was a coward. And I live with that.'

It was a lot to take in. Terri moved to his chair, knelt in front of her father and looked into his face.

'Thank you for telling me, Dad. For sharing how you feel. But I can see you and Mum love each other, even if you *are* different personalities.'

She had often resented the way Tina spoke to her father. But lately, Terri had noticed something new between them. Something gentler.

'I've watched Mum over the past few months. The way she cares for you. No fuss. No complaints. No bluster. That's love, Dad. And let's face it, you married the best fritter maker in Glasgow. That has to count for something!'

Terri saw his features relax, as if the guilt had loosened its grip. He even managed to laugh at her attempt at humour.

'You may not be a saint, Dad, but you'll always be my hero. And Joe Reilly knows a wedding ring won't change that.'

She rested her head on his lap. He stroked her hair. They stayed like that, sharing the silence. Bonded by unconditional love.

Then Terri got to her feet. 'It occurs to me, Mr Coulter, you never did answer my question. How are you today?'

Alec's eyes were closed now, sweat on his forehead, jaw muscles visibly working to control the pain.

'Please don't tell me you're fine,' she said gently. 'I know you hate taking medicine, but the doctor left morphine. Please let me give you some.'

He opened his eyes.

'To be honest, Teresa... and it seems to be a night for honesty... I haven't been great today. Feels like a bloody rat is gnawing away inside me. I'd like to kill the bugger.'

He never swore. Terri's throat tightened.

'Maybe I'll have a spoonful, just to keep you happy. I don't want to be a misery-guts when your mother gets back.'

Terri fetched the morphine. As she measured it into a spoon, Alec called her name.

'Thank you for listening. I wanted you to understand… in case something happens sooner rather than later.'

He paused, gathering himself.

'It's not always like this. Some days are good. That's why I save the morphine. And I want to be awake for our chats. I look forward to them.'

She fed him the syrup, concentrating on keeping her hand steady.

*Don't spill the medicine. Don't spill the medicine.*

'And by the way,' Alec added, eyes closing, 'I have no intention of going anywhere before you get married. I won't see you walk up the aisle, but I'll be around long enough to make sure Joe Reilly makes an honest woman of you.'

*Don't spill the tears. Don't spill the tears.*

'He's a good man, Teresa,' Alec whispered, then drifted into sleep.

Terri stood in the kitchen of 35 Beechgrove Street with an empty spoon in her hand and an empty ache in her heart. She didn't spill the medicine, but she couldn't stop the tears from spilling.

## 26. Maureen. Belfast. 12*th* April 2021
### Back and Forth

The sound of Barbara Dickson wafts through my headphones: *Another Suitcase in Another Hall*. I smile, aligning myself with the title and the line, 'Where am I going to?' I could change the words to *Another Rucksack in Another Lounge,* but it doesn't have the same ring.

This time, the departure lounge is in Belfast Harbour rather than an airport.

My brother Joe phoned on Sunday.

'Maur, you have to come back. Mum's not good. She took the news about Aunt Maureen hard.'

My Aunt Maureen, known as Sister Mary Christine, a Servite nun for seventy years, died on Saturday. Mum has known her as a sister-in-law even longer and kept in regular contact. Colette and I visited Aunt Maureen with Mum at the convent in Bognor Regis just before Covid. She was ninety-six then, sharp-witted and engaging, despite her age and frailty.

'I know, Joe. As soon as I heard the news, I thought of Mum. I knew she would be devastated, especially coming so soon after Martin's Mum. I spoke to her last night. She was very tearful.'

I could hear the anxiety in my brother's voice.

'She's hardly eating, Maur. I think she needs you.'

\* \* \*

There was no hesitation. No choice to be made. But no available flights either. So here I am, a day later, aboard the eleven o'clock sailing to Cairnryan, travelling to Scotland for the final time before Mum dies. There is no escaping reality now.

I settle at a small table in the lounge and retrieve my laptop. The ferry is busier than the crossing in June. Now that vaccination is available to all age groups and older people have had their boosters, it is hoped restrictions will be lifted, and life will return to some form of normality. But not for me. I stare at the screen, desperate to write something. My life will never return to normal. I am about to lose my mum. The lifting of Covid restrictions will not help that pain.

Mum and I have stopped delving into the past. It was time. We both sensed it. Mum sleeps more now. Asking about the past began to feel contrived. We simply enjoy the time we have. No agenda. Often, no words. Just togetherness.

Mum still insists on a daily top-to-toe wash, as she has done since those scullery days in the Gorbals. 'A cat's lick,' she calls it. At least she doesn't have to stand in a basin.

Afterwards, she sits on the chair outside the bathroom while we tackle the challenge of dressing and preparing for the day.

'Maureen, look after your back. I can do that bit.'

I kneel on the floor and say, 'I'm fine, Mum. I'll put the tights on your feet and the trousers on your ankles from here. Then we'll pull them up together.'

Basic stuff. She struggles to her feet from the chair. I struggle to my feet from the floor. This is usually accompanied by hoots of laughter at the absurdity of what we call *the blind leading the blind*. But we manage. No fuss. No stress.

The same goes for our adaptation of the ileostomy bag change every two days. Mum begins the process in the bathroom, and I finish it on the bed. It gives her some independence and self-respect and keeps her safe. Episodes of *the Blackness* are increasing. A fall could mean hospital. That would be disastrous, not just for Mum, but for all of us. Hospital means separation. During Covid, that's unthinkable.

The laptop screen stays blank. I expect my thoughts to turn into words. They fail to comply. I want to document the small details. Not because I think anyone else will care. But I care. What if I forget? Shared intimacy is special. It takes trust and has nothing to do with being a nurse. When Mum came to Ireland, I used to help her into the bath and let her soak for as long as she wanted. We had great chats and laughs, me perched on the toilet seat, Mum submerged in bubbles, discussing the problems of the world, and the family.

I pour coffee from my flask and close the laptop. Clutching my mug in both hands, I smile and think of those happy times. The couple at the neighbouring table look over. I think my smile may have decided the memory deserved a laugh-out-loud moment.

## 27. Maureen. Perth. April 2021
### *The New Routine*

**13th April 2021**

Babies like routine. As they grow, their routine adapts to reflect new stages. That's the theory, anyway.

Our lives are filled with adaptations. Some changes are minor, others major or catastrophic. The phrase *'The only constant in life is change'* is attributed to the Greek philosopher Heraclitus. This pandemic is a good example: simple routines like shopping, socialising, travelling and attending appointments have required changes we never imagined. As we approach the end of life—if it doesn't come suddenly—routines adapt to the changes in body, mind and spirit. Comfort and care become the priority.

I reached Perth yesterday, thankful to be here. Today was Mum's last day downstairs. Her last day to get dressed. Her last day out of bed. It feels as though the Grim Reaper is somewhere in the shadows now, waiting to pounce. This stage in Mum's illness came both suddenly and slowly, dramatic yet inevitable. I came to Scotland ten months ago to care for my mother and preside over her imminent death. That was the remit, the commitment, the fear. But death faded into the background, and we settled into a cocoon of normality. We embraced life with stories and lattes, with laughter and dancing, with unexpected outings and shopping trips. There were tough days, physically and emotionally, but no tangible end in sight.

Until today.

On reflection, the stairs had already become a challenge. *The Blackness* was descending more and more frequently. We leaned on each other, stopping often to rest and wait for the dizziness to pass. Mum accepted it with her usual resilience. We tackled it together. Another adjustment in our evolving normal. Eventually, Mum began using the downstairs toilet to empty her ileostomy bag, something she hated because of the lingering, peppery odour.

'It has to be done, I suppose,' she said the first time.

After that, she never mentioned it again. Acceptance. Resilience.

Today began as usual, though everything took longer: washing, dressing, getting downstairs. Our latte and morning chat were closer to lunchtime than coffee time, but that didn't matter. It was *our* time, not dictated by the clock.

Barney came in after work and chatted to Mum for a while. She was tired.

'Why don't we go upstairs and Barney can say goodnight before he goes home?' I suggested.

At the top of the stairs, our first regular Blackness bus stop is an ottoman where Mum stores sheets. But the Blackness did not lift. Mum was swallowed into its depths, relentlessly. No respite this time. She slumped on top of me, her voice barely audible, slurred.

'Maureen… Blackness… I can't… I just can't.'

'Barney, I need you,' I shouted, trying not to sound as panicked as I felt.

I did not succeed. He galloped up the stairs and appeared at my side in seconds. Without a word, he cradled our tiny mother in his arms, carried her into the bedroom, and laid her down on her bed with love and tenderness.

Once lying flat, she recovered quickly and was back to herself by the time Barney was ready to leave.

After a goodnight kiss, she said, 'I'm fine, you know. Now, get yourself home. Lorna will be waiting for you.'

She did not see him cry as we hugged at the front door, both aware this was a watershed moment. The beginning of the end. Barney the GP and me, the nurse. But in that moment, just a brother and sister, holding each other, trying to bear the weight of what was to come.

\*\*\*

## 14th April 2021

I straighten my shoulders before opening the door to Mum's bedroom to begin the first day of our new routine. The final chapter.

'Morning, Mum. It's a lovely day. Not as good as this time last year, but lovely anyway.'

I pull up the window blind. Mum sits up in bed, ready for breakfast. She has a way of manoeuvring herself and will not allow me to help, worried about my back. I sort the pillows, a traditional nursing task, and settle the tray on her lap.

The courtyard is bright in the early sun. Mum makes no mention of going downstairs. Neither do I.

We chat about this and that. Even confined to bed, Mum insists on colour coordination. Fresh pyjamas must match her cardigan and hairband. She dabs at her mouth with a napkin.

'I think I'll wear the green cardigan today, Maureen. My outfit for Sarah's wedding last April was going to be green.'

I swallow hard at this.

'Good idea, Mum,' I say. 'We'll send Sarah a WhatsApp message to tell her you're wearing green in her honour. I'll leave your clothes on the radiator to warm and put on a wash while you finish breakfast. Then I'll join you for a cuppa. How does that sound?'

What a joy to see Mum's face beam at the simple idea of coffee and a chat.

I lift the laundry basket from the floor and leave the room.

'Watch your back!' she shouts.

I smile. Always the mother.

\* \* \*

## 15th April 2021

I bring my coffee up to the bedroom and sit beside Mum as she nibbles at her breakfast. It is clearly an effort. I have avoided the subject long enough:

'Mum, do you think it's a good idea to go downstairs today? It wasn't nice to feel so dizzy the other night. And the *Blackness* doesn't seem to bother you when you're in bed.'

I leave it there. Mum gazes out of the window, then turns to me and says, 'I think I'll stay in bed for the time being, Maureen. It's nice and close to the bathroom, and we can bring a few chairs into the bedroom if we need them for visitors. I like looking out at the trees. But you might bring up my vase of Alstroemeria and leave them on the dressing table where I can see them.'

And that was that. No looking back. No self-pity. No regret. Just acceptance. Resilience.

\* \* \*

### 18th April 2021

The pressure-relieving mattress from Sligo is now on the bed. There will be no pressure ulcers on my watch.

Meals are bird-sized now, but Mum still enjoys her latte. I cut up toasted cheese or bits of cake into tiny sections. The cappuccino from Costa, courtesy of Barney, Lorna and the girls, still feels like a treat for us both. Mum likes a morsel of cherry Bakewell tart, always ensuring Barney gets the large piece with the cherry. It's tradition now.

Our morning and evening routines are unhurried, but continue to reflect the meticulous attention to cleanliness and appearance expected of Terri Reilly. I hand her cleansers, toners, serums, moisturisers and cotton wool. She applies each one carefully. When I pass her the face cloth and towel for personal hygiene, I am reminded of bed baths long ago at Glasgow's Western Infirmary.

Before sleeping, Mum protects her hair with a pink hairnet. We have agreed that curlers are off the menu for now. Colette can deal with the hair issue when she arrives. One of Mum's simple pleasures is having cream massaged into her feet and legs. My hands brush over the lumps, bumps and holes left by cancer.

'Oh, that feels good, Maureen,' she says and I'm struck again by how such a small act can bring such comfort.

Then the final steps in our bedtime ritual: I remove and clean Mum's false teeth, store her tiny hearing aid batteries, and turn on the radio, loud enough to hear without aids. Very loud.

I kiss Mum goodnight and we exchange the words of the old rhyme:
*Good night, sleep tight*
*Don't let the bedbugs bite.*
What a beautiful new routine. What a privilege.

As I lie in my bed across the landing, I think of the families who were deprived of showing and receiving this kind of love at the end of life because of Covid.

*Thank you*, I whisper to the Universe as I close my eyes.

## 28. Terri. Perth. April 2021
### Reflection: Hindsight and Foresight

**19th April 2021**

I've been in bed for a few days now. It makes life easier for Maureen, not having to get me dressed and help me downstairs. In all honesty, it's easier for me, too. But I feel lazy, lying here being waited on hand and foot. I've been thinking and dozing. Dozing and dreaming. And I must say, I'm enjoying it.

Thankfully, after we settled on the September wedding, everything fell into place. The ceremony was lovely and we had a wonderful day. Of course, I missed my father, but we were blessed he lived to see us married. For some reason, the final memory I shared with Maureen wasn't the church or the reception. I told her about our honeymoon train. I wanted her to know how happy I was with Joe. And that journey has always been a vivid, special memory. It felt like the right way to end our story time together. I didn't tell Maureen it was the last story, but I think she already knew. It was time to leave the past in the past.

The nurse came with a commode yesterday, so I don't have to worry about the *Blackness* when I get up to the toilet. It's not ideal, but needs must. The nurse also asked Maureen if I wanted to be resuscitated. What a silly question.

'Of course,' I said to Maureen. 'They asked me the same question in the hospital and I gave them the same answer. Life's precious. Of course I want to be resuscitated.'

I never thought I'd see the day I'd be entertaining in my bedroom. Sitting up in bed like the Queen of Sheba. It's one thing, family coming and going, but I've had my Keep Fit friends as well as Fraser and Elaine from along the road. Fraser has already seen me at my worst. Like the times I've had to call him when something broke down before I was properly dressed or had my face on. He brought me a wee glass of Jamaican rum because he knows I'm partial to a drop. I drank the lot.

'Better than any bunch of grapes,' I told him, and he laughed. They have been so good to me over the years. And my sausage rolls are a big hit when they go away in their caravan.

I must have been dozing or daydreaming because Maureen is beside me.

'Do you fancy some music, Mum?' she says.

We've been listening to a lot of music since I've been in bed. Maureen finds anything I want to hear on her mobile phone. The two of us have done so much talking about the old days and now I get to listen to all the old songs too. Colett's CD is still on the machine downstairs. We had some great laughs, singing and dancing to my favourite tunes.

I wanted to hear *The Minstrel Boy* again. And Bob's your uncle, there it was. It was my father's song and always makes me cry. But today, it feels soothing, reassuring, like he's with me in the room. I know that sounds daft, but it doesn't matter.

Lying here, I've been thinking about my mother and father a lot. Maybe it's reliving my memories with Maureen, maybe it's the music. I'm not sure. I don't remember my mother having a song. It annoyed her when we were in my grandmother Annie's house and the Coulter family would sing. And then Joe's family were all musical and that annoyed her even more. But when I think about it now, I understand. She was probably intimidated. I felt the same way myself at times. I wouldn't perform in front of the Coulters and certainly never sang at any of the Reilly gatherings. But I knew I had other skills. I never thought I had to sing to prove I was as good as them. My mother was a different kettle of fish. When she felt daunted, she attacked. Her modus operandi was always to attack first and think later. It got her into a lot of trouble, but it's all she knew. Dad tried to explain it to me before he died, but I didn't think about it properly. Until now.

My father was my hero. Always. And my mother embarrassed me when I was young. I loved her, but she was coarse, mouthy and loud. I hated that. But when I think of her now, I realise she was also kind and caring. She let my dog, Major, stay for a year, even though she was terrified of him. She took in a pregnant girl when the house was already overcrowded. And she nursed my father at home for months on her own before he died.

My father wasn't perfect, even if he was my hero. So many times, I wanted him to stand up to Tina. Make her send me back to school. Defend me. But he never did. He took the path of least resistance. He told me that himself. It was just a different era. My parents both did their best.

My father died when I was on honeymoon. He was only forty-seven. That's ten years younger than my youngest son is now. My mother was a widow for nearly forty years. I made sure she never wanted for anything. But I never told her she had done her best. I wish I had. The funny thing is, when I think about it, I'm not as different from her as I always liked to believe. I probably inherited some of her no-nonsense attitude to life.

God knows, I wasn't always a good mother, or even a good wife myself. I made a lot of mistakes. I got a lot wrong. Joe would be amused if he could hear me. He used to say, 'You're right, Terri,' when he didn't mean it. And I'd say, 'Of course I'm right, Joe.' And we'd both laugh. It was a family joke. No one's always right. Not even me.

## 29. Terri. The Honeymoon Train. 2nd September 1952
### A Whole New Start

The whistle blew and the train pulled slowly out of Glasgow Central Station, belching clouds of thick steam and coal smoke in its wake. Family members waved enthusiastically from the platform. Then Mr and Mrs Joseph Reilly pulled up the carriage window and plonked themselves into their seats, giggling like teenagers. They watched as the busy station, then the familiar industrial buildings and red sandstone tenements, faded into the distance. They were on their way, heading to Southampton and instead of taking the ferry, they were to board a flight to Guernsey for their two-week honeymoon. It was all very exciting. Their very first flight. Joe described himself as 'faintly terrified' when he told Charlie, but Terri couldn't wait. If they were going to embark on a new life together, it should start with an adventure, she reasoned. They had the carriage to themselves, an unexpected bonus.

Terri moved closer to Joe, her new husband. She lifted her left hand and admired the thin 18-carat white gold orange blossom wedding ring, twirling it a few times.

'Our honeymoon train, Joe. Peace at last.'

She cuddled even closer to him. It was hard to tell where one stopped and the other began. Joe turned his head and looked into her eyes. Terri felt as if invisible wires connected them, his love flowing like a current. He didn't blink and she didn't look away.

'You seem pensive,' she said, sweeping a stray auburn curl from his forehead. 'Penny for your thoughts.'

'Well, apart from feeling like the luckiest man on the planet, I was thinking about my pathetic, lovesick letters when you were in New Malden on holiday. It's a wonder you didn't send me packing there and then.'

'It's a wonder indeed, Mr Reilly. But your letters were rather romantic, even if they were sometimes a little over the top.'

'Over the top? *Moi*? I can't imagine what you mean, *Madame!*'

Terri sat forward in her seat and, in what she hoped was a pretentious voice, announced:

'...As often as I breathe, I think of you. There's not one moment of the day when you stray from my mind, and I damn the convention which places you and me at opposite ends of the country..."

Joe laughed and Terri joined him.

'I am deeply flattered that you memorised my letters, Mrs Reilly. And yes, perhaps a tad effusive.' Then he paused and added, 'Though I take back not one single word.'

'Don't get carried away with yourself, Mr Reilly. I memorised a line, not a whole letter. But you should still be flattered. Anyway, it worked, didn't it? After all, I married you.'

Joe took both her hands in his. He wasn't laughing any more.

'You did. And as well as being the luckiest man alive, I am also the happiest. You looked stunningly beautiful in your wedding dress as you made your way towards me. And I knew how hard it was for you to have your brother, not your father, walk you down the aisle. But you were strong and magnificent, just like you always are. Of course, I couldn't cry in case I set you off. Also, I forgot to put a clean hanky in my suit pocket."

'It's just as well you didn't take out a big hanky as I walked up the aisle, Joe Reilly. Considering the noise you make when you blow your nose, I might have marched back down again.'

Joe liked nothing better than a bit of banter.

'I am mortally offended at your less-than-kind innuendo, *Madam*. And had you retreated down the aisle, I would have had to charge you for the flowers, which, though I say so myself, matched your dress rather well, considering I had never clapped eyes on it.'

His playful tone became gentle again. 'But I never had any doubt you would be a vision of loveliness, the epitome of elegance. And of course, I knew you would choose a sculpted collar that would show off your beautiful neck.'

'Did you indeed, Sir? And were you also confident I would choose a tightly fitted lace bodice to hug the contours of my slim waist?'

Terri was aware that she was flirting outrageously, but she was married now and savouring the feeling of freedom from propriety. She fluttered her lashes, doing her best to look innocent and stifle a giggle. Unfazed, Joe responded, like an actor in one of his Gilbert and Sullivan productions.

'*Madam*, I beg you to spare my blushes. I can only reveal that, though I remember nothing of the wedding reception or the simpering, smiling guests, I have forever committed to memory every detail of my beautiful bride as she approached me, her dainty hands peeping from long, modest, lace sleeves.'

He paused, just long enough for Terri to think he had finished speaking. Then, with a dramatic flourish, said, '... delicate hands that were wrapped around her exquisite bouquet of expertly chosen flowers.'

There was no holding back this time and the pair of them collapsed into a heap of unrestrained, happy laughter.

Terri looked at this man who was now her husband and she knew why she loved him. He was clever and funny. And he could be sarcastic at times. But he was also thoughtful and kind, sensitive and loving. Life would never be dull. As her Dad had said, 'He's a good man, Teresa.' And he was right.

'The flowers were indeed exquisite, Joe Reilly. And I never had any doubt that you would choose large white lilies to perfectly match my dress. Or that you would craft them into the most beautiful bouquet ever held by a bride.'

Then Terri thought of her father. Her precious, irreplaceable father. 'Joe, I am so pleased we stopped on the way to the reception to show the bouquet to Dad. I know he saw me in my dress before I left for the church, but I wanted him to be the first to call us Mr and Mrs Reilly. Seeing him in his good suit, enormous on his tiny frame and knowing the effort it must have taken to put it on was nearly too much for me.'

The pain had threatened to overwhelm her and Terri forced herself to concentrate hard, not allowing Alec to see her distress. If he could hold onto his pride and composure, then so could she. Even when her heart was gripped by a sorrow too deep for words and a hole that would never be filled. Hard as she tried now, there was no way of stopping the hot tears. Without a word, Joe handed her his pressed white handkerchief.

'I remembered to bring it on honeymoon.'

Terri wasn't ready to speak yet. She accepted it, dabbed her cheeks and eyes gently, and returned it, grateful Joe didn't make one of his sarcastic remarks.

The train lurched from side to side as it rattled along the west coast towards Carlisle. They would change at Crewe and then Birmingham before finally arriving in Southampton. It was a long journey, but they didn't care. It was part of their adventure. Joe's father had suggested Dun Laoghaire in Ireland for a honeymoon, but there wasn't a snowball's chance Terri would have agreed to that. They decided on one of the Channel Islands. The travel agent had given them brochures and the photographs of Guernsey had won them over. Rugged cliffs, sandy beaches, winding coastal paths and cobbled-stoned old towns. It sounded perfect. After the hectic lead-up to the wedding, Terri was looking forward to them having time to ruminate, reflect and plan. Her father had told her about the wartime museums and fortifications, and she wanted to discuss them when they got back.

The wedding was held on a Tuesday, when shops closed for the half-day, causing minimum disruption for Mr Reilly and his staff. The reception was a blur of speeches, food and talking to people Terri didn't know. Her mother had done well, exhausted from nights without sleep and reluctant to be away from Alec. It must have been hard for Tina to be at her only daughter's wedding without her husband of nearly thirty years. But she seemed to have had a good time and Terri was pleased.

Joe sat back in his seat and closed his eyes. It always amazed her that he could have what he called *forty winks* in the middle of any day. Mr. Reilly did the same. The countryside flew past with flashing images of fields with cattle, clumps of forest, threading rivers and occasional farmhouses. Terri was reminded of the train journey from Brighton after she had demobbed. She had looked out at the passing scenery and wondered what life held in store for her. She never imagined this ending. Or rather, this beginning. That day, her father had turned up at Central Station, wearing his good suit and a new hat. He had held her in his arms and said, 'Welcome home, Teresa. Welcome home, my Darling Girl.'

When she hugged her fragile father on her wedding day, he had whispered, 'Welcome to your new life, Teresa. Welcome home, my Darling Girl.'

As if he could read her mind, Joe opened his eyes and handed her back the hanky he had been holding in his clenched fist.

'You know me so well,' she said.

'I have a feeling I know you not at all yet. But I look forward to having the rest of my life to rectify the situation. In the meantime, I will simply say, O Teresa Reilly, I love you.'

## 30. Maureen. Perth. April 2021
### *Contentment*

My dad's headstone is inscribed with the words 'Estoy Contento'. They perfectly encapsulate him because he was a man who appreciated the smallest pleasures in life. His love of the Spanish language and culture came late in life, but it embedded itself in his soul.

However, a similar epitaph would not suit my mum. Terri Reilly, a dynamo who loves to work, to travel, to dance, to shop, to socialise and so much more. Now, as I sit beside her bed and watch her struggle to eat the slice of orange and handful of Rice Krispies, I know the time will come, probably very soon. We will have to find the words for the headstone, where she will be buried beside my dad, her beloved husband, Joe. I have no idea how we will sum up this legend. She may be physically frail, but her zest for life is undiminished.

'Let me help you sit up, Mum. It will make it easier for you to eat.'

'Watch your back, Maureen,' she says. Always concerned.

'I'm fine, Mum,' I lie, struggling to my feet.

Once propped up on pillows, I smooth her thin hair and replace the pink hairband that keeps it neatly in place.

'Colette'll kill me when she sees my hair,' Mum says, and we both laugh because we know it is true. My sister will comment on Mum's straight hair and lack of makeup when she video-calls later this morning. Normally, Terri Reilly hates to be seen without her hair curled and her face made up. But in a silent agreement, she and I both know that glamour is a bridge too far today. It will take too much energy. Energy is needed for other things.

Mum turns her head to look out the bedside window. Her white, shrunken face accentuates the prominence of her jutting cheekbones, but when she smiles all I can see is her essence, her beauty, her grace.

'Isn't it a beautiful morning?' she says and before I can reply, she adds,

'I love to watch the branches of the trees in the garden swaying and rustling in the breeze. It's so peaceful.' She turns back to look at me, 'Does that sound daft?'

'Sure, why would it sound daft, Mum? It is indeed a lovely spring morning.'

The two of us stare out the window, taking in every detail of the world beyond, aware of how closely nature mirrors life. Precious and fragile. For some reason, I am reminded of the first few lines of a poem by Derek Mahon. I cannot remember where I first heard them, but they stuck with me...

*'How should I not be glad to contemplate*
*the clouds clearing beyond the dormer window*
*and a high tide reflected on the ceiling?'*

I say the words out loud. Mum smiles and I smile back. Living in rural Ireland, surrounded by fields and trees, I realise how rarely in all our years there, my mum has remarked on the beauty of nature.

'I'm very content,' Mum says without taking her eyes from the window.

I do not want to break the spell with clumsy words. I take her hand in mine. 'Yes.'

Colette video calls later in the day and comments on Mum's hair,

'I'll be back on Friday, and we'll get those curlers in and make you look better.' Then she asks, more seriously now, 'How are you feeling today?'

Mum responds with her usual, 'Ok. Ok,' and smiles in the general direction of the phone screen.

'Put me on to Maureen. I'll chat to you later. Love you, Mum.'

Mum hands me the phone and closes her eyes, but not before saying, 'Love you too, Darling.'

Colette's voice is tense. She looks strained and anxious.

'Mum doesn't sound good, Maur. Is she ok? Did you not manage to get her curlers in?'

My heart aches for my sister because she is desperate to be here, but can't. She teaches musical theatre and her students are sitting exams. I do my best to sound reassuring.

'Mum's ok, Colette. We're here discussing nature and quoting poetry. She's in good form. Honestly. And you'll be here in a few days. Mum would hate for you to leave your kids high and dry. You know what she's like.'

'True,' Colette agrees. 'She keeps telling me to play it by ear and everything will be alright. But my ears don't want to play anymore, Maur. I just want to be there.'

I laugh and it breaks the tension.

'Yes, one of Mum's favourite expressions. Play it by ear. But she's right, Colette. Everything will be alright. Just concentrate on getting your students through their exams. You'll be with us in no time.'

Mum has repeatedly stated that Colette is not to let the school down by leaving early. Her sense of duty has never waned and overrides any longing to see her daughter.

'It's so hard, Maur. Don't let anything happen before I get there, will you?'

'I'll do my best,' I say and end the call. It's a big ask, and I can only hope and pray that Mum can hang on.

Another day has ended. Mum is still with us, sleeping peacefully next door. I try to capture the day's events in my journal, like collecting butterflies. This morning was the closest Mum and I have come to any discussion about *the end*. She has never wanted to talk about death or dying, except in a general way. The word *contentment* is rarely used in the same sentence as *Terri Reilly* because there is always something she wants to do or somewhere she has to be. And yet, during this past week, she has never objected to staying in bed, never asked to go downstairs. Her acceptance is not passive, her resilience is not forced. They are the embodiment of *playing it by ear,* Terri Reilly-style. I think again of Dad's epitaph: Estoy contento. This morning, for the first time, I believe Mum is saying, *Estoy contenta*. And Dad, I imagine, is smiling to himself, remembering how he always said she would leave the world kicking and screaming.

I am struggling to write. The enormity of Mum's simple and beautiful words, 'I'm very content,' hit me again like an emotional sledgehammer. It feels like a final declaration. The lump in my throat swells, more like a rock than a pebble now.

The remainder of Derek Mahon's poem, *'Everything Is Going To Be All Right'*, comes into my head:

*'There will be dying, there will be dying,*
*but there is no need to go into that.*
*The lines flow from the hand unbidden*

*and the hidden source is the watchful heart.*
*The sun rises in spite of everything*
*and the far cities are beautiful and bright.*
*I lie here in a riot of sunlight*
*watching the day break and the clouds flying.*
*Everything is going to be all right.'*

I concentrate on every breath. My chest hurts from the effort of holding back the tidal wave of grief I know is coming soon.

*In, out, in, out. Breathe Maureen. Just breathe. It's not hard. In, out, in, out.*

The moment passes. My breathing calms. I say the words out loud. Words of reassurance to Colette. Words I pray are true. Words I will hang onto with clenched fists. Soothing words penned by Derek Mahon.

*Everything is going to be all right.*

### 31. Maureen. Perth. Wednesday 21st April 2021
### The Gift that Keeps on Giving

The end, when it comes, is a gift. Not a blessing. Not in that well-meaning way people say 'it's a blessing' when a loved one dies, freed from pain or a life without purpose. No. This is different. This is a gift. A beautiful gift.. The final hours of Teresa Coulter, who became Terri Reilly, always Mum to us, went something like this.

I open the curtains to welcome spring into the bedroom. Mum looks tiny in the double bed, head on the pillow, chin tucked under the sheet, but her smile is big and beaming, matching the brightness of the early sun.

'Morning, Maureen. Another beautiful day.'
'It is indeed, Mum. Would you like any breakfast?'
'No, I don't think so. I'm quite happy as I am.'

I do not encourage or cajole. I have no idea how I know today is different. I just know. I bring a cup of tea upstairs and sit at the bedside. I wish I could remember the details of our chat. I can't. I spend the morning in and around the bedroom, and what I remember is music. Lots of music. I sing and Mum smiles, nodding in appreciation, recognising every song. I join Max Bygraves and belt out:

*When it's spring again, I'll bring again,*
*Tulips from Amsterdam.*
*With a heart that's true, I'll give to you,*
*Tulips from Amsterdam...*

I search for Burl Ives and sing along with his renditions of 'Big Rock Candy Mountain' and 'The Ugly Bug Ball', songs I have not heard since childhood. I dance to Fred Astaire's 'Top Hat, White Tie and Tails', and nearly do myself a mischief during Glen Miller's 'In The Mood'. Mum's bedroom overlooks the courtyard. If neighbours glanced up and saw a woman prancing around her dying mother's bedside like a disoriented gazelle, they could be forgiven for thinking it bizarre. Maybe even inappropriate. But it feels right to me. After sixty-five years as mother and daughter, after months of caring and sharing, of memories and stories, of fears and frustration, lattes and laughter, a deep, unspoken understanding has settled between us. We allow ourselves to be enveloped in a lifetime of familiar melodies. Some of the music Mum requests is hard for me to listen to without becoming upset: *Songs of the Hebrides* by Kenneth McKellar, an LP played by my parents until it was worn thin; 'O Gin I were a Baron's Heir', sung by my dad to his beloved wife at family gatherings; Vera Lynn singing 'We'll Meet Again'. I swallow and sing. Occasionally, I lick salt tears from my lips. Mum looks like a little dancing bird under the covers as she moves in time to the music, eyes closed, singing an occasional line of a song.

I struggle to hold back tears, while Mum just keeps smiling. No matter how emotional the song, she beams her radiant smile. It is all the more surprising because, for Mum, music that stirs memories usually comes with a box of tissues. Today, I see only serenity on her face, as if the music has reached into her soul, each song painting a different scene, familiar, comforting, warm. A peaceful calm permeates the room. I can almost touch it. Colette video-calls, as she does every morning, but she is perplexed when Mum appears distracted, unable to engage in conversation.

'What's wrong with Mum, Maur? Did she have breakfast? Why won't she talk to me?'

The panic in her voice intensifies with each question. How can I explain what is happening here in this room? I take a moment to gather myself. I tell her Mum is just tired, that she'll be better later. But I feel disloyal. A hypocrite. I want to shout: *Come now. Jump on a plane. Mum is dying*. But what would be the point? Colette's flight is already booked for the day after tomorrow. I phone my brothers, Barney and Joe, to tell them Mum's condition has changed. Paul and Jules left yesterday after a week here. My brother knew it was goodbye, but wanted it that way: quiet, dignified. No need to summarise a lifetime of love.

Barney, Lorna and I spend the rest of the day in the bedroom, like hospital visitors. We chat quietly in the background and continue to play a variety of music while Mum drifts in and out of sleep. Even with her eyes closed, her frail hands move in time to songs loved and remembered, her feet dancing beneath the duvet. I look at her and wonder:

## Impossible to Fill

*Where are you, Mum? Are you with people you knew and loved from long ago? Another time, another place?*

I hope so. I am reminded of a song I wrote for Mother's Day nearly twenty years ago:

*She never walks when she can run,*
*Won't sit it out if she can dance,*
*Lives every day as if it's her last chance.*

The memory makes me smile, albeit a watery one.

'You haven't changed a bit, Mum,' I whisper. 'Why lie still when you can dance? Don't ever stop dancing.'

And I know she never will.

In the early evening, we talk about this and that, nothing in particular. Like swans, we are outwardly composed, but underneath the surface, we paddle furiously to survive the waiting. In my career, I've often seen families sitting like this around a bedside. Waiting. Watching. Worrying. Wondering.

*'Is the end near, nurse?'*
*'How will we know?'*
*'Will there be a sign?'*

Trapped in that strange limbo between life and death. Like an airport departure lounge with only one destination and no scheduled flight time. And in that space, a confusion of emotions becomes a kind of prayer:

*'Please don't let them die.*
*Please let it be soon.*
*Please let it be yesterday, last week, last year.*
*Please don't let them suffer.*
*Please don't let them die.'*

I think of those families now and realise we are in that same limbo.

Our conversation drifts to my cousin Lorna's son, Fraser, who is like a grandson to Mum. He has an important interview tomorrow. Suddenly, she opens her eyes, pushes herself up on her elbows and joins in as if it were any other day. Clear, coherent and animated.

'Of course, he'll be the best person for the job. You know, Fraser could take computers apart at the age of seven or eight. Could build a new one from the bits and pieces. He might only be nineteen, but he's as smart as a tack.'

We look at one another, bewildered. Here she is, our mum, sounding like she has no intention of going anywhere. I brim with relief and hope. Maybe Colette *will* get here in time.

* * *

Joe arrives from Inverness around nine o'clock. Barney and Lorna leave an hour later. Barney hugs me tightly. 'Let me know if anything changes.'

Joe is exhausted after a day's work and the long drive. He spends some time with Mum, then heads to bed. I lie beside Mum. We hold hands. I have no memory of what we talk about or even if we talk at all. I only remember the feeling of togetherness.

At some point, I recall saying something like, 'Rest, Mum. I'm right here beside you. You don't have to sleep. Just close your eyes and rest.'

I remember wanting her to feel safe.

Mum's hand is thin and fragile in mine, but when her bony fingers wrap around, I am the one who feels safe. I doze fitfully. I become aware of Mum's arms moving in the air, as if she is conducting an orchestra. But this is not a happy, musical gesture. She is unsettled. I know something is wrong. I get out of bed and kneel beside her.

'Mum, are you feeling a bit unwell?'

She nods her head.

'I think I'm going to phone the nurse. Is that ok with you? She left some medication here and I think it'll make you feel better. What do you think?'

'That's fine, Maureen. That's fine.'

She closes her eyes again, her expression troubled, as though she is trying to fight off the feeling. I wonder if the dreaded *Blackness* has descended, but I don't ask.

I call for Joe. He comes running into the room—half asleep, fully awake, frightened.

'It's ok, Joe. Everything's fine. Mum's just a little unsettled. We both think it's a good idea to phone the nurse. Maybe you should give Barney a buzz.'

I take a deep breath to keep my voice even and controlled. I try not to think beyond the phone call. The nurse answers immediately. She says she is on her way.

'Joe, it might be better if you had trousers on when the nurse arrives.'

He looks down at his underpants. 'Oh yeah. Good call, Maur. By the way, I didn't get Barney. I'll try again.'

Mum's face is pale, but her voice is steady, her words clear. 'Maureen, can you sit me up the bed a bit?'

'Of course, Mum.'

Joe hears us talking. By the time I'm tucked under Mum, ready to move her, he is back in the room. Decent, if not fully dressed.

'Wait for me, Maur. Watch your back.'

He drapes himself across the double bed, tenderly lifting one side of Mum's tiny body while I concentrate on the other. She sits up. I fix her pillows.

'That's better,' she says.

Then she gently leans her head on my shoulder.

And dies.

I have no idea how I know instantly. But I do

A few seconds pass. I place my mum's head gently back onto the pillow.

'She's gone, Joe. She's gone.'

Her eyes are closed. I close my own and cry silent, burning tears.

'No, Maur, you're wrong. She's here. She's just asleep. She can't be gone. She was talking a few minutes ago. She's still here.'

I think I say, 'No, Joe. Mum has gone. But it's ok. It's ok.'

We repeat these phrases to each other several times, trying to make sense of the moment. But there is no sense. It's hard for Joe to take in. To comprehend. It is hard for me, too.

As a nurse, I have witnessed death. I recognise the familiar sounds that often herald its arrival: the rattling, the gurgling, the gasping, the whispers. I have listened to shallow breathing, laboured breathing and the long, lonely pauses that stifle breathing at the end.

I thought I was prepared.

But not for this.

No slow decline. No fading. No transition. Not even a final sigh.

One moment, Mum was here. The next, she wasn't.

I tell Joe there's something special about her eldest and youngest child being with her at the end. Words muttered through tears and noisy sobs. We cry together because there is nothing else to do. We immerse ourselves in grief. And love.

Our mum, the indomitable, irreplaceable, one-of-a-kind Terri Reilly, has left us.

She died—or, more accurately, she *lived*—every moment of her life until 1:50 a.m. on the morning of 22nd April 2021.

Rest in peace, my beautiful Mum. I will miss you forever.

The nurse arrives a few minutes later. She is taken aback and apologises for not being with us sooner. It has been less than 15 minutes since the phone call. She is kind and unobtrusive. Barney arrives. My heart aches for him. He has spent so much time with Mum since she came to live in Perth. He and Lorna have cared for her and supported her through this final terminal diagnosis.

'It was so fast, Barney… fast and peaceful.'

He understands. His gratitude and love outweigh any regret that he was not with his Mum.

\* \* \*

And thus begins the process of informing the people who need to know. We split the phone calls and pray we don't forget anyone. There are so many practicalities after a death and no matter how much time you have had to prepare, it's overwhelming. The three of us sit huddled in the living room with mugs of tea, plates of toast and a lifetime of memories. Mum's chair—her office—is empty. Each of us has imagined this moment. It is still hard to absorb. We are like actors in a play who have forgotten their lines. Floundering. Adrift.

We start with the onerous task of informing our other two siblings. Paul knows the moment he lifts the phone. No words needed. His pain is palpable—a lonely grief that rebounds and engulfs our own.

Telling Colette in France is one of the hardest things I have ever done. She and I have spoken so often about our fears, our feelings. Colette, more than any of us, has anticipated Mum's death with trepidation for years, not months. A terror not tied to illness, but to the inevitability of time and age. The mere thought of living without her mother's presence.

*'How will I manage, Maur? How will I survive? I won't cope. I'll fall apart. She can't die. She just can't.'*

And now, I can feel my sister's heart tearing apart with every piercing scream on the other end of the phone.

## 32. Maureen. Scotland/Ireland. 29th May 2021
### The Final Journey

My son, Paul, has arrived in Perth. He will drive me back to Sligo, along with everything I am bringing home. The car is close to bursting. Bags and boxes of miscellaneous missives and misfits are jammed behind the front seats. We cram, push and pile what we can, abandoning the rest for my brothers and Fraser, the neighbour, to deal with. Time, tide, and P & O Ferries wait for no man, and a month after Mum's death, it is time to leave The Falconry, 25 St Boswells Place. We have cleared and cleaned the house, distributed and bequeathed Terri Reilly's possessions. I have said my farewells to Mum in every corner of her home, the home we have shared for the past year. Although not looking over my shoulder, I heard her whispering,

*Someone might be glad of that, someday, Maureen.*
*That's too good to throw out.*
*I loved that, you know.*
*You'll be sorry if you don't take that home with you.*

And so it continued. I could hear Mum's voice and feel her presence, as if we were together in the house. Trying to let go of the past. Trying to let go of each other. Or maybe it was just me trying to let go.

I squeeze into the cramped passenger seat next to Paul. I see the tears in his eyes as he grips the steering wheel and turns towards me.

'You ok, Ma?'
'I am, Paul.'

And I truly am okay. Much more okay than I thought I would be on this day. The day I leave my mother's home, her world and her life behind.

We turn out of the courtyard and I gaze up at the window where Mum always stood to wave goodbye. I feel a jolt in my chest as I imagine her there, hand raised in a blown kiss. I am filled with love rather than sadness, which surprises me. It feels as if she is waving for the final time. Giving me her blessing. Encouraging me to leave, to return to my own home, my own life. This time, I will take her with me. Never again will I have to feel the emptiness and ache of looking back and waving to the tiny shape in the window frame. My mum is right here in my heart, where she will stay. Always. This is the world of *after*.

Harder than leaving the house is leaving Perth and those who were part of my life here. Barney, Lorna and the girls have been my go-to support system during the past year. My cousin and her family, the 3 Gs, have also been there for me. I said an emotional farewell to Fraser and Elaine, who became so much more than neighbours to Mum, always on hand to help her and her madcap relatives, especially me. I have built a temporary life in Perth, navigating my way around like a resident, getting to know the people who were important to Terri Reilly. As a family, we worried and wondered about how our mother would adapt to retirement at the age of seventy-eight. After almost a year of coming and going to Perth, I am reassured that she survived very well without the flower business. She was genuinely accepted into the community and formed true friendships during the latter part of her life. What a surprise. What a joy. They have become my friends too and I will miss them. I came to Perth to look after my dying Mum, but the reality has been very different and unexpected. I learned something every day, and I gained something every day, through the simple human act of loving and being loved.

* * *

## The ferry to Belfast

The weather is calm and the ferry is on time. Paul and I climb the stairs onto the lounge deck to find a quiet corner. We are both exhausted. Paul's only day between travels was spent packing boxes and then packing the car. After something to eat, he drifts off to sleep in preparation for the final leg of the journey to Sligo.

The final journey. The last of so many journeys for me. The final leg of this final journey with Mum. And what a journey it has been!

My laptop beckons. The urge to write claws its way through fatigue. There are words that must be written. If not now, they might vanish into the haze of exhaustion and emotion. For now, I feel a fragile relief, calm, logical, resigned. Yet I know that grief will catch me off guard over and over again. Recounting the serenity and dignity of Mum's death has been a kind of shield against the pain of loss.

'It was a gift,' I say.

'It was her time,' I say.
'She lived a vibrant and full life,' I say.
'She lived every moment right up 'til the end,' I say.

These facts are all true. But I don't tell them about my fear of life without her. I don't tell them I would do anything for one more day, one more latte, one more chat. I don't tell them how much I long to hear her laughter, to see her radiant smile and feel its warmth, its comfort, its love. How can I explain that her absence feels raw, a wound that may never heal? I don't tell them any of these realities because that would be selfish. Even if I am unable to verbalise my thoughts, documenting them helps. The process stops me from imploding. After all, writing brought me closer to Mum, and writing is how I make sense of the world. This is my world now. I retrieve my trusty laptop and begin typing. No order. No censor. No internal editor. Just words.. My fingers move without a plan or intended destination.

I nudge Paul in time for the announcement: *Drivers, return to your vehicles.* He looks drained and weary as we settle back into the car.

'We'll stop for a coffee and chips or something, Paul.'

He grins. 'Good idea, Ma. I'll check the nearest place on Google Maps.'

\* \* \*

Paul pulls into the carpark of a Kentucky Fried Chicken restaurant somewhere near Belfast. This is not the kind of food I usually eat, but it is hot and tasty. The coffee is not too bad either. We open the windows. The car still smells of vinegar. We ignore it and sit back, making the most of the food and the break.

'Mum, can I ask you a question?' Paul says.

I put the chip I am about to eat back into the bag.

'Of course. Fire away.'

I wait and speculate.

'I was thinking about how great it was that you were there for Mama over the past few months. Is it too soon to ask you what the best bit about looking after her was? For you, I mean? I know it was good for Mama. Look, if it's too soon, it's fine. I was just wondering.'

## Impossible to Fill

'Not too soon at all, Paul. A good question. And one I've asked myself more than once.' I think maybe it was *not* looking after her. It was just *being* with her. Yes. I think that was the best bit.'

'I get that,' Paul says. And I know he does.

He gulps a mouthful of coffee and lays his plastic cup on the dashboard. 'If you had to describe the past year with Mama in three words, what would they be?'

I am not so quick to answer this one. 'My God, Paul. That's an A-level question. You've caught me on the hop.'

'Sorry, Mum. I didn't mean to…'

'No… No….,' I want to give you an answer… Just let me think for a minute.'

I munch on the last few chips. Paul waits. We stare at the windscreen. It feels like being in a therapy session. The answer comes to me in the silence.

'Listening, learning, laughing.' I sound glib, but feel pleased with myself. I love a bit of alliteration. Then, without warning, the other words tumble out—uninvited. The ones I've been trying to find since Mum laid her head on my shoulder and left me.

'I suppose I learned about acceptance and resilience… from listening to Mum's stories. Being together. Laughing together. And I learned it's okay to make mistakes. Life's not really about success or failure… it's about doing your best, getting on with it, not giving up.'

I can hear the quiver in my voice, but I'm not quite finished.

'The stories made me see we're all part of each other. Mum's past isn't just hers. It's mine… and yours… and one day, it'll be your family's too.

'Wow, Ma! That's such a lovely thing to say. But I'm so sorry. I shouldn't have asked such a stupid question. You're not even home yet. What an idiot! Are you alright?'

I look across at Paul. His face is serious, his eyes full of concern.

I realise I am crying. Tears drip onto the empty chip box in my lap.

'These are happy tears, Paul…Honestly…You missed your vocation as a therapist. Now, let's get home.'

Paul finds a refuse bin, and we drive out of the deserted car park. He is not quite finished. 'What you said is so true. Mama always had a positive spin. Never gave up on anything.'

He hesitates and then, without turning his head, says, 'But the same is true of you, Ma. Don't forget that.'

I swallow slowly and deliberately. 'Thank you, son,' is all I can manage and we sit together for the rest of the journey in what is known as *companionable silence*.

\* \* \*

**Sligo, Ireland. night of 29th May 2021**

The house is visible from the end of the road, like a lighthouse in a dark sea, guiding us home with its warm, unwavering glow. Every light in every room blazes a welcome. We turn into the driveway and Martin pulls open my door, barely waiting for the car to stop. We cling to each other. Not a face mask in sight.

'I'm here, Martin. I'm finally home.'

He carries the first of the bags into the house. I stand at the front door and gaze up into the clear, ink-blue sky above Glencar Valley.

Goodnight, Mum.
Thank you for sharing your stories.
Thank you for a year I will treasure forever.
Thank you for memories I never could have anticipated.
I learned about you. And I learned about myself.
I'll never fill your shoes. But I learned that's ok too.
In time, I'll also learn how to let go.
But, until then, I'll just *play it by ear*.

## HERE'S TO...

## LATTE, LAUGHTER, AND LOVE!

## *Epilogue*

*Dear Mum,*

*There is a Glasgow expression: I said I'd dae it an' I done it! More accurately, we did it together, and I wish you were here to hold this book, your book, our book.*

*There were so many times I wanted to give up, but I could hear your voice in my head:*

*'Get on with it, Maureen. You can't quit. My friends are waiting.'*

*And I kept going.*

*You were with us at home for almost two weeks before the funeral. During that time, Colette organised your clothes into bags, chatting as she sorted, aware of your spirit and silent approval. It felt strange, yet normal. It was her way of coping, of grieving for you. Family came and went. It gave us time to let go.*

*Your fellow Soroptimists helped to pack, move, store, distribute and sell your stylish outfits and accessories in a pop-up shop, raising over £5,000 for the projects you cared about. I know you would have been delighted. We also gave a brooch and scarf to family and friends, near and far. Many wore them proudly at the funeral, including your big sons.*

*Two days before the funeral, Covid regulations relaxed, allowing fifty people to attend. I still think you had a hand in it! Colette and your granddaughters sang in the church. Paul played a piece he had composed in your honour on his bagpipes at the graveside. Then, as the sun broke through the clouds, we clapped along to The Radetzky March, just as you had requested. It was the perfect balance of joy and sadness.*

*We counted over a hundred pairs of shoes in your wardrobe, many of them neatly stacked in their original boxes. They were all too small for my feet, yet too big for me to fill.*

*Never stop dancing, Mum.*

*I will love and miss you always,*

*Maureen*

## Author's Note

I set out to document my mum's memories, not to write a memoir. But the telling and listening to those memories took on a life of its own. They became the story of our final months together and changed us both in ways we never could have imagined.

The book was written in three strands, woven together as scenes rather than chapters, reflecting how the story itself evolved. Although some of them have been fictionalised to give historical context and texture, the details are true to the original memories shared. They give a flavour of Mum's life rather than a blow-by-blow description. As she would have said herself, *the stories are a C to a Z rather than an A to a Z.*

Mum's reflections are a creation of my imagination, based on recorded conversations, numerous coffees, and the closeness of our mother-daughter relationship. I hope I have captured at least a little of her personality, character and wit. Family opinions and recollections of her favourite expressions and sayings were invaluable.

The letters quoted in this book, are all from the original letters Collette and I found, in a box in my mother's shed.

I have done my best to ensure the accuracy of the facts. Along the way, I discovered that much of what I thought I knew was contradicted by research.

Finally, the names used in the book have not been changed, and I have tried to portray each with honesty and respect. Writing it has been a privilege, a challenge and a joy in equal measure.

## *Acknowledgements*

Without sounding like an actor at the Oscars, the first thing to say is how many people played a part in the finished book.

**Technical and publishing team**

To Michèle (Jasami Publishing & Productions), who told me I had a book at our first meeting, then made it happen, reassuring me all the way.

To Manon, developmental editor, for her hard work, editorial advice and constructive guidance.

To Joy, cover designer and photographer, for her talent and patience when I continually changed my mind.

To Nicola (Butterfly Books), editor and proofreader, for her experience, expertise and motivation.

To Pauline, for her editing skill, vision and confidence in me.

To Avril, Mary, Evelyn and Des, my beta readers, for their invaluable feedback. And to Des in particular, for his insight, oversight and tough love when needed. You were with me from the start and got me over the line.

**Specialist contributors**

To Mark, for sharing his military knowledge, and to Anne, for driving me to the former Barrhill Campsite in Skelmorlie, where I stood in a field and felt the Clyde coast wind in my face.

Thanks also to the Mitchell Library, Largs and District Historical Society, and the many voices in Glasgow's online history groups, whose memories and photographs helped bring the streets of the Gorbals, Bridgeton and Maryhill to life.

## Friends

To friends near and far, who kept me going by checking in and cheering me on. Clare, you smiled at me from the photo on my wall, and I felt your presence.

## Family

In so many ways, this book is about family love. I have no way of adequately thanking you all. I could fill another book with the ways in which each of you have supported me.

To my brothers, Paul, Barney and Joe, unstinting in your care for Mum and your help to me. Thank you for reminding me that Mum's stories mattered and for your significant input. important contribution.

To my sisters-in-law, Lorna and Jules, who gave of their time and themselves with unwavering commitment and love. Roisin, Mum would have been thrilled for you and Joe, and for the gift of your wedding bouquet on her grave.

To Mum's fifteen grandchildren, who each expressed their love for her in different ways. She cherished every one of you.

To my sister and closest friend, Colette, always at my side. You are the yin to my yang, my go-to person, partner in hijinks and laughter, and so much more. You were the breath of fresh air Mum needed, with her in the best and worst of times, and part of so many stories. Mum will never be gone while you are alive!

## Mum's network in Perth

To Barney, Lorna and the girls, who enabled Mum to live independently for as long as possible, and who were there for us both during those final months. Thank you for the many journeys to and from the airport. Your home felt like my own.

To my cousin, Lorna, and her family, Chris and Fraser, for your thoughtfulness and loving generosity to Mum, and to me. And to Lorna's mum, Teresa, my dad's sister and Mum's great friend as well as her sister-in-law. They shared many a happy outing, as well as a sausage sandwich in Morrisons, before Teresa's death in 2017.

To Fraser and Elaine, more than neighbours, ever ready to come to Mum's aid with good-humoured kindness.

To Mum's Soroptimist friends and Keep Fit pals, who gave her retirement years a richness we never expected. And especially to Mary, her late-night telephone buddy. Listening to their girlish laughter always lifted my spirits

**My own family**

Finally, to my own family, who bring me the greatest joy and deepest pride: Mark, Paul and Sarah. Thank you for the countless ways you sustained me throughout the long process of writing this book. To my son-in-law, Niall, whose card with encouraging words meant so much to me.

And to Martin, my long-suffering husband and the wind beneath my wings, who has been with me every step of the way. You never gave up on me, never doubted that one day I would write a book. In my desk drawer I keep a handwritten page dated Friday 7th June 2013, which says: 'I want you to write the first page of your book today.' It took me another few years, Martin. Thank you for believing in me when I didn't believe in myself. This book is as much yours as it is mine.

*The Moving Finger writes; and, having writ,*
*Moves on: nor all thy Piety nor Wit*
*Shall lure it back to cancel half a Line,*
*Nor all thy Tears wash out a Word of it.*

Omar Khayyám, The Rubáiyát of Omar Khayyám,
trans. Edward FitzGerald

*Photo of the original book purchased by*
*Terri in Alexandria, Egypt in 1949*

*About the Author*

A native of Scotland, Maureen is married to Martin, whom she first met at Glasgow Central Station, a setting echoed in several scenes in this book. She is proud mum to three grown-up children and now lives in County Sligo, the beautiful northwest of Ireland.

Maureen spent many years in nursing and midwifery before retiring as an assistant director of public health nursing. She has always enjoyed writing and gained an MA in English Literature at Glasgow University. Her essays and poetry have featured in local anthologies, and she is known among friends and family for composing light-hearted verses to celebrate weddings, birthdays and retirements.

While raising her children, Maureen worked with radio stations in Edinburgh and Sligo as a presenter, also producing short documentaries on human interest topics. When she is not writing, Maureen loves to sing and dance and has been involved with Musical Theatre in Sligo for many years. *Small Shoes, Impossible to Fill* is her first book, a labour of love, with another already in the pipeline.

Printed in Dunstable, United Kingdom